70

(Φ562)

HOW TO CATCH 5000 THIEVES

HOW
TO CATCH
5000
THIEVES

BY *Gerard Luisi*
AND *Charles Samuels*

THE MACMILLAN COMPANY · NEW YORK

First Printing

The Macmillan Company, New York
Collier-Macmillan Canada, Ltd., Galt, Ontario
Divisions of The Crowell-Collier Publishing Company

Printed in the United States of America

Library of Congress catalog card number: 62-21211

I dedicate this book WITH HEARTFELT GRATITUDE
TO *LILLIAN*, MY WIFE, WHO WORKED WITH ME ON HUNDREDS
OF INVESTIGATIONS, AND NOW AGAIN HAS PROVED INDISPENSABLE
TO ME IN THE ASSEMBLING OF THE MATERIAL FOR THIS BOOK
FROM THE FILES, RECORDS, AND NOTES I HAVE KEPT DURING THE
HALF-CENTURY I WORKED AS AN INSURANCE DETECTIVE. I ALSO
WISH TO EXPRESS HERE MY THANKS TO ALL LAW-ENFORCEMENT
AGENTS IN THE UNITED STATES.

Gerard Luisi

Lake Park, Florida.
March 20, 1962

Though the facts in this book are all true,
in many cases I have changed names of criminals
and also persons involved with them —
for obvious reasons.

CONTENTS

HOW TO CATCH 5000 THIEVES

THE
HAPPILY VIOLENT LIFE
OF AN
INSURANCE DETECTIVE

1

FOR FIFTY years I was the sort of private detective the world knows least about: an insurance detective. My work was investigating claims of loss for companies that sell protection on almost every sort of property, and bond employees of banks, brokerage houses, department stores, and many other businesses.

You won't have to get very far into this book to understand why so little has been published until now about my trade. Publicity about their inner workings is the last thing these great casualty insurance companies want.

But this book is no exposé.

I do intend, however, to show how the public might be saved millions of the dollars they pay each year in premiums to these companies. It is not a matter of the companies' honesty, but the elimination of old-fashioned business habits. The public has the right to know, for instance, how great a fortune it pays each year because the companies so often find it easier and sometimes more profitable, to pay off claims ranging from dubious ones to those that are outright frauds than to investigate them. There are other practices that merit overhauling, to put it mildly.

One good reason I would not write an exposé is that I am not that ungrateful a man. I've had a happy and adventurous life working for insurance executives. And I know no group of men I like better or whose personal integrity I respect more. I've made a good living at it, have been able to travel widely, meet colorful

1

people on all social levels, and educate my children at the best schools and I've quite enough money left over to live comfortably in my old age.

I need envy no man his career.

I cannot imagine one more thrilling than mine. In my time I have conducted or supervised about thirty-five thousand investigations of claims for great amounts and small, and I have caught about five thousand thieves.

Thirty-five thousand investigations, and never a moment of boredom. Fifty-odd years of going to the office, never knowing what wild experience might await me there. The telephone, a horror that harasses and haunts many business people, was to me always like some generous friend summoning me to investigate fantastic capers, outrageous swindles, ingenious new angles.

Like most people, I prefer to believe that most of my fellowmen and women are honest. But I caught and exposed so many persons who outwardly seemed to be in every way decent, respectable people who were trying to cheat the insurance companies that it was not always easy to keep on believing that. I had to keep reminding myself that for every fraudulent claim there were perhaps a thousand honest ones.

The real eye-popper was discovering how many would try to cheat, and chance disgrace and a prison term, for a frivolous reason: to get the money to redecorate their homes or for a trip to Florida. Some middle-aged, middle-class women reported their jewels lost, strayed, or stolen so a daughter could have a catered wedding or a son could attend an Ivy League college. Bookkeepers, clerks, theater cashiers, executives of corporations — scores of them — devised new ways to steal or tried to improve on the old ones.

The so-called Upperworld bred plenty of thieves also. I had a case in which one of Wall Street's biggest operators got up in the middle of the night to steal his wife's jewels for the insurance money. While he was at it he grabbed the jewels of his guests, who happened to be Lord and Lady Mountbatten. I am convinced I could have proved it if my employer, Lloyd's of London on this particular job, had not preferred to settle.

Another extraordinary case involved a stockbroker. He stole his wife's jewels and collected the full amount of the insurance. I was suspicious enough about this Wall Streeter to put a shadow on him — but he never let down his guard. A few months later I read in my newspaper that this gentleman and a girl friend had been shot to death. They were necking in his car in a lonely part of the woods just outside New York. When the bodies were found the girl was wearing jewelry worth thousands of dollars. Because of this, the police knew that the murderer either was not a thief or had been frightened off right after the shooting.

On a hunch I got out the claim loss. It listed a diamond necklace, brooch, and ring. So did the newspaper story about the murders.

They turned out to be the jewels we'd paid the claim on. The stockbroker's widow got them back on returning the money the company had given her husband.

My work was full of these little plot turns.

I handled one case in which a dozen New York millionaires abruptly decided overnight to move their mistresses into new "love nests." They were all afraid that one man, a liveried chauffeur, planned to blackmail them.

Not long after that, one of our outstanding industrialists told me to drop my investigation of the alleged theft of $175,000 worth of jewels belonging to his young wife. He asked me instead to check on her past. He offered to double my fee. He said he did not care how long it took.

The job took months, led me across and up and down the country. When I got the story, I hated making the report. The gorgeous-looking girl he had married was still in her early twenties. Nevertheless, before meeting him she had been a thief, a bigamist, a big-money gambler, and the inmate of a whorehouse on the Mexican border. He cried like a heartbroken child when he read my report.

I had the pleasure of cracking one of the very first killings perpetrated by a member of Murder, Inc.

One year I rode alone across the country in a train compartment with a punch-nutty prizefighter who had turned stickup man, not daring to close my eyes for fear he might try to strangle me.

I had a part in the trapping of Gerald Graham Dennis who was called the "Prince of Thieves" and the "World's Smartest House Burglar." I once outwitted the crooked district attorney of a Midwest city who was trying to act as a fence for a gang of jewel thieves.

Down through the years my work brought me into contact, sometimes of a violent nature, with three generations of goons, blackmailers, burglars, stickup men, safecrackers, hijackers, pimps and their tarts, con men, swindlers, and jewel thieves, professional and amateur. It is my belief that 25 percent of the robberies of jewelers and jewel salesmen that you read about in the newspapers are faked by the "victims."

On the other hand, I have investigated claims of jewel losses made by many of the great stars of the stage, screen, and opera, some of them during the years when fake jewel robberies were the stock in trade of theatrical press agents. Not a single such claim I handled was a fake. However, one of the most popular stars the opera world has ever known asked me to stop my investigation. The reason seemed to be that one of his in-laws was the thief.

On many occasions I was called to work for, sometimes against, celebrated society ladies. Their fine manners did not always show. I investigated women on all the other social levels, many of whom had no manners or morals at all. Quite a few displayed the ferocity and resourcefulness of alley cats.

Though fascinating, I must admit that my trade is not one for a nervous man. Most of the time I found it wise to carry with me quite an assortment of weapons—two revolvers, a stiletto, and sometimes a blackjack. Come to think of it, a lot of people who are not nervous at all might not care to be in my business. But I loved every minute of it.

The so-called aristocracy of the underworld has surprised me on more than one occasion. Consider my relationship with Arnold Rothstein, the gambler who was supposed to be able to fix anything in New York and who was also accused of having fixed the 1919 World Series. I have heard that he was the Big Bankroll of everything crooked in the big town from Wall Street's bucket shops to dope-peddling syndicates.

I am not in a position to deny any of this. Rothstein may well have been everything people called him. But time and again he gave me clues in baffling cases, helped me recover a great fortune in stolen jewels and other valuables — because I had done favors for two friends of his that saved them from prison.

Furthermore, I could not have accomplished anything if not for the cooperation of the F.B.I., police in communities all over the country, in Canada and in Europe, United States Postal inspectors, and the members of our other law-enforcement agencies. I could have done nothing without their help, the use of some of their facilities, and most of all their know-how. And without them I could not have done the one thing in which I take the greatest pride. This was the saving of hundreds of men and women, first offenders, from going to prison. In every case this required the consent of the police and the district attorney. I almost always got it.

I quit only when I was no longer able to do my own legwork. A couple of years ago I retired for good, and moved with my wife to Florida. I say for good, but I don't know what's good about it.

No man ever retired with greater reluctance. Certainly no police detective or private detective ever regretted more than I did having to put away his shield and the other tools of his trade, his revolvers, blackjack and, in my case, the stiletto.

Writing this, my life story, is the closest I can come, I guess, to reliving it.

*

IF there is such a thing as a born detective, I'm one.

Raffael Luisi, my father, was a member of the Italian Secret Police before I was born. Other boys had George Washington, the Three Musketeers, and Teddy Roosevelt and his Rough Riders for heroes. I did not need them.

I had my father.

When I told him that I had decided to become a detective, he taught me the things I would have to know, including the most important thing of all: how to handle criminals — when to be gentle with them, when to get tough. What I learned from him saved my life many times.

One of those times was in 1912.

When I mention any such year as 1912 my grandchildren stare at me as though I was talking about the Stone Age. I confess that it now does seem a little remote even to me.

There were still a few horsecars on the streets of New York in 1912. Beer was a nickel a glass, whiskey ten cents except at the better places, which charged fifteen. Lillian Russell was still the great American beauty, George M. Cohan the best-loved man on Broadway, but the new sensation was young Al Jolson, prancing the stage in blackface, singing "When the Midnight Choo-Choo Leaves for Alabam' " at the Winter Garden.

Out-of-towners coming to New York still could find there the city whose gallant knights and shopgirls O. Henry wrote about, the glittering and romantic heroes of Richard Harding Davis, the bootblacks and newsboys Horatio Alger loved so much. In the year 1912 the *Titanic* sank, and Wilson was elected President. The city was shocked by the Herman Rosenthal street murder; the old folks were also fretting over the women's suffrage movement, the Turkey Trot, which had become all the rage, and the demands of labor unions for a living wage. But what really convinced these older citizens that the country was really going to hell in a horse and buggy was the popularity of afternoon dances at which certain shameless women checked their corsets at the door before flinging themselves into the arms of their favorite lounge lizards.

I myself had plenty to worry about that year. I recently had been made Chief Investigator of the Burglary and Fidelity departments of the Ocean Accident and Guarantee Corporation, Ltd. And that summer there had been a series of baffling larcenies by servants. Neither I, the detectives employed by other companies, nor the police had so much as a clue.

One day toward the end of the summer I was called into the general manager's office. I found executives of many other companies with him. I knew some of them, and he introduced me to the others.

"What about these larcenies committed by servants?" he asked. "Why haven't these thieves been arrested?"

I didn't think my theory would make any of them happy, but I offered it. The servants, it seemed to me, were working under the orders of some master thief, a very clever and cunning man. "He must also be cautious and very lucky," I added. "If one of his people has made a mistake so far, the brains of the New York Police Department, not to mention all of us insurance investigators, know nothing about it."

My boss naturally asked what gave me the idea that there was a mastermind running the wholesale thefts by servants. I explained that most veteran thieves were like carpenters and other craftsmen in one thing at least: they have their own individual way of doing a job.

"Veteran detectives," I went on, "often take one look at a loft robbery, a safecracking job, a house burglary, and tell you what crook pulled it off. And when an arrest is made he proves to be right.

"Now, these larcenies were not committed by the same thief, but they certainly look as though the same man planned all of them. In most of these thefts, a housemaid was hired. But sometimes it was a butler, sometimes a couple.

"In each instance the same procedure was followed. The servants get the jobs through reputable agencies or by answering newspaper 'Help Wanted' ads. They offered excellent references which described them as 'honest, reliable and hard workers.'

"Yet in from one to several days, the 'honest, reliable' servant disappeared with jewels, clothes, and silver."

By this time the executives in the room were sitting on the edge of their chairs. We solved the mystery when we hunted down some of the servants so highly recommended and had the robbed employers look them over. Each of the victims said the same thing: "This is not the servant who robbed me." Somehow or other this ring of servant-thieves had got hold of the references of honest servants. They stole some, made copies of others.

None of the jewelry, furs, fine clothes, antiques, silverware and household furnishings, including one large and expensive Oriental rug, had been located. This though we'd been covering the pawnshops and all known fences for weeks. I was asked about that.

"It is possible," I said, "that whoever is running this servant ring has found a way to get the loot out of town and sell it in another city. The thieves may have someone breaking up the jewelry and melting the settings to prevent it being identified.

"It is also possible that the man who runs the ring is keeping most of the loot in some hiding place of his own right here in New York, with the idea of disposing of it when he feels it is safe to sell it."

One of the executives asked if I could suggest something new that their companies might try. I did have just such a suggestion. It was that the companies jointly set up a Central Investigation Bureau to cope with these surprisingly successful servant thieves. Each company would pool all of its reports and information and, whenever necessary, contribute the services of its New York investigators, and pay a share of the expenses.

It took the rest of the afternoon for us to work out the details. I was appointed head of the bureau, was to devote all my time to trying to stop the ring's operations. I was to have the full time help of John (Spider) Allen of the National Security Company. He had recently retired from the New York Police Department. I couldn't have asked for a better man, or a harder worker than Allen. He'd been given his nickname because of his scrawny build. But he happily took on crooks twice his size in rough-and-tumble battles. The companies' other men would be available, I was assured, whenever we needed their help.

After talking it over, Allen and I decided to compile a record of the servant robberies that had been reported to the various companies of the pool since the beginning of the summer. We used big white index cards. On these we set down the known facts, how and from whom the job was obtained, how long the servant worked there, from whom the references came, a description of the property stolen, and so on.

After studying all of this information, we hoped to have a clearer picture of how the mob of thieves operated. But it told us nothing whatever about the phony references. The pattern remained about the same, though in some instances the servants had explained that their former employer was traveling in Europe for the summer and could not be contacted.

But the index cards revealed other facts that might prove helpful. The ring apparently had stolen valuables from more than a hundred different homes. But these were almost all apartments in the same fashionable West Side neighborhood of Manhattan, in the West seventies and eighties, between Central Park West and Riverside Drive. After comparing the various descriptions victims had given of the thieves, Allen and I agreed that the larcenies had been committed by ten different persons, nine young women servants and one man who hired out as a butler.

The man, of course, became our Number One suspect as the mastermind. He was described as being about thirty-eight years old, of slight build, with dark hair and a bushy black moustache. He had a thick German accent.

The women were all of the familiar drab German servant type. They would work from morning to night for ten to fifteen dollars a month and board. Eight of the nine were young, in their early twenties. Each had participated in from two to four crimes.

The ninth woman had been the servant in dozens of the thefts, either working alone or with the man, as a couple. She had a very high forehead. She was about thirty-two, of average height and weight, was a good cook of plain food and a good cleaner.

One case indicated that this woman could turn vicious and violent when caught in the act. A wealthy old woman, Mrs. Sidney Bernheimer, had hired the woman with the high forehead one morning late in June. That same afternoon Mrs. Bernheimer left her new maid alone in her apartment, saying she would return shortly before dinner. However, after being out only for an hour she was caught in a shower, changed her plans to shop, and went home.

In her bedroom she found the new maid and another woman busily stuffing her jewelry, furs, and dresses into two large suitcases. Mrs. Bernheimer demanded what they were doing. The two women immediately turned on her and beat her over the head. She fell unconscious across her bed. She was still there on the bed, gagged with a handkerchief, her hands and feet bound with her own silk stockings, when her husband came home that evening.

The doctor who treated Mrs. Bernheimer said she probably had fainted as much from shock as pain. The thieves had carried off considerable loot, about $4,000 worth of jewelry, the couple's best clothes, much lingerie, and about $5,000 in negotiable bonds that Mr. Bernheimer had carelessly kept in an unlocked drawer of his writing desk.

Allen and I had just completed our index of the cases when another woman, whose home Ocean had insured, was robbed by a newly hired maid. This crime followed the pattern of the others. Among other things, Mrs. S. Ganz said that the girl had put on a new blouse when she started work.

"I showed her to her room," she said, "and when she came out I noticed she had changed into a new blouse." I searched the closet and the drawers of the dresser of the maid's room without finding anything. While going over the room with a fine comb, I found a price tag stamped $2.95. The name of the store wasn't on it. I also found a new toothbrush. Nothing was on this either to indicate where it was bought.

Putting both in my pocket I started for the precinct police station. I wanted to talk to the detective who'd been assigned to the case. Maybe he had some ideas. On the way to the station house I passed a small women's apparel shop.

There was no reason for me to think the blouse was bought there. But having nothing else to work on, I had nothing to lose by asking. You can do hundreds of things like that on an investigation without any of them helping. But if you overlook nothing your luck is bound to turn sooner or later.

It happened this time. The store owner told me the tag was the sort he used. One of his salesgirls recalled selling the blouse early that morning. But she didn't know the customer, and had never waited on her before.

"But I think that woman lives somewhere around here," she said. "I've seen her in the neighborhood more than once." Her description of the customer tallied with the one Mrs. Ganz had given me.

The next day, before the store opened, Mrs. Ganz, the precinct detective, and I were in a car parked across the street. We waited there all day on the chance that the servant might walk by. She didn't.

We were there the next morning. On the afternoon of the second day, Mrs. Ganz in great excitement pointed out a plainly dressed young woman.

"That's the maid who robbed me," she said.

We arrested the girl and brought her into the store. The saleslady said she was the customer who had bought the blouse.

But Sophie Beckendorf denied she was the girl Mrs. Ganz had hired. She had never seen Mrs. Ganz before, she insisted. In her furnished room there was nothing that had been stolen from Mrs. Ganz or the other women.

We questioned her all night. But it was only at four o'clock the next morning that she began to talk. And what she told us, it developed later, was only part of what she knew.

Sophie said that she had been in the country for less than a year.

Though she now admitted being the servant who had taken Mrs. Ganz's valuables, she denied having worked in any other homes that were looted. This we doubted because the description several other victims of the ring had given us fitted Sophie.

But we were more interested at the moment in getting her to tell us about the master crook than in having them identify her.

Sophie finally cracked — a little — on this. She had turned over everything she'd stolen, she said, to a woman whom she knew only as Lottie. She'd met Lottie in an employment agency, and the older woman took a motherly interest in her and promised to help her find work.

Lottie also introduced her brother Hans to her. He seemed to fall in love with her at first sight, Sophie told us. Before she knew what was happening, Hans — again Sophie would not give us the last name — was begging her to marry him. She had accepted him on the spot. All that delayed the wedding was his temporary lack of money. Hans was eager that they start off life together with a nice home and a little business that he could run.

The next day Lottie brought Sophie the Help Wanted ad Mrs. Ganz had put in the paper. Lottie convinced her that she should steal from her new employer, and turn the loot over to Hans. He could sell it. Maybe he would be able to raise enough that way to buy the little business he had told her about.

So she had turned thief, and given everything she took from Mrs. Ganz's apartment — two gold watches, a bar pin set with fifty-two diamonds, and a coral necklace — to Hans and Lottie.

"Where?"

"On a street corner."

But Sophie would tell us no more. She was booked for grand larceny. We again went through her furnished room, this time with extreme care but found nothing.

I spent hours trying to figure out our next move. When I had a plan I discussed it with Allen, Police Detective–Sergeant Martin S. Fay, and the assistant district attorney, who was to prosecute the case against Sophie Beckendorf.

They all thought my plan was feasible, and well worth trying. It consisted of planting four women detectives in different employment agencies that the ring had not used, so far as we knew, to get jobs in homes they planned to loot. Though at that time I had no women on my staff, I had used them before on other assignments. They had worked for a reputable private detective agency run by a friend of mine. He was able to help me out again on this occasion.

Each of the four women he sent me was in the early twenties, was plain-looking, could speak some German, and would pass without question as a domestic. By that time we had good physical descriptions of both Lottie and Hans. If they walked into one of the agencies, the girl we had planted there would recognize them. The girls had their instructions. The managers of the agencies had been informed of what we were doing. They were only too glad to cooperate.

In a few days the woman with the high forehead, whom we still knew only as Lottie, walked into an agency where we had planted

May Leukroth. May was twenty-two years old, a high-school graduate, and intelligent. When not employed as a detective, she worked as a substitute stenographer. And she was single, which meant she was also free to work nights.

When May Leukroth saw Lottie walk in, she smiled at her, shyly. Lottie, after registering at the desk, sat down next to May. She said, "You look worried."

May said she was worried. "I just got here and I've never been in a big city before. I don't even know what work I'll have to do if I do get a job."

Lottie encouraged her to talk.

May explained that she'd lived all of her life on her family's farm in western Pennsylvania. Her folks had not wanted her to come to the great city. But she'd been lonely there, and didn't even have a beau. But now that she was actually in New York, she was scared to death.

Lottie asked the new prospect that day to have lunch with her. During the afternoon she suggested that they meet the next day. "I'll get you a job," she told May. "Don't worry about that — or anything else."

On being informed of all this, I got down to the agency fast. The manager gave me Lottie's application, which he had set aside when May signaled him. I had a photostat made of this. Lottie had registered under a name I had not come across before but by comparing the handwriting with that on applications at other agencies that had resulted in larcenies, we saw that Lottie was using a different alias at each place.

But the next day when the two women met, May had great news. She had found a job in a rich man's home. This was the apartment of a wealthy insurance executive who was as eager to trap the thieves as I was. We were all set — or thought we were. We were going to put a tail of two men on Lottie when she left May and let her lead us to Hans and the others in the ring.

On meeting Lottie next day, May took her, with the shadows following, to her new job so that her newly made friend could see for herself what fine luck she was in. Lottie seemed deeply impressed by the luxurious home, May reported.

"Will you be able to get out tonight to meet me?" Lottie asked.

May was sure she could. When Lottie left, the shadow men followed her to a house in the East twenties. She did not come out until the time came for her to meet May on a street corner. And she was alone.

On meeting May (I learned afterward), Lottie explained: "After I left you I kept thinking about what you said about being lonesome. Now I have a surprise for you."

In a moment or two a man, fitting perfectly the description we had of Hans, joined the women. Lottie introduced him as her brother. "He's lonesome too," she told May with a sisterly wink. Soon after, she excused herself.

Hans didn't waste any time in starting a romance. He took May to a movie theater, and to a restaurant afterward. During the show he tried to put his arm around May. She objected, but only half-heartedly as though she liked him well enough but wanted him to understand that she was a decent girl. He told her he was a bank clerk and lived in a furnished room with a very old-fashioned family. These people did not like him to have visitors. He said that was why he had to meet her on the street.

And now we had a tail on Hans as well as on Lottie.

We could have picked them up at that point, but thought one or the other would lead us, if we were a little patient, to other members of the ring, and also to the loot.

Meanwhile, the romance was proceeding with the same speed as Hans's wooing of Sophie Beckendorf. He was in love with her, he was soon telling May Leukroth. He was a good actor, she told me; he actually had tears in his eyes as he swore that he loved her as he'd never loved anyone before. And he was eager to marry her, he said. But it was too embarrassing to explain why they would have to wait. It made him ashamed whenever he thought of it.

In rushing these romances with servant girls, Hans could be fairly sure of himself. In most homes these drudges were treated wretchedly, worked fourteen hours a day, and were given tiny rooms for their $10 to $15 a month. Any marriage at all seemed preferable to their miserable lot as servants.

But it was Lottie who made the important move, as she had with Sophie Beckendorf.

The next time she saw May, Lottie explained that her brother had lost everything he had in the world on the stock market. With a sympathetic sigh, May exclaimed, "If I only had some money . . ."

Lottie had a good suggestion of how she could help Hans. May's new employer had some valuable jewelry, didn't she? Why didn't May borrow it? Hans would then pawn it, use the money he got buying shares of a stock he'd been tipped was about to double in value. He would quickly sell the stock, and get the jewelry back so that May could replace it before her boss even noticed it was missing. The money Hans made on the stock would enable them to be married and get a home in the country.

"After that," Lottie said, "you'd never have to work again as a servant. Maybe, after a few years, you would be able to have a servant girl of your own to order around."

By that time we had picked up and questioned six additional servant girls who were members of the ring. Each of them met Hans at a different street corner, and handed him a package. We arrested the girls after he left them. It was almost time to bring him and Lottie in.

But we wanted to find out, if possible, whether he was using a fence. Such a receiver might lead us to a fortune in stolen goods.

I got some good jewelry and gave it to May to pass on to him. That afternoon I was with the shadow man who followed Hans when he left May. He walked to a jewelry store, and went in. He stayed there for fifteen minutes.

Right after he left the shadow man followed him, and I went into the shop. I tried to sell two rings to the man behind the counter.

He was suspicious, and said he didn't buy secondhand jewelry from friends, no less strangers.

"Stop kidding!" I told him. "If I didn't know you were okay, would I have come in here? And don't try to take advantage of me. I know just about what I should get for this stuff."

He remained unconvinced. "Who did you say sent you here?"

"I didn't say," I told him. "But that guy who was just in here told me you were okay."

"What guy?"

I described Hans and the jewelry May had given him. This was a long shot. But it worked.

"You don't deny you bought that jewelry from him, do you?"

"No," he said.

At that point I showed him my shield. It was easier going after that. I even got the badly shook-up jeweler to hand over the jewels he had just bought from Hans. I put them in an envelope, and sealed it. Such an envelope is called a "police stop." I brought this and the jeweler to the nearest station house, and got in touch with Detective Fay. We decided the time had come to arrest Hans and Lottie.

But when we got to their home we found that Sam Friedner, our shadow man, was in a frantic state.

A few minutes before, Hans and Lottie had come out of the house with a lot of luggage and got into a taxicab. There was not another cab in sight. Friedner had been unable to follow them.

But he'd got the cab's license number.

If we didn't move fast it seemed that the master thieves would make their getaway. But it isn't always possible to move fast. Sometimes it is not possible to move at all.

A call to Headquarters obtained for us the information that the cab driver was John Williams. We called the company that employed him. He worked out of Pennsylvania Station, we were told.

We hustled over there, and enlisted the help of the terminal's police. But Williams was not at his regular hack station, and did not show up there for more than two hours. Meanwhile we'd almost gone out of our wits. We had come so close, missed by so narrow a margin. It seemed certain that Williams had driven the fleeing couple out of the state. If he'd taken them to a railroad or some ship we might never locate them again. They'd be gone for good along with thousands of dollars' worth of valuables.

Williams finally drove up. He steadfastly denied that it was his cab that had taken the couple from the East Twenty-second Street house.

In the end, with the help of some tough talk from the Pennsylvania Station's private police chief, Williams admitted that he had been lying. He said, "That man gave me $25 tip and made me promise that I would not tell a soul where I'd taken them."

"And where did you take them?" I asked.

"To the Elsmere Hotel," he said.

"The one in the Bronx?" I asked. He nodded.

Sergeant Fay, John Allen, and myself all breathed a sigh of relief. Once checked in, it was likely that they'd remain there overnight or longer. But there was also the chance that they'd checked in just long enough for Williams to drop them and drive away, and then would take another cab, meaning that the second driver would have to be found.

So we got into Williams' cab and told him to get us up to the Elsmere fast. It was a third-rate hostelry, the sort that would be called a hot-pillow joint today.

The Elsmere was on a shabby street corner and had three floors. On the ground floor were a saloon, a back room with tables, a retail and wholesale liquor store. There were twenty rooms on the two upper floors. These were rented for an hour or a night, usually to happily unmarried couples, or to prostitutes and their customers.

Two weeks before a man had been killed at the bar. When the bartender, William Butler, saw us come in, he groaned. He knew Sergeant Fay, and feared no good could come of another visit by a policeman. In fact, he made no secret of the fact that he was sick of cops. He played deaf and dumb when Fay asked him about the couple who had checked in with a lot of luggage.

The sergeant was getting indignant when Louis Mondschein, who owned the hotel, walked into the barroom and asked what the trouble was.

When informed, he told Butler to take us to the room the couple were in. It was Room 9, on the second floor.

"Knock on the door," Fay told Butler, as we followed the bartender up the stairs. Mondschein wandered up after us.

When Butler rapped on the door, the man inside asked gruffly, "What do you want?"

"There's a leak downstairs," the bartender said. "I better check your pipes."

The door opened an inch or two, and I rushed in, followed by Allen and Fay. The couple had been getting ready for bed. Hans had his nightshirt on. Lottie was naked except for a short brassiere that covered only her breasts. She stepped behind the head of the bed as we rushed in.

Hans's clothes were lying on a chair next to the bed. Sergeant Fay started to search these for weapons. He found none. We told the pair to dress for the street. Out of curiosity, first Mondschein, then Butler drifted in.

That meant seven persons, six men and the woman, in that small bedroom. While dressing, Hans made a sudden move toward the pillow. Fay, Allen, and myself, thinking he was reaching for a gun, all jumped him at once. But it was his wallet that he'd placed there. Allen handed it to him, and Hans slipped it into his pocket.

The couple began talking quietly to each other in German. I

told them to cut it out. I also saw Hans tugging at two rings he was wearing, and ordered him to keep them on.

All of this time I had my hand on the gun in my pocket. Hans was about ready to start for the station house with us. But Lottie still had her dress to put on, and her coat. The dress was lying on a small bed table. She reached for it. But instead of the dress she came up with an automatic in her hand, and began firing.

Her first bullet hit me in the groin. Lottie deftly passed the revolver to Hans, who kept pumping bullets into us. I must have been hit a couple of more times in the next two seconds. I heard somebody near me scream. It was Mondschein. The room was turning blue with gun smoke.

Plucky John Allen jumped at Hans again. This time he got one arm around the gunman's neck and tried to reach for the weapon. Unfortunately, he did not make it, and grabbed only Hans's wrist. Quick as a flash, Hans turned the gun on him and shot once. Allen's grip loosened and he fell across the bed.

Now I had my gun out. But my hand was trembling. And Hans's next bullet caught me in the kneecap. I sank to the floor, still trying to aim, though I felt faint and dizzy.

Then I remembered something my father had told me twenty times — "If your hand is shaking, do not aim for the head. Aim for the bigger target, the chest."

And that's what I managed to do. Rising on one knee, I exchanged shot for shot. Hans hit me again and again. I heard Mondschein yell with pain. Hans also shot Sergeant Fay. But I managed to get Hans three times, the last time in the heart. As he fell, and his gun clattered to the floor, I looked around the room for Lottie. She seemed to be reaching for something under her dress, and came up with another automatic. I fired three times more. She fell to the floor. Neither she nor Hans moved after they went down.

I staggered out and started downstairs, followed by Fay and the two hotel men, all on their hands and knees. Allen apparently was unable to move. I knew I was terribly wounded. But I didn't know how many bullets had hit me or where. Somehow we managed the stairs with people who came rushing up to help us. They led us to chairs in the back room, told us ambulances were on the way, and a priest. Men went upstairs to see about Allen.

My chest felt wet. With quivering fingers I opened my shirt, and looked down. Blood was pouring out of the left side of my chest, directly over the heart. I looked down again. There was a pool of blood forming at my feet. It was dripping down my leg. I was sure I was going to die. But I got my shirt open again, and this time I saw that the bleeding on my chest had stopped. At least that's what I thought I saw.

The ambulance men seemed to take forever, but at last they arrived and carried us out. A grotesque thing happened just before Fay was taken out. His gun fell and exploded. The bullet narrowly missed hitting Father Wallace, the priest who was giving him the last rites. But I did not see that. I had passed out.

Only when I regained consciousness the next day did I learn the score. Hans and Lottie Vogel, supposedly man and wife, had died instantly. The doctors were unable to do anything for poor John Allen. He died the morning after the shooting. The two hotel men's wounds proved to be only superficial. But Fay and I remained on the critical list for almost a month. We were in the hospital for six weeks.

When I left, I still had six bullets in my body. The surgeons at the hospital told me I'd have a better chance to survive if no attempt was made to probe for them. Now, having enjoyed perfect health during the fifty years since, I am inclined to agree that they were right.

A few hours after the shooting Police Inspector Joseph Faurot went to see Hans and Lottie at The Morgue. He said that Hans was a Pole with a long record; his real name was Joseph Von Plaszynsky. Newspapermen had nicknamed him the crying thief some years before. Once, on being arraigned for larceny, the gentleman had won his freedom by producing a wife and four children in court. He said they would starve if he was in jail and unable to support them. Telling the story made Hans cry like a baby. On following him outside, reporters saw the notorious thief give money to the woman on the steps of the Criminal Courts Building. She thanked him and then left with the four little ones. She had rented them and herself to him for his performance in Court. Hans joined an attractive young woman who had been watching the little drama.

The smiling woman, Inspector Faurot believed, was Lottie, Vogel's real wife, who now lay on the next slab to his at The Morgue.

Sophie Beckendorf told a lot more about her relations with the

Vogels on hearing that they were dead. She changed her story and said she had met Lottie a year and a half before, when she went to work as a maid with a family named Schwarzchild. Lottie was the cook there, and after she introduced the girl to Hans, she told Sophie: "You are a fool to work so hard washing floors and doing other dirty work. All you need do is steal enough to get Hans started in his own business so he can marry you."

The references Lottie wrote for Sophie at the beginning were fictitious. "If the new boss asks how to get in touch with the old boss, say that the whole family is traveling in Europe, and can't be reached for some time."

Lottie also inserted ads on Sophie's behalf in the matrimonial newspapers then published. These described the younger woman as "a young widow who wishes to get acquainted with an aged man, a widower preferred."

As far as I ever learned, no old men fell for this bait.

Sophie now admitted committing larcenies in four different homes. Once she brought the jewelry from one of these jobs to Lottie, and was told, "We can't get much for this junk. Get better stuff for us next time."

Sophie kept insisting that she'd never kept a bit of the jewelry she stole or was given a cent of the proceeds by the Vogels. By an odd coincidence she was indicted on November 18th, the same day that the man-and-wife team died in the gun battle at the Elsmere.

Apparently none of the six other girls was given one penny for turning crooked. I still believe it possible that Hans exerted some hypnotic influence over them, for none of them had ever stolen a thing before they met him. And I never heard of any of them getting into trouble later on.

Sophie was sent to prison for eighteen months. The six other young women servants were either given short terms in the Workhouse or placed on probation.

No less than $15,000 worth of jewels and clothing were found in the Vogels' luggage. But the big discovery came when safe-deposit boxes Vogel had rented were opened by the authorities. Keys to these had been found in the master thief's pocket. All told, something more than $60,000 worth of stolen property was recovered.

The insurance companies were pleased.

So was I — once I got out of the hospital.

A BORN DETECTIVE 2

IT WAS in 1906, when I was twenty-one, that I got my license to work as a private detective in New York State. At the beginning, I took every sort of legitimate case I could get, except divorce jobs. Bernard S. Deutsch, who later became a leading city official in the La Guardia Administration, kindly let me use his office until I was able to open my own a year later.

I was not a private detective long when another lawyer asked me to recover the diamond stickpin, gold watch and chain, and $20 in cash that one of his clients, a Mr. Thompson, had been robbed of in a Raines Law hotel.

This was in the red-light district in East Harlem, which was located just south of the Little Italy where I grew up. It could be described as a sort of uptown Tenderloin. Crime was rampant there, and murder commonplace. Both sides of Second and Third avenues, the main boulevards of the area, were lined with brothels, gambling houses, saloons, and these Raines Law hotels. The hotels were given that name in honor of New York State Senator Raines, who in the nineties had fathered a law which he naïvely hoped would reduce Sunday drinking. The law stipulated that only hotels that served food could sell beer and whiskey on the Lord's Day. The saloonkeepers, intent on not losing their profitable Sunday trade, promptly circumvented his law by converting their establishments into hotels. They did this by putting beds in all rooms on their upper floors and offering them for rent by the day, week, month, or hour, the chief takers being prostitutes and their customers.

Those barkeeps who served no food placed a tiny cheese sandwich on each table. These were never replaced, and in time got so hard that even mice and the hungriest of bums were never tempted to touch them.

Mr. Thompson explained to me that he had been accosted on Second Avenue the night before by a streetwalker whom I recognized from his description as Big Mame, a blowsy old-timer in the business. While he was in bed with her his money and jewelry disappeared.

That mystified Mr. Thompson, though anybody in the district could have told him he had been pillaged by a panel thief. I had him go down to Second Avenue with me and point out the woman. It was Big Mame, all right. It figured. Her pimp, Joe Spaghetti, had worked the panel end of the deal. He had done two stretches already for petty larceny.

This old-fashioned type of thievery was simplicity itself. The victim is taken by the streetwalker into a room where there is only a bed and one chair to put his clothes on. While they are in bed, a wall panel slides open. The hand of a man — in this case Mr. Spaghetti's — reaches in and goes through the man's pockets.

Few victims ever complain even to their lawyers after being robbed in this compromising and ludicrous manner. Mr. Thompson was an exception. That evening I bade him good night, but promised him nothing except that I would let him know if I got his property back for him. After he turned the corner, I caught up with Big Mame and bawled her out for stealing from a client of mine.

"I didn't take nothing from him. Two dollars was all the cheapskate slipped me," she said.

"You kept him too busy to notice Joe Spaghetti reaching through the hole in the wall for his pants."

"Joe didn't have nothin' to do with it," she said. Big Mame looked terrified, something that didn't move me deeply. Prostitutes are all the same. Any threat to the happiness of the pimps they adore frightens them to death.

"Let's not waste time," I told her. "Just find Joe. Tell him that Jerry Luisi wants the watch, the stickpin, and the $20 he stole last night from my client. I'll wait for just ten minutes." I glanced at the saloon on the nearest corner. "Tell him I'll wait for him there, in Barney's."

Mame hustled off to find Joe. While waiting, I used Barney's toilet. I expected no trouble. Invariably pimps are brave only when they are chastising and bullying the pitiful women whose earnings support them. But like Mr. Thompson, Joe Spaghetti proved an exception to the general rule.

When I came out of the toilet I found this repulsive little man waiting for me. He was scowling and there was blood in his eye.

"What's the idear of telling Big Mame you're gonna t'row me in the can?" he asked. I started to explain what I'd really said. But before I could say anything he came up with a gun.

"I'm gonna put a slug in you right now," he told me. And he sounded as though he really meant it.

"You'll get two bullets from me for every one of yours," I told him. The thought of anyone in his trade threatening me infuriated me. I guess that was what made my nose bleed just at that moment. When I felt the blood trickling over my mouth, I touched my lip, and with astonishment looked at the blood on my finger.

He was watching me closely.

"Jesus!" I said, and reached for my back pocket. He thought, of course, that I was getting out my handkerchief. But I pulled out my gun instead. When that little pimp of a sneak thief saw the revolver in my hand, he was all through. It was child's play to take away his gun.

"Now, Joe," I told him, "your ten minutes are up. Have you got that jewelry and dough on you?"

"Of course not," he said. "I didn't have no intention of giving it up."

"Well, get going. I want it," I told Joe Spaghetti. "This time you got five minutes."

He was back in five minutes, and turned over to me the watch and chain, stickpin, and $20. He left without a word, and I followed him out.

Big Mame, always a hard-luck gal, had the misfortune to come along just at that moment. When Joe Spaghetti saw her he lost his temper, and slapped her savagely across the face.

"What's the idea, you fat old whore, of making trouble for me with Mr. Luisi?" he demanded. "He wasn't gonna t'row me in the can at all." Poor Mame started blubbering and sobbing. As Joe led her away, he kept snarling at her: "Fat old bum. I don't know why I keep you in my stable."

As I watched them move on, it never occurred to me that another man might have been afraid even of a contemptible little rat like Joe Spaghetti — with a gun in his hand. In those days, as I remember it, I was not afraid of anything, including the biggest of them, the toughest and trickiest.

One reason, I guess, was that I'd grown up in a junglelike part of the city where every day you had to expect anything and everything: a challenge to fight the biggest boy on the block, a trap by a half-dozen members of an enemy gang.

Another reason was the inordinate pride I took in being my father's son. Long before I was born he had been a secret agent of the Italian police. I wanted to be the kind of man he was.

*

My father, Raffael Luisi, was born in St. Angelo le Fratte, a small town in the province of Potenza, in southern Italy. Our name originally was Luis. In the eighteenth century his great-grandfather, Monsieur Francis Luis, a French soldier, had fallen in love with Italy. This French ancestor of mine married an Italian girl, settled there, and never left. In time Luis became Luisi.

My father, as a sixteen-year-old student at the University of Naples, joined the forces of Garibaldi, the great Italian patriot whose dream it was to unite all Italy. His older brother, my uncle Giuseppe, joined Garibaldi's opponents, and they fought on opposing sides during the fight for control of St. Angelo le Fratte.

Suddenly, in this battle the two brothers, who had always been inseparable companions until then, found themselves facing each other. Giuseppe raised his gun. So did my father. But neither was able to shoot. With wild brawling going on all around them, they just stood there, staring at each other, and feeling foolish. Finally, my father turned his weapon around and slammed Giuseppe over the head with the butt, knocking him to the ground unconscious. That was the last he saw of his brother during the battle. When it was over, he went looking for Giuseppe. Unable to find him, he supposed that his brother's comrades had dragged him to some safe place.

My father went home. His parents, my grandfather and grandmother Luisi, were dead, and he and my uncle lived with their married sister. But Giuseppe did not come home that night, or the next. When the fighting was over, my father and his friends searched everywhere for Giuseppe for weeks, but without result. They could conclude only that Giuseppe had died from the blow and that his comrades, swearing themselves to secrecy, had buried him.

But the story turned out to have a surprise ending. Thirty-five years later, long after my father brought his family to New York, he got a letter from Giuseppe. It told how my uncle had escaped. Fearing arrest, Giuseppe had gone to sea, and shipped out to South America, where he settled in Brazil, married and prospered. He had six daughters now, all beautiful.

My father went back to the university to complete his studies, then became one of Garibaldi's confidential aides. Later he served in the same capacity for many years for King Humberto.

He became a great hero to all Neapolitans in his early twenties — this by a single heroic feat. One day my father was in the Silvio Spaventa prison in Naples on official business. While in the office of the commandant he heard shouts of "Stop the murderers! They will escape!" coming up from the dungeons below.

My father seized a saber from the wall and rushed to the head of the stairs up which the convicts had to come to get out. There turned out to be more than a dozen of them, all brigands. Some of them had already been tried and condemned to death or life imprisonment. Others were awaiting trial. They were all desperate men ready to face death for the chance of escape. They had either fashioned stilettos for themselves or had had them smuggled in.

And there my father stood, all alone, like an Italian D'Artagnan, determined to stop them, and hacking, slashing, and stabbing away until the carabinieri and turnkeys were able to come to his assistance. By that time three brigands lay dead at his feet and a half-dozen of the others were severely wounded. It was not too difficult to disarm the rest and herd them back into their dungeons. My father was not lucky enough to escape all the stilettos. There were wounds on both arms, and two more on his chest.

This happened soon after he married my mother, Sylvina Altiere, of Muro Lucano, a small town built on the side of a mountain and situated about fifty miles from St. Angelo le Fratte. He had gone there on secret government business, met, fell in love with, and married my mother.

He was away from home a great deal, and they lived with her mother. All of their four children, my brother, two sisters, and I, their youngest, were born in our Grandmother Altiere's hillside home. My birth date was April 5, 1884. The Altieres had lived on that hill for centuries. And like all second sons of Muro Lucano families, I was named Gerardo in honor of the local saint.

We emigrated to America when I was only four, so I remember almost nothing about my birthplace. In New York my father went into the business of importing Italian cheeses, salami, wine, and olive oil. A prudent man, he had come here alone to investigate possibilities. After six months, he was convinced he could do well and brought us to this country.

This was in 1888, when the flood of immigrants from Europe was rising to its fantastic crest. The Germans, the Irish, and the Scandinavians had preceded us; now it was the turn of the Italians, the Polish and Russian Jews, the Austrians, and the Hungarians. New York was becoming the great melting pot, the most cosmopolitan city the world has ever known. In 1890 the United States census figures revealed that New York had half as many Italians as Naples, as many Germans as Hamburg, twice as many Irishmen as Dublin, and two and a half times as many Jews as Warsaw.

As we all know, the oppressed, the weary, and the underprivileged brought with them their enormous energies, ambitions, and the sweetest of all dreams, the one of freedom. Unfortunately, many of them also brought from the Old World their feuds and their prejudices, their fears and age-old superstitions.

Immigrants from different lands, once here, moved as close as they could get to the countrymen who had preceded them. They wanted to hear their own language spoken, to eat food, and see faces and furniture that would help them forget they were thousands of miles away from the Old Country.

But of all these strangers from far away, huddled together, none felt so lost in America, where they'd heard everyone was rich and walked on streets paved with gold, as did my own people. The Italians, for one thing, had a double language difficulty. In addition to not understanding English, they were unable to understand one another. This was because the dialects spoken in the various parts of Italy differ so greatly that they are incomprehensible to most other Italians.

So it was that one could find, in New York's many Little Italys people who came from the same province living in every flat of a tenement. If they all were from the same town, they liked it even better.

We, whose first American home was in East Harlem's Little Italy, moved into a house in which all of the other tenants came from Potenza, including quite a few old friends and neighbors from Muro Lucano!

The tenement was on East 110th Street. Its apartments were called railroad flats because of the long hall from which you entered each of the three bedrooms, the front parlor, and the kitchen, which was in the rear.

None of us called that tenement a walkup because we did not know there were houses that had elevators. It was also a walkout. It had no indoor toilets. We all used outhouses which were in the backyard. Our flat was heated by two stoves, one in the kitchen and a handsome, big-bellied affair in the parlor.

Like many another old fellow who grew up on the streets of New York I remember my childhood as pure paradise. Except, of course, for the hours I had to be in school.

When the day came for me to start my education, my mother, a devout Catholic, brought me to the parochial school in the neighborhood. I came running back home that day, wailing, in Italian, "I can't go to that school. They don't speak any Italian there."

Next day I was taken to the public school in our neighborhood. The teachers there used the children who had been in the country longer as interpreters. But I quickly learned enough English to communicate with the teachers person to person.

There was always excitement on the streets of our colorful Little Italy, new adventures each day, and danger — what normal excitement-eater of a boy could ask for anything more?

The greatest glory of our street was its horsecar line that ran crosstown to the banks of the Hudson River and terminated on the corner nearest us. On finishing a trip the driver and conductor would retire for a drink of beer before starting back on the return trip. Meanwhile we boys were really living it up, chasing one another through the car, pulling on the signal cord, and doing everything else short of overturning the rickety vehicle.

And my real education as a boy was acquired on those colorful streets of Little Italy, always jammed with pushcarts with fruits and clothes piled high upon them, and jabbering housewives haggling with the peddlers over prices of the meat, produce, and vegetables. In and around them we kids played marbles, tops, hide-and-seek, cops and robbers, three ol' cat. The bad boys of Little Italy raided the pushcarts, and stole everything they could pry loose from the large houses in which lived the well-to-do members of old Bronx families. They stole brass doorknobs, and brass plates from the letterboxes. When the family was away they got into the cellar and stole copper wire and sections of pipe, and sold them for a few cents to junk dealers.

Less than a mile north of us was the awesome "Murder Stable." According to Herbert Asbury, author of *Gangs of New York,* this was "the scene of more killings than any other spot in America with the exception of the Bloody Angle of Doyers Street, in Chinatown." And just south of our Little Italy there was constant warfare between the Red Peppers and the Duffy Hills, marked by more violence and many gang murders.

We fought with each other and, in kid gangs, with the gangs from the other blocks. The big street wars, however, were those we waged constantly with the freckle-faced Irish Micks and the Dutchmen, as Germans were derisively called at the time, who lived on the streets that surrounded our Little Italy.

They were tough kids, those Micks and Dutchies, but we liked to think we were tougher. One of the streets in our Little Italy was called "Murder Row," and the day that there was not at least one killing on that block, the police of the Old Fourth Ward regarded as a holiday.

The bad boys of Little Italy tormented and taunted the police, threw snowballs at them in winter, and sometimes dropped cans on them from rooftops in the summer.

I was one of the good boys, something which was not due to nobility of character but to my parents' vigilance. They had no intention of letting me and my brother turn into daring little hoodlums. And when they were unable to keep an eye on us, those of our neighbors who had similar ideas about their own youngsters functioned as their espionage agents, reported our misdemeanors, and the bad company we were keeping. My parents did the same service for them. At times I found this system quite irksome.

I will never forget the day a gang of these tough little guttersnipes challenged me to throw a potato at a young patrolman. He was on the other side of the street.

Eager to impress them, I took the stolen potato one of them pulled out of his blouse and heaved it at the cop. He turned just as I was throwing it, and the potato hit him right on the neck.

It was only then that I thought of what my mother, father, and the cop would do to me for that. The other boys ducked into a cellar as he started across the street. But I stood there in a state of complete paralysis. Many a time I had seen policemen grabbing boys by the neck and slapping them with mighty whacks for doing much less.

But this young cop had a puzzled look on his face as he came up. Instead of slamming me around, he asked me in a quiet voice why I had thrown the potato at him. I explained that the other boys had dared me to.

To my amazement he did not even threaten to tell my parents. Instead he lectured me on how wrong it was to do such things. I burst into tears, I suppose out of relief and gratitude. If he had told my mother and father they would have walloped the life out of me.

Eighteen years later I was down at Police Headquarters discussing a blackmailing case with Deputy Commissioner George S. Dougherty when the same policeman, now a captain, walked in. The commissioner began to introduce me when I stopped him.

"I have met the captain," I said, asking him; "Don't you remember me? It was while you were attached to the East 104th Street precinct. You lectured me about hitting cops with potatoes."

"You are the little guinea who hit me that day in the back of the neck?" he asked. "When I walked over I couldn't make up my mind what to do — then I saw how scared you looked. You were too scared even to run."

I agreed but explained, "I was far more scared of what my parents would do to me than of you, the young cop."

As in all Italian families of that generation, my father was head of the house and the supreme ruler. We, his four children, never questioned his right to make all the decisions for us until we became twenty-one.

Though also acknowledging his authority and when necessary bowing to it, my mother was a stern, domineering woman, very quick and generous with her slaps. Even when I was fifty years old she thought she still had the right to slap me. Sylvina Altiere Luisi's temper was of such a volcanic character that often when she exploded Father would smilingly shrug, put on his hat and leave, returning only when he thought the storm was over.

One of the brightest of my memories is of the music that constantly filled the street of our Little Italy. Singing in the flats, the barbershops, the cobblers' stores, the wineshops. Singing to the accompaniment of mandolins, guitars, harmonicas. Couples would sing old Neapolitan lovesongs for pennies in the backyards in good weather, Christmas carols during the holiday season.

And there always seemed to be hurdy-gurdys in the streets. Our sisters danced to this music. We would have liked to, but we were afraid we'd seem like sissies. Hurdy-gurdys, yes, and organ grinders, some with monkeys who begged for pennies and tipped their hats politely on getting one. And what New York street boy ever forgot the hokeypokey man selling his small mounds of ice doused with juices that were every color of the rainbow?

The holidays were the days I recall with the greatest emotion. Then we felt closer to one another than at any other time. Each year I could feel love gathering all around me as Easter and Christmas and the New Year's approached. My mother and sisters began their preparations weeks in advance. They started their work by getting on their knees and scrubbing the floors, walls, every corner of the house, until it was spotless and shining.

Whole days were spent by my mother just in the preparing of all sorts of pastries for these great occasions. These would be stuffed with eggs, salami, or cheese. Eels were served on Christmas Eve, and huge platters of spaghetti covered with my mother's homemade sauce. On the other great holy days the evening meal began at five o'clock with the serving of antipasto imported from Italy, and ended only at midnight with the table covered with great bowls of fruits, figs, nuts, and candies.

There was one day in the year when peace reigned throughout Harlem's Little Italy. That was July 16th, on which the Feast of the Lady of Mount Carmel was held. Then we would all parade the streets, behind bands, proudly carrying huge lighted candles, floats on which stood sacred statues and on which money was pinned by the pious and impious alike.

It was *the* gay day, observed by much feasting. At the stands on the sidewalks souvenirs of all kinds were sold, mostly religious. Pushcarts were out by the score, and from their vendors you could buy Italian sausages, both hot and sweet, garnished with onions and green peppers, red peppers, garlic — according to your taste. Some of the woman cooked great pizzas in their basements, and the good Italian wine flowed for all on that day as it did for the rich ones on other days. You could buy hot chestnuts, and figs that hung on strings from the top of the stands.

The mobsters lay aside their stilettos, their guns, and their grudges. The day before there might have been a murder, but the victim's friends would wait until the day after for revenge.

My father would get out his accordion at holiday time and play tunes that my sisters would sing. Relatives would visit us, and partake of the wine and cakes and Italian coffee that were always on hand. We would play lotto and dominoes.

When the weather was fair most of the men in the neighborhood would play boccie in a backyard or empty lot. I do not recall my father ever playing boccie or cards. He was on friendly terms with the other men, and I know they respected him. They never addressed him as Raffael. It was always Signor Luisi. He never drank more than one or two glasses of wine, even during holidays or weddings.

He taught me to swim in a floating swimming pool that was moored in the East River at the foot of our street. We all lived a simple, happy life. Our recreations were simple too, consisting of excursion boat rides, trips to Central Park, to Fort George with its shooting galleries, merry-go-rounds, and other delights.

We, foreigners in a strange new land, never felt like aliens, never felt alone. Our life centered around the family; we knew nothing more in those days, and wanted nothing more.

Not that it all remained perfect.

It was one thing for our parents to choose the boys we could play with when we were young. But when we were a little older our mothers selected the girls we could go out with, or tried to.

My mother certainly tried to pick out a wife for me. She, like so many other Italians of her generation, was very old-fashioned. If a girl in Little Italy went out with a boy without a chaperon and he did not marry her, the neighbors immediately branded her as a whore. On hearing my mother talk like that, I asked her more than once, "What makes Rose a whore?"

"She goes out with boys who don't marry her."

My mother never stopped trying to choose a wife for me. I am afraid that looks and intelligence and the usual virtues, aside from virginity, counted for little with her. What she wanted was a frightened little mouse who would not demand a home of her own, but who would do the washing, scrub floors, and cook under her matriarchal rule.

For here, as in Hell's Kitchen, the East Side Ghetto, over in Irishtown and on Sands Street, Brooklyn, and in all the other slums around the town, an incredible mixture of humanity was boiling up and bubbling. For if we had our thugs and extortionists and our killers, we also had boys growing up in the same dreary, filthy houses with them who became great business executives, outstanding lawyers and judges, doctors of great skill. And here is a mystery for the sociologists to solve. Why didn't we all turn out badly, brought up as we were, amid poverty and neighbors hopeless enough to break your heart?

Some of these slum boys who became such useful and important citizens had brothers who died in prison or in the electric chair. I can't answer the riddle as far as they are concerned. But I do know why I, my brother, and many of the other boys we played with as children were able to live decent, honest lives when we grew up.

For whatever we achieved we could thank our parents. Consider my own mother and father. My mother was a terror for discipline, quick-tempered and as quick to punish. My father left the punishing to her, but his behavior and bearing made us all proud of him and eager to win his approbation.

When my father felt he had mastered English, he quit the importing business and went into the real-estate business. We moved to a home on Fifth Avenue, the same Fifth Avenue where Frick, Andrew Carnegie, and steel and copper and oil kings were building their mansions, and trying to create a new American society. But we were at the other end of it, on unfashionable Upper Fifth Avenue, at 111th Street, a block north of Central Park.

On leaving high school I worked for my father. When I was eighteen I told him I didn't care for the real-estate business, but wished to become a detective. That day he began training me for the career I never afterward left or wanted to leave. He taught me how to care for and handle weapons. My shooting lessons took place at an amusement park on the Upper West Side. They had .22

rifles and .22 revolvers there, and after a while I became a crack shot. There were many lessons in throwing the stiletto. These did not end until I was able seven out of ten times to hit a postage stamp up to a distance of twenty feet.

He showed me how to twist the stiletto after stabbing a man if it was necessary to inflict greater injury.

My father taught me how to use a sword cane for self-defense. He gave me his when he was satisfied with the way I handled it. He taught me the hundred devices one needs to master to be a good shadow man. He tutored me in undercover work, investigation of all sorts of crimes, how to detect telltale signs of guilt in the faces, gestures, and other movements of suspects.

"Never bully a thief," he told me again and again. "Never lie to crooks. Never threaten one. At the same time, never make them any false promises. Never promise them anything that you are not sure you can deliver. Keep smiling, be friendly.

"Be kind to them. Treat them as though they were human beings, not just crooks. While questioning them, ask them often, 'Do you want a drink of water? Do you want to go to the toilet?' Offer them cigarettes, cigars. Get them coffee, sandwiches if they are hungry.

"But they must never suspect that you are soft-soaping them. On the other hand, never let them suspect that you are trying to outwit them. Do not accuse them of lying unless you feel they are and are asking them direct questions, such as 'Did you steal this?' or 'Did you murder this man?' And then only when there is nothing else left for you to do.

"Never draw your revolver unless it is necessary or because your life is endangered. But when you do shoot, shoot to kill. If you notice that under the tension your hand is shaking, do not aim for the man's head, but for his chest. That gives you a larger target, one you are less likely to miss."

And it was this last bit of advice that had made the difference between life and death in that Bronx hotel room. He lectured me often that fear was only mental, and managed to convince me of it. This, keeping the fear out of my eyes and hands, may have saved me from being shot by Joe Spaghetti and many another nervous gunman.

He told me, "Never, under any circumstances, let anyone interrupt you when you are examining a criminal."

I thought of that sage bit of advice one day many years later while I was questioning a thief, and had him ready to break. We'd been at it for hours, since I got to the office that morning. Then, my secretary who was taking notes, stopped, turned to me, and said: "Mr. Luisi, will you excuse me? I have an appointment for lunch." It took me five hours after that to get him back to where I was when she remembered her appointment. I did more than excuse her. I fired her at the end of the week.

There was one more thing he said that proved not always possible to manage: "Don't let anyone else question a suspect during your examination, except by prearrangement."

The police, of course, often think of a few questions they wish to ask whether you have finished your own quiz session or not.

After getting my license in 1906 I spent four years as a free lance. In addition to my other jobs during that period I organized the International Detective Agency, and for good measure the National Secret Service Bureau and Information Service, Inc.

The latter I established when I had a request for twenty night watchmen to patrol sections of Staten Island. This was the most sparsely populated part of the city. There were not enough policemen there, a large group of homeowners felt, to protect their property and there had been too many house burglaries. My twenty men were uniformed, and worked with the consent of the police officials. After my night watchmen appeared the number of burglaries dropped sharply.

At this time the New York police were having their hands full trying to cope with the criminals and ex-convicts who recently had arrived from Italy. Many of these were or had been members of either the Mafia, the Sicilian secret society, or the Camorra, the one Neapolitans belonged to. Many of these criminals were in the country illegally, having jumped ship. Though actually, until the end of the first decade of this century there were few restrictions placed on immigration. Not until 1910 did an amendment to the Immigration Act of 1907 forbid the admission of criminals, paupers, diseased persons, and anarchists.

In Italy the law had not been able to protect poor, hard-working ignorant Italians. They couldn't believe that in their new country, whose language they could not understand, they would be protected either. Italian pushcart peddlers were afraid to complain when these menacing fellow-countrymen of theirs shook them down. One reason so many murders and other violent crimes remained unsolved in the Little Italys was that no witnesses could be induced to talk. They feared the police less than the gangsters who had followed them to New York and "signed" their threatening letters with a hand outlined in black ink.

It was in the turn of the century years that newspapers first began to publish stories saying that the Mafia — or the Black Hand as it was then called — had established an international organization. The headquarters of this underworld empire was in Sicily and it had branches in many cities in the United States. There were Italian-born policemen on the New York force, but not enough to cope with these criminals who kept getting bolder. Italian gangs here were believed to be circulating counterfeit American currency. Much of it was said to be manufactured in Italy, and shipped here in the false bottoms of cans of olive oil and other food products. More of the currency was reported being turned out in the so-called Murder Stable not far north of our Little Italy, and in cellars on the East Side.

One of the most notorious of these Italian-American criminals was Ignazio Lupo, alias Lupo the Wolf, counterfeiter and mob leader who would rent out his thugs and terrorists and murderers to other Italian secret societies for rather modest fees. William J. Flynn, Chief of the United States Secret Service, traced no less than sixty murders to Lupo's gang.

By 1902 Lupo's gangsters, among others, became even more daring and savage. They threw bombs, and continued to counterfeit money. They put the men they tortured and murdered in boxes, sacks, and barrels and sometimes shipped them out of town. They slit the tongues of those they suspected of talking too much. This served both as a trademark and as a warning to others.

Members of the gang themselves were not immune. The eighteen-year-old stepson of Giuseppe Morello, Lupo's most trusted aide, had his tongue slit, and was tortured and murdered for gossiping about gang secrets.

On April 12, 1903, Lupo's villainous mob committed a particularly atrocious murder. This time they wanted the body to be found where they left it on the East Side. Detective-Sergeant Joseph Petrosino, the Police Department's most efficient, most feared and toughest Italian-American cop, was among those assigned to the investigation. Deputy Inspector Arthur A. Carey in his memoirs described the crime in these words:

The man's body had been jammed into the barrel over the top of which had been thrown an overcoat. Around his throat, tightly wound, was a coarse burlap sack of foreign manufacture. The dead man was young and fairly well dressed. His left hand and right leg protruded from the barrel, making it obvious that his murderers had intended that the body should be discovered so that it might be a warning to others.

The body was still warm. The head was almost severed by an ugly wound running from ear to ear. A razor-sharp knife had been used. A watch chain dangled from his vest; the watch was gone. Both ears had been pierced for earrings, the mark of a native of Sicily. In one of his pockets I found a crumpled note in the handwriting of a woman. Petrosino translated it:

"Come in a hurry. You understand that it is most urgent."
It was unsigned.

The victim turned out to be Benedetto Madonia, recently a member of Lupo's gang.

Carey, with the help of Petrosino and other Italian-American detectives, solved the crime. They arrested Lupo the Wolf, Petto the Ox, and other criminals. But when brought to court their witnesses repudiated the statements they'd made previously. The Black Hand had been able to get to them and frighten them into silence.

The Wolf was later convicted of counterfeiting, and sentenced to a federal prison for thirty years. But the murders and extortions in the city's Little Italys continued.

Slowly the fear of Black Hand kidnappers and killers and shakedown men spread from the Italian colonies to other people living in cities and towns where one or more "Little Italys" had been established.

Some daily newspapers began running articles in which the impression was given that all Italians were criminals. People began worrying about patronizing Italian barbers and cobblers, and imagined that Sicilian ditchdiggers were capable of kidnapping children, bombing their homes, and other acts of viciousness.

The anti-Italian feeling probably reached its peak after Petrosino, now a Lieutenant of Detectives and head of the Italian Squad, was murdered in Palermo, Sicily, early in 1908. Police Commissioner Theodore H. Bingham had sent him there to get information about the records of criminals who were in America, continuing their careers.

I knew and admired Petrosino, and had warned him of the danger of a man like him, whose face was well known, venturing alone into the Italian island; so many of the men he had helped deport were waiting for a chance to revenge themselves.

"Ask the commissioner to send another man with you. At least you'll have some protection in Sicily."

But Commissioner Bingham refused the request, whether this was to avoid the extra expense or for some other reason, I never learned. In any event, Petrosino was killed one night as he was crossing the public square in Palermo. The crime, which never was solved, caused a sensation all over the world. Congress sent a committee to investigate. They reported that a Palermo police official was asked how he managed to have so few crimes in his own city.

"Why, sir," he answered, "our criminals have all gone to America."

Italian-Americans, without quite knowing what to do about it, had been outraged by editorials in the English-language newspapers that either hinted or said outright that Italians were a "criminal race." They were also puzzled by the endlessly repeated story that the Mafia was an international organization.

One day a group of fifty prominent Italian-Americans asked me to find out whether any such international organization existed, or if there was in the United States a national Mafia, whose Black Hand gangs operated in different cities. If so, they wanted me to see what could be done about stamping it out.

When I accepted the assignment, I told them I did not believe there was an international Mafia. The investigation, financed by these fifty men, permitted me to hire as many aides as I considered necessary. I used only Italian-born investigators. Some of them had been carabinieri in the old country.

I began my investigation by sending out an appeal to Italian-Americans living all over the country for cooperation. Any of them who received a threatening letter from a member of the Black Hand or other secret societies was asked to send it on to me. I promised that if they did this, they would be protected from the extortionists. But I emphasized that they should mention to no one that they had passed on the letters to me.

In the next few days I got no less than eight threatening letters myself. All contained death threats. All were written in Italian. Judging from the handwriting the authors had the same difficulty a nine-year-old child does in forming letters. But I did not hold the threats lightly. Here is an excerpt from one of the letters:

> Don't you want to stop? You are being watched night and day. Stop hunting blackhand men with your detectives. This is the second letter. Don't go where you have been! Watch! You will die! Take up some other business.

This letter, and most of the others, instead of a black hand, had a crudely drawn picture of a coffin at the top, and at the bottom a crossbones and skull and a revolver.

I won't pretend that I was not impressed. I knew that these writers would kill me and everyone working with me whenever they got the chance. They were savage, half-civilized creatures, and not the less dangerous because they sincerely believed that they were entitled by long-established custom to extort money from their fellow Italians. They would not hesitate a moment before murdering me any more than they had in Petrosino's case.

Almost as disturbing as the letters was the amount of confusion about my motives and role there was among some ordinary everyday Italians. These men seemed to be convinced that I, not the Black Hand, was making the trouble. I got a good hint of this kind of thinking the day I ventured into an East Side barbershop. The barber, while shaving my throat, talked in Italian to the fellow presiding over the next chair:

"That fella, the detective, will drive us all crazy, making fuss, making trouble. I would like just one chance to shave him. I would cut his throat."

And he gestured by drawing the blade of his open razor from one of my ears to the other, narrowly missing my throat. Needless to say, I never let him shave me again, nor did I stop there for a few moments to begin his education on the subject of my investigation of the Black Hand menace.

After I had worked for some time in New York, a group of Italian-American businessmen in Pittsburgh asked me to conduct an investigation there and in the mining towns nearby where there were many poor Italians being preyed upon. I also conducted an investigation in and around Erie, where there had also been much of the same sort of extortion.

The families threatened were all but scared out of their wits. The letters they had received contained threats to kidnap their children and disfigure, cripple, or murder them and their wives, slitting their tongues if they went to the police.

But I was able to induce many of them to tell their stories of having been forced to pay tribute to these monstrous goons. I did it by doing some of the things my father had taught me. I began with the advantage of being able to speak their own language. Having grown up in a Little Italy, I knew enough of all the different dialects to get by. Before approaching such a family I would find out what part of Sicily or southern Italy they came from. I would read everything I could find about their native town and province. When I talked to them I sounded as though I had been born there myself.

I told them how homesick I was for Italy, the sunny land where we were born. It would mean so much to me, I said, to have a plate of homemade spaghetti or, better still, *pasta e fagioli*. Soon I was eating a dinner with these sad, good, harassed people, and enjoying a glass of wine with them.

In almost every city — Cleveland, Pittsburgh, Erie — and mining town I went, as in New York, I gave the local police information that enabled them to arrest some of the human vultures who had been terrorizing these hard-working families of immigrants, as well as wealthy Italian-Americans.

But always, when the chips were down, when my friends the informants had to face their enemies, they faltered, recanted, and were too frightened to testify. They were afraid, and who could really blame them? These people had been peasants in Italy, underfed, exploited, always hungry. They had never gone to school. They were superstitious, believed that they could be bedeviled and destroyed by the power of the evil eye. They did not believe, I repeat, that the forces of law and order in the United States could protect them from evil. The same forces in their native land had never done so.

But even for a man like me who understood the problem, it was a maddening and frustrating experience.

And a curious thing happened to me while I was making that investigation. When I began it, as I mentioned, I did not believe that there was a national Black Hand or Mafia organization in the United States, or an international one outside Italy.

However, as weeks and months passed, I became far less sure. At one time I became fully convinced that there was a nationwide Black Hand organization in this country.

Every community where there was a Little Italy or Italian-Americans with substantial incomes also harbored parasitical groups, extortionists, writers of blood-chilling letters who were capable of carrying out their threats.

They used the same methods in every case.

Nevertheless, before I finished my work — the job occupied me for more than a year — I reverted to my original theory that there was no national or international underworld empire, only separate gangsters in each town, working independently. (In more recent years such eminent journalists as Herbert Asbury and *Life* magazine's Herbert Brean arrived at the same conclusion about the Mafia men of the present day.)

The fifty men who had sponsored the investigation were pleased to hear this, but disappointed when the men arrested on the evidence I and my assistants had gathered were released.

The fight went on, and still goes on.

And there was a tragic aftermath to my investigation. Among my Staten Island night watchmen were several who had been carabinieri in Naples or Sicily before coming to the United States. They and some of the others had helped me in my investigations of Italian counterfeiting rings in Harlem and elsewhere in the city.

One of the hardest-working of these men was Thomas Maresca, who was in his early twenties. He lived in Brooklyn, and had received almost as many threats from members of Italian gangs as I had. One of these read:

Dear Friend Thomas Maresca,
 Kindly don't do what you have done. Stop chasing us; you're always going after the poor laborers. You are always watched. This is the second letter. You will suffer and your life is sweet. You and your friend Gerard must stop!
Stop or otherwise you will go to paradise.
What nice wine — red, RED.
                                    The Seven Brothers of Brooklyn

This was a counterfeiting mob, and seven little scraps had been torn from the top, bottom, and sides of the one-page letter.

Maresca thought he knew who these seven brothers were.

Maresca also got threats from the counterfeiters in Harlem he had helped investigate. Like Brooklyn's Seven Brothers, this gang also thought of themselves as poor laborers. One of their letters read:

Dear Friend,

Don't Prosecute. It's enough what you have done. Don't disturb the peace in Harlem. Go after the crooks, not after the poor workingman. Don't enter the café on First Avenue any more. If you value your life, don't let us see you any more. Goodby and take good care of your life.

Society of the Laborers

One night in 1909 Maresca, in uniform, was patroling the streets of Tompkinsville, Staten Island. He saw a stranger coming out of a house, and thinking he was a burglar, gave chase. But he lost the fellow in the dark. A few days later he encountered on a street a man who resembled the suspect. But on attempting to arrest him, Maresca was shot and later died in a hospital. An arrest was made, but the suspect was freed because of lack of evidence.

It was through the job in Staten Island that I got my first full-time job with an insurance company. One of the subscribers, and the man to whom I made my weekly reports, was F. A. W. Ireland, an attorney at the Ocean Accident Guarantee Corporation. One day he asked if I would be interested in joining the company as an adjuster.

That meant I would have to close my private office, and Ocean's starting salary was only $100 a month. I was a married man, but in 1910 a couple could live comfortably on that and even save a little money.

The Ocean was a big company, a branch of a British corporation that had opened its New York branch fifteen years earlier, and had enjoyed a solid success writing casualty insurance. It was still growing. There would be chances for advancement, probably, for a young man like me who enjoyed working hard.

I had another reason for ending my career as a freelance private detective. My mother never stopped worrying about my being in such hazardous work. Every time I went to see her she carried on about it, and told how she had worried constantly about my father being killed by brigands or other criminals.

But, as you have seen from reading the Vogel story, her idea that working for an insurance company meant a quiet life could not have been more mistaken. When she found that out she wanted me to give up my job with the Ocean. I refused.

She begged me to try to find work that was less dangerous. She sobbed as she described the ordeal of waiting up all night for my father. He also had assured her that he would not get hurt. But he had come home many nights heavily bandaged. She dreaded to think that my body would one day bear as many scars as his had. I told her, however, that I loved my work and could not give it up even for her.

When she saw that she could not change my mind, she bowed her head. "I will pray for you every day, my son," she said. "I am a religious woman, and maybe God will heed me."

And she handed me, with tears in her eyes, a medal of St. Gerard, who was born in Muro Lucano, and became its patron saint. I have never neglected to wear that medal in all the years since. Though I am not a deeply religious man, I have always believed in God, and sometimes, after escaping great personal danger, I have thought that perhaps my mother was right and that He did listen to her that day — and kept an eye out for me.

One of my first jobs as an Ocean employee was adjusting claims of Italian laborers at the Ashokan Reservoir which was then being constructed in the Catskill Mountains as part of the great Croton chain of reservoirs. It furnishes much of New York's water supply.

For its day, it represented a great engineering project. It is the largest of New York's twenty-four reservoirs. Two thousand persons, including the inhabitants of seven villages, had to be moved from the valley before the dam could be begun. Sixty-four miles of highway had to be discontinued and forty miles of road built. A section of the Delaware and Ulster Railroad had to be relocated on another route for which ten new bridges were built.

Construction began in 1907 and was finished in 1912. The dam was 12 miles wide from east to west. Its waters covered 10,000 acres; the marginal property surrounding it amounted to 5,000 additional acres. The average depth of the water was 50 feet and up to 190 feet in other places. It sends 500,000,000 gallons a day into New York.

Of the two thousand persons who were compelled to move, a great many, understandably, objected to being uprooted from their homes and farms. They refused to sell their land and it had to be condemned.

An even more sensitive problem was what to do about 32 cemeteries in which there were 2,800 graves, some of them 200 years old. But that was settled by moving the remains and reburying them elsewhere.

Ocean was one of the companies that insured the construction companies building the dam from damage suits brought by their employees. A great deal of the work had been done by 1910, of course, but there were plenty of injured workmen to talk to. Many of these were Italians, *cantadino*, or peasants. Not speaking any Italian, my predecessor naturally had got nowhere with them. I did not know how I would fare myself.

One of the problems my predecessor had been stymied by was the matter of getting into some of the hospitals where injured workers were taken. And during my very first try I could see what his problem was like. The receptionist sternly informed me that I would not be permitted to see the patient I inquired about.

"Would you let me see the head nurse?" I asked meekly.

She gave me a withering look, but she did call up the head nurse, and told me that I could see her: "But it's against rules for anyone but a relative to see patients. You're wasting your time. She'll tell you that."

When I walked into the head nurse's office, I knew I was in luck. She turned out to be the former girl friend of a lawyer I knew.

"Hello, Jerry," she said. "What are you doing here?"

I told her.

"When are you going to take me to dinner?" she said.

"When I get some information," I said.

It was against the rules. But she made an exception of this case. And when I returned to the office she had out on her desk a record of all the dam-building accident cases the hospital had handled up until then. I read it, and the executives of the company were both delighted and amazed when I was able to submit a report to them.

They asked me where I got it, but I just smiled.

"I think that you will find it authentic," I said. "But I cannot embarrass the friends who were kind enough to get this data for me. I promised never to tell a soul. If their employers knew, it would cost them their jobs."

*

I REALLY loved that job, even in the winter.

But I wished almost every day that I could give the injured workmen more substantial amounts than the company allowed. An injured finger got from $5 to $10, and a broken rib $15. The workman who lost an arm was offered $200; $500 was given for a lost eye or leg. If he was killed, his widow got $2,000 from us by way of compensation.

Most of these rates were about what the underworld thugs charged for inflicting similar injuries or very sudden death. In very few cases did the injured persons refuse the company's offer. The Italians came to like me, and nothing I could say stopped them from calling me "Dr. Luisi."

My friend, the nurse, made things a lot easier for me. She called up nurses she knew in other hospitals and asked them to relax stringent rules against visitors, when possible, when I called. The real trick, she explained, was getting in to see the patient first whenever I could. If he agreed to talk to me, the hospital authorities would not interfere.

At least once I met a man from my native town who was recuperating from an accident that broke two of his ribs. He turned his back, but on recognizing speech in his native dialect he turned around again.

What he wanted most in the world was Italian food. After talking to his doctor, I arranged for him to be served a big plate of spaghetti that night, and once every two days after that. This townsman of mine was so delighted that he refused to accept any money at all from my company. It was enough, he said, that the contractor was paying him the $1.50 a day that he had been getting on the job. In a couple of weeks he left the hospital and a few weeks after that was able to go back to work.

In Italy these people had been paid the equivalent of three cents a day. They had lived in huts. So the poor accommodations furnished them in the Catskill project seemed very comfortable. Most of them were married, and their families lived in shacks. The mattresses were on the floor in some of these. Others had bunks the workmen had made themselves. They had been hungry most of the time in their native land, but here they and their families could have all of the spaghetti, *pasta e fagioli,* bread, cheese, and wine they wanted, as well as venison, for they shot deer, and they trapped rabbits for stews. They picked dandelion greens for vegetables.

They enjoyed a freedom they had never known back home. They played cards and boccie, sang to the tune of the concertinas, guitars, and mandolins the musicians, all of whom played by ear, had brought with them. They were good family men. Those who had wives and children in Italy saved every cent possible to send home for their fares to the Promised Land. The wives on the project made a little extra money doing the wash for those without their wives and for the bachelors. Much has been written about the small-town and farm people's joy and elation at discovering New York. But I have often wished more could be written about the wild and wonderful emotions stirred in the New Yorker's breast when enjoying his first real look at the country. Except for short boat rides and other one-day excursions, I'd never spent much time in the country.

But now its beauty was mine.

Such natural beauty: shimmering green everywhere, the forests, the lovely mountains covered with pine trees in summer and crowned with snow in cold weather. And I'd never breathed such wonderful air. Sometimes I would be unable to control myself, and I'd sing at the top of my lungs all the old Italian songs I had learned as a child.

I can't say that I was ever mistaken for Caruso. I sang best on my way to the commissary where I ate with engineers and officials of the company. The food was unlike anything I'd had at home — corned beef and cabbage, Irish stew, hash, pigs' knuckles and sauerkraut — and each meal, at least at first, came as a surprise. They would have been wonderful meals even if I'd had to pay for them. But they were all free, part of our contract with the contractors who had bought their insurance from Ocean.

Two or three nights a week I slept up in the Catskills. Few automobiles were used because of the bad roads. I got around by horse and buggy. Sometimes I walked for miles when no transportation was available. It wasn't always comfortable work, particularly in the winter when the snow was piled several feet deep and the temperature sometimes went below zero.

Often I was hours late for dinner because I'd had to stay too long on the job. On some cases I would have to get statements from as many as six or seven persons, witnesses. I never thought much of the discomfort or the inconvenience. It seemed to me that they were doing me the favor. Why should they suffer any inconvenience? I recommended settlement on 99 percent of the cases.

I had an experience in 1911 that was almost like a dress rehearsal for the experience with the Vogels the following year. And this case began in the same way — with a series of larcenies by a maid, this one a Negro.

I discussed the case with Captain of Detectives Cooper who was then in charge of the Old Fourth Ward where these thefts had been occurring with such frequency. He agreed with my suggestion that an ad be placed for a maid in the Help Wanted columns of the New York *World*. That was where she learned of the jobs she got with the families she later stole from.

In each case the girl had presented written references. None of the women who employed her had bothered to check on these, even by telephone. None of them could remember the name and address of the person who had written it. But the first chance she got, the girl would grab jewelry, silver, and other valuables and make off with them.

One of my friends in that part of the city was an insurance broker. I explained the situation and suggested that we try to trap the girl by inserting a "Help Wanted" ad in his name. He was agreeable, but said I must guarantee there would be no roughhouse in his apartment and that if anyone answered the ad I would do the interviewing.

We put the ad in two Sunday newspapers the victims of the robberies had also used. I arrived at the apartment before nine on the Sunday morning the ad appeared. I did not have long to wait. At eleven o'clock the apartment house's telephone operator phoned to say there was a girl downstairs wishing to speak to someone about the job.

We had her come up. As soon as she walked in, I recognized her as the girl whom the robbed housewives had described. She also had on a coat and was carrying a bag that had been reported stolen.

I never made a quicker arrest. She showed me two written references. I pulled out my shield and told her she was under arrest. To my surprise, she broke down at once and started to cry. She was not a bad girl, she said. It was her boy friend who forced her to steal.

"Have you given your right name?" I asked.

"No, I haven't," she said with a sob, and gave me a name and an address that was in Harlem, and proved to be correct.

"Where is your boy friend?" I asked.

"I haven't seen him for three or four days," she explained. "He told me he was going down to Baltimore to sell the jewelry I got for him."

"Did you give everything you've stolen to him?"

She shook her head. She had quite a lot of stolen articles in her room he'd not yet had a chance to dispose of. We went in a taxi to the address she'd given me. It proved to be a boardinghouse. She turned over to me two suitcases full of silverware, jewelry, and furs. I then took her to the Old Fourth Detective Branch and turned her and the stolen property over to two of the men there who had been assigned to the house robberies.

I talked again to the girl after the detectives left the station house to go about some other business. Apparently wishing to make a clean breast of everything, she explained that there were four other pieces of stolen jewelry at the boardinghouse that she'd forgotten to get. The landlady had them.

"Is the landlady a fence?" I asked.

"No, she doesn't know they are stolen. She was just holding them for me."

Because the landlady had come into the girl's room while I was there, she would know me. When I went back and gave the land-lady the note, she lost no time in giving me the jewelry. She said she had no idea the gems were stolen — they proved to be a brace-let, necklace, and two diamond rings worth $8,000. Needless to say, I did not believe her. But I had the rings, which was what I was principally interested in.

It was my hard luck that, just as I was about to leave, four husky, rough-looking Negroes should come in.

"What are you doing here?" one of them asked.

Before I could reply, the landlady said, "He's come for that jewelry Myra left with me."

I started to leave, and got as far as the hall.

One of the men, who had not come inside the landlady's apart-ment, said, "Brother, you better give back that jewelry!"

Before I could get out my stiletto, the four of them rushed me. I was pushed to the top of the stairs in the dark hallway. One of the men made a grab for me, but, miscalculating the distance between us, pushed me instead. My back was to the stairs, and I started falling. Instinctively, I grabbed for the stairs with my right hand and threw my leg over the banister, swinging myself around.

The men were coming down after me.

I rode down that banister in record time. My legs were wide open, and before I could brake myself, I had crashed into the post at the bottom. The pain in my testicles, which had smashed against the post, was agonizing.

Wincing with pain, I turned around. The leader of the four men was by then only two or three feet from me. I pulled out my .38. The moment they saw it they started racing up the stairs. I shouted to them, "Stop, or I'll shoot!"

They just kept on going, and I wasn't sorry. The pain was so intense that I doubt that I could have handled one of them, let alone four. I got off the banister, hearing no more from them, and weakly made my way to the street.

The streets of Harlem are swarming, day and night, with people who are not overfriendly to white men, particularly one with a gun in his hand. It was my great luck to find a cab that took me to the station. The desk lieutenant immediately saw how pale I was, and asked whether I was hurt.

I asked him to send upstairs for one of the detectives so I could turn over the stolen jewelry to him. When the detective came down, I described the four men who attacked me and told him that I did not believe the landlady was in collusion with the maid. He sealed up the jewelry in a police envelope and wrote out a receipt for it.

I do not remember how I got home. But when I did, I telephoned my doctor.

After examining me, he said:

"I know your injury is painful, but if you'll stay in bed for two weeks you'll be as good as new."

The men were never caught. I think the maid's boy friend was one of them. She, poor creature, pleaded guilty and was sentenced to the reformatory as a first offender.

Nobody, reading that tale and the Vogel story, will be surprised that during the rest of my career I always went as heavily armed as

I thought the circumstances warranted. I carried a derringer in my vest pocket or shirt pocket, and the stiletto on ordinary jobs. But when investigating a hijacking, a big-money burglary, or professional bank robbery, I sometimes carried two guns: the small derringer and either a .38 Colt Police Positive Revolver or a .45 in my holster. I even went armed when my duties required me to wear a tuxedo.

THIEVES
I HATED TO CATCH

3

LIKE everyone else who lives a long time, I have encountered in my day many snobs, many asses. But the peerless example of both in my memory book was one Gerald Mortimer who came fresh out of the Harvard School of Business Administration to work for Ocean during my own early days there.

Mortimer could drop names faster than a comedian-juggler can drop breakaway props. But the name he dropped most often was his own.

An ancestor of his had been on the *Mayflower*.

His mother was among the doughtiest of all the Daughters of the American Revolution.

His father was a banker of great wealth, vast wisdom, and impeccable taste. Collectors from London, Boston, and New Orleans traveled thousands of miles to inspect and delight in the family's heirlooms. When Gerald was a child his parents had made extraordinary efforts to shield him from all contact with the vulgar boys and girls of the lower classes.

The baffling oddity about this tireless braggart was that all that he said was true. If such things make an aristocrat, he surely should have been one. Yet he broke another first rule for gentlemen by lording it over the company's office boys and other minor employees, while bootlicking and fawning over the executives. He would invite heads of departments to lunches and dinners, and would buy choice seats for them at the big Broadway hits. Some of the executives felt compelled to reciprocate, and Mr. Mortimer thus established a social relationship with them. They were intelligent men, but most of them had come up through the ranks. For all I know, they may have felt flattered by the eagerness of this go-getting socialite to be their friend.

The rank-and-file people were not at all impressed by Mortimer's grand airs. They ignored him as much as possible. His first job at Ocean was as an adjuster. He was promoted twice because of the expansion of our Workmen's Compensation Department.

More and more states had been enacting this legislation. In fact, nothing ever expanded the casualty insurance business like this fine stroke of social legislation. In most states employers were given the choice of buying insurance or setting enough money aside to pay compensation to employees who were injured in accidents while working. Very few businessmen preferred the latter choice.

Unfortunately, this noble law also opened the door to swindlers, great and small, inside and outside the business.

We were opening new branches in various western states and enlarging the department at the home office. Mortimer was given the job of handling the dealings with the New York State Workmen's Compensation Bureau. Soon afterward he was made Chief Investigator of that department, with an eight-man staff working under him. He also could issue company checks up to $1,000 without countersignature.

By that time I had become Chief Investigator of the company's Burglary and Fidelity departments. But other department heads were authorized to call on me for help whenever dissatisfied with the way their own claim agents, adjusters, and investigators were handling their assignments.

As far as I know, I was the first investigator in the field to be assigned to probe the ethics of men who worked for the same company. Some of them were found to be doing crooked work, and were discharged. Needless to say, this won me no popularity contests among my fellow employees. Even the honest ones, who were in the vast majority, looked at me askance, feeling I was keeping an eye on them. They were right. I was doing this at the urging of Frank G. Morris, Ocean's assistant manager.

Suddenly Mr. Mortimer began asking me to his lavish lunches and dinners and inviting me to the theater. His boasts amused me. And when he began asking questions, trying to appear casual and indirect about it, concerning my methods in cases involving company people, I had a second reason to be interested in him, particularly so because he was spending far too much money. Besides the fancy meals, his clothes were far too expensive for anyone who earned about $200 a month. It was possible, of course, that he had some source of additional income.

But that seemed unlikely. For one thing, this man who boasted about every other material thing never mentioned a legacy or his investments. He was also delaying his marriage to a society girl he'd long been engaged to. They had agreed not to marry, he explained, until his salary was large enough for them to afford the sort of luxurious home and social life they had always been accustomed to.

I am afraid that my answers to his questions about my working methods when company men were suspected were unsatisfactory. For each time we were out, he again asked,

"What is the first thing that usually arouses the company's suspicion of a certain man?"

"His spending habits. His boss starts to wonder about him when it is noticed that he is spending more than his income warrants." Each time I said this I couldn't help thinking that the beautifully tailored suit he was wearing must have cost a great deal.

"But what do you do first?" he would then ask. "How do you start your investigation?"

"There is no one particular approach. Each case presents a different problem and consequently must be handled differently."

"But how do you manage to find out the facts about such a man's personal life?"

If I merely shrugged, he would add, "I have heard you have caught more than one dishonest employee."

"As I have told you, Mortimer, there is no trick about it. The dishonest person in the insurance business or any other business always makes a mistake sooner or later. No matter how careful he tries to be, he will leave at least one clue. And it is through this that he is caught, not because of any brilliant trick on the part of the investigator."

His curiosity up to a point was understandable. Everybody is interested in methods of detection. This was particularly true of my fellow insurance investigators. But it was Mortimer's habit of never missing a chance to ask the same old questions that made me wonder if he might not be one of the boys worth watching.

Mortimer had been with Ocean for five years the day Mr. Morris called me into his office to ask about him. With Mr. Morris was Everett F. Warrington, superintendent of three departments at Ocean, including Workmen's Compensation.

"What's your opinion of Gerald Mortimer?" asked Mr. Morris.

"I have nothing against him," I told them. "But I have noticed the expensive clothes he wears and also his freehanded spending. Both seem out of proportion to his salary."

Morris turned to Warrington, "Tell Luisi what you have found out." Warrington was a lawyer, thought like one and was the last man in the company to make unwarranted charges. But he had been puzzled by something he noticed accidentally in the file in Mortimer's department where the records of reopened cases were kept.

In New York State Workmen's Compensation Law there was provision made for persons who after returning to their jobs found they had come back too soon. Weekly payments to them were resumed if their doctors certified they were unable to work and that this was due to the original accident.

Warrington had gone to the reopened cases file that morning to get the papers on a case which had been referred to him. He was surprised at the number of other cases which recently had been reopened. Mortimer, in those cases which he had glanced at, had handled the entire matter personally.

At this point Mr. Morris suggested that Warrington and I better discuss the matter further at dinner that evening. After dinner we went back to the office. Warrington picked out a few of the reopened cases for me to look at. All had been handled by Mortimer. But that was the only odd thing about them. All of the necessary forms were there and appeared to be properly filled in.

"I think we might look in Mortimer's desk."

I found in a drawer some telephone numbers. No names or anything else were jotted down next to them. Much more interesting to me were some savings banks deposit slips, none filled in. They were mixed in with his office papers. What attracted my attention was that these slips were from three different downtown Manhattan banks, all many blocks from our office. One was two miles away.

The next day I visited officials of the three banks. None of them had a Gerald Mortimer among their depositors. But there was a way to find out whether he was banking at any of the three under a fictitious name. I hired three investigators and let them have a good look at Mortimer. Each was then spotted at one of the banks in a place where the tellers could see them.

The tellers were told to watch for a signal from the spotter. If my man took off his hat and waved his hand, the teller was to close his window on completing the transaction and take the slip just given him to the bank manager.

I also put a night and day shadow on Mortimer. The night man reported that each evening he walked about three blocks from the office. There he took a taxicab to Grand Central Station, where he caught the train home. On alighting at Yonkers he took another taxicab to his home. Reports of the morning shadow revealed that he also took two taxis each morning on his way to work.

The night shadow also found out that Mortimer on two or three evenings each week went to a poolroom where gamblers hung out and played in pool games in which he bet as much as $5 on a single ball. He also made heavy wagers on horse races. But he was no great ladies' man. He went out only with his fiancée.

Within a week one of my bank spotters saw Mortimer come in and go up to a paying teller's window. The man there got the signal. On completing the transaction, he closed his window and brought the slip to the manager of the bank.

It was a deposit slip with several Ocean company checks attached. They amounted in all to $74.20. Each had been issued to a different man and covered his workman's compensation for one week. The $74.20 deposit was to be credited to the account of Mortimer Gerald, his name reversed. By the end of the day we knew that he was using the same reversed name dodge at the two other banks and that at one of these he had rented a safe-deposit box as Mortimer Gerald.

Warrington and I, checking his files at night, by that time had found thirty-five cases Mortimer had reopened and was issuing weekly checks to. Only two of the thirty-five were bona fide reopened cases. On the other thirty-three cases he himself made out the application for renewal of compensation, forged the workman's signature, and also that of the man's doctor. He used a disguised hand when signing for each workman. But he endorsed the checks as "Mortimer Gerald" in his ordinary hand. Each week Mr. Mortimer issued a check to this man and pocketed it, instead of mailing it out. He tried to avoid suspicion by not keeping the payments going for too many weeks in any one case. From time to time he closed certain cases, and reopened others to replace them.

At this time weekly compensation checks in New York averaged only about $15. But in a little over two years, Mortimer had managed to swindle the company out of about $75,000. It may have been more. But that was the aggregate amount we were able to trace.

With the evidence gathered, the time came to confront Mortimer with proof of his guilt. I have never believed in using old-fashioned police methods, brutality, or bullying tactics, or such devices as brilliant lights shining in his eyes to get a suspect to confess.

But I always felt I should have the advantage of surprise if I hoped to start a thief talking. This case, like many another, required a little stage-managing, in my opinion, and I used Mr. Morris' office for my set. I had a dictograph hidden there with an outlet in the adjoining office where two court stenographers would take down everything that was said.

Morris, Warrington, my secretary, myself, and the two court stenographers all got to the office early on the morning chosen and made certain everything was in readiness. Just before Mortimer arrived, I sat in Morris' chair. I had him standing on one side of me, Warrington on the other. The girl sat near the desk with pencil poised over her pad. We were all facing the door through which he would come.

As soon as we got word he was at his desk, Morris sent for him. Mortimer entered, with his admiring smile all set and ready. But he lost it on seeing the four of us, and said an odd thing:

"Luisi, I didn't think you would take advantage of me in front of these two gentlemen."

It was difficult to know just what he meant by that, but it was obvious that he preferred to talk to me alone. I asked the others to leave. They did, but lost no time joining the two court stenographers in the next room.

There was no point wasting time with Mortimer. I showed him the evidence we'd accumulated against him: the canceled checks on which he'd forged so many different names, a record of the amounts he had deposited and withdrawn at the three banks during the past two years. He had less than $5,000 left in each bank. When his safe-deposit box was opened later on, he proved to have less than $3,000 in that.

Many white-collar thieves who find themselves in Mortimer's position say that they are relieved that the jig is up. As they tell the whole story, they sometimes sob and cry as they think of their folly.

If Mortimer was relieved, he neither told me nor showed it. When I asked, "Do you wish to deny that you stole all this money?" he replied, quite calmly:

"You know damn well I'd like to deny it, but what would be the use?"

His story was one I'd heard before and was to hear ten thousand times again. He'd got a hot tip on a horse, and bet more money than he could raise. The horse lost. It was to pay off the bookie that he'd put through the first fake check. Losing more money gambling, he'd continued. It seemed like child's play, something he could get away with forever. With no confederate needed, he had no one he need fear would betray him.

Before signing a formal confession, he asked me if he could send for his lawyers. I expected him to call in the help of respectable lawyers, of the sort he must often have met in his parents' home. Instead he summoned two shysters, brothers who knew their way around every angle and loophole in the lawbooks.

We had Mortimer arrested. Despite the total amount of his thefts, he could only be held on petty larceny and forgery charges. In no instance had he made out a fraudulent check for more than $99.99, and larceny in New York became grand larceny then only when the amount involved was $100 or more. When his parents agreed to make full restitution, he was let off with a suspended sentence.

While these arrangements were being made, I noticed that Mortimer and the two lawyers seemed to be pals of long standing. I asked the lawyers about that.

"Oh, we've known him since we were all kids growing up in Yonkers," one of the brothers told me. "Every day he could sneak away from that swell neighborhood he lived in, he'd come to play with us on our street, which was in that town's crummiest neighborhood."

Figure that out, if you can. As a boy Mortimer had furtively sought out the company of poorer boys. As a man, while snubbing his inferiors at the office, he still wanted to impress and win the approval of the roughnecks who hung out in a Yonkers poolroom. There was only one way he could do that — by being a big and flashy

bettor, and stealing the money at the risk of prison and disgrace
to his family.

The mind of any ordinary man is a mysterious thing, but the
mind of a thief is often a riddle.

*

EVEN though Gerald Mortimer was not liked by the other claim
agents and investigators, I felt that same wave of resentment against
myself the moment word got around that he had been fired and
arrested as a result of evidence I'd collected.

That is why I hated, after a while, to catch other insurance men
who had turned into crooks. Some of the fellows who gave me the
cold shoulder were men I'd eaten fifteen-cent lunches with when
we were beginners. We had enjoyed drinking at cafés and eating
together in better places as we moved up to better jobs.

Some historians say that the United States is a country whose
greatest heroes are lawbreakers. I don't know whether that's true.
But what I was made to feel, each time I investigated another insurance man, was that my fellow Americans sure didn't like cops.

The men who ran the insurance companies felt differently, of
course. They had no sympathy for men they trusted with responsibility and who turned crooked when they got the chance. That
these men were, by and large, underpaid was to them no argument.
In fact I take great pride in the number of erring insurance men
and other white-collar workers I saved from prison. Sometimes I
had to argue my head off with their bosses. Always it was worth it.
I have letters of warm gratitude, scores of letters, from men for
whom I obtained freedom. Some were written years afterward.
These men were not criminals in any true sense. I have difficulty
recalling a single instance of such a man getting into trouble after
being mercifully treated. Which proves a point I made at the time
of their trouble: they'd already been punished enough.

*

AFTER the first few years my success as a investigator for Ocean
resulted in offers from executives of other companies. My company agreed to let me take on these outside assignments, providing
it did not interfere with my regular work. In a very short time I was

making more than my regular salary on these outside jobs. This was another sore point with some of the other investigators.

I would not say even now that I was more intelligent than they were. One of my great advantages was my willingness to work harder than they, and to give everything I had to whatever job I was doing. I thought nothing of working twenty-four hours at a stretch. I've worked as much as forty-eight hours without closing my eyes, changing my clothes, or eating anything substantial. This is how absorbing I found the game of matching wits with thieves and men of violence. I did not ever, of course, choose such grueling work marathons. But keeping at it, without cessation or rest, to wear down the other fellow often made the difference between winning and losing.

On more than a few occasions my bosses at Ocean suggested or urged me to accept assignments from other companies. It was our general manager, for example, who called me in one day in 1916 and said he wished me to undertake a confidential investigation for Joseph Frelinghuysen of New Jersey, who was then running for the United States Senate. Frelinghuysen was head of a group of fire-insurance companies whose headquarters were in our building.

"Give a whole week to the senator's problem," my boss said, generously adding, "two whole weeks, if necessary."

I just looked at him, quizzically, wondering if it could be possible that he didn't realize that an investigation, properly done, could take months. Well, I thought, I might not have to give him those good tidings after I spoke to the senator.

Joe Frelinghuysen was the sort of old-fashioned, fire-eating senator you seldom see around anymore. To many of his constituents he symbolized the spirit of their country. He could rock crowds with a Fourth of July speech, the same old one each year, but it was his personality and appearance, complete with shock of white hair, square face, and flashing eyes that got them. And his sincerity was a great asset. He believed every word he was saying — at least while he was saying it.

And in a way he was the America of that day in person. His folks had been here back in colonial days; members of his family had fought in all our wars. He himself had served as a cavalryman in the Spanish-American War. Frelinghuysen had distinguished himself in the New Jersey Senate by fighting successfully for much-needed farm legislation, and he was father of that state's automobile-insurance law. His success as a businessman equaled his political success. He was only twenty-one when he organized twenty-one underwriters into a group that took over an insurance company, and his business interests had grown and flourished ever since.

But when I called on him the senator was terribly upset. And I could understand why when he explained his problem. Here he was, in the middle of the most important political campaign of his life and his suspicions had just been aroused by something he had noticed. So many fire claims were coming from his Newark office that he felt that his employees must be investigated.

A distressing situation, but the senator's agitation convinced me that something more than suspicion of employees was troubling him. And so I asked him that day, "How far do you want me to go?"

"The limit!" he thundered.

I still was not satisfied. I had been on jobs before in which the victim was furious because he suspected a relative or lifelong friend had been robbing him. Later the same man would cool off and order me to stop the investigation. Unfinished investigations always have left me with a sense of frustration.

So I asked, "Regardless of whom is involved — your broker, investigator, a top executive in your company?"

Senator Frelinghuysen fixed me with an astonished stare. "Could it be possible that you know something already about these claims?"

"No," I told him, "I was just trying to find out how far you wished me to go. Suppose somebody quite close to you is involved?"

"I don't care if it's my own brother."

I asked the senator if he would have some employee he trusted get together the folders containing fifty recent or current claims from Newark, bring them to my office and work with me on them. These were delivered that afternoon. I found nothing in them that hinted of collusion, misrepresentation, or fraud. Some claims had checks attached to them, were ready to go out to the Newark office for distribution to the assured persons. Only the last-minute orders of the senator had held them up.

There was one exception, however: a $700 claim for a fire loss in a home that was described as being in "a good residential section," and expensively furnished. A rug and the living-room furniture had been ruined.

And there was my lucky break.

I'd been in that very neighborhood on a case only a short while before. Good residential section! It was one of the worst slums in the state.

I took the check, some notes on the case I'd made, and a list of recent fires in Newark homes insured by the company, and went off to Newark.

In the application the assured man had described himself as a salesman in an "auto supply store." No one at that store had ever heard of him, I was told.

My second call was at Newark Fire Headquarters. The official records there revealed that the fire department had been called out on all fires on my list. But the official records showed far less damage than the claims had reported.

My third stop was at the "expensively furnished home" in the "good residential section." This proved to be a tenement flat in the middle of the slum I'd visited not long before. The assured man's wife opened the door for me. I showed her the $700 check and explained I was from the insurance company. She invited me in. I told her I could give the check only to her husband. And the agent must be present. But I expected the agent to join me in a few minutes. She suggested I wait there for her husband and the agent. I was very happy to do so, and seated myself in the living room.

The place was filthy. The furniture consisted of broken-down chairs and a sagging sofa. No junkman would have given seven bucks for the lot. And none of it looked scorched.

My hostess spoke only in broken English, but she spoke a lot of it. As I waited for her husband to come home, she explained that the agent was her cousin. "He is a good friend of the manager, a good friend of the adjuster, too. He is doing good business."

"But where was the fire that you had here?" I asked.

She laughed, and took me to a closet. There had been a fire all right — in a corner of the closet. A few newspapers had been burned there. I could see the charred scraps of pages in the little heap of ashes.

"Where is your husband working?" I asked.

"On a downtown street."

"On a street?"

"Yes, he is a fruit peddler."

I took out the proof of loss, which had her signature.

"Is this your writing?" I asked.

She looked at it, and nodded.

"You were lucky not to have had anything damaged in the apartment."

"We sure were," she said.

At this point I said I could wait no longer for the agent. But I told her I would be back. By that time, of course, I was fairly sure that one or more of the key men in the Newark office must be in on the swindle. Most of them lived as well as worked in Newark. It was impossible that they were unaware that the neighborhood was a slum. Yet they'd approved this $700 claim. It seemed certain that it was but one in quite a series.

But I'd have to work very fast if I was going to arrest them. For some reason I felt that Mr. Frelinghuysen, running as he was for so high an office, might change his mind at the last minute about having the whole matter aired. I telephoned him.

"I haven't changed my mind, and will not!" he shouted into the mouthpiece. "I told you to go ahead. Arrest everyone you think guilty."

I hurried over to Newark Police Headquarters, told my story, and was assigned two detectives. We got back to the tenement before the pushcart peddler did, and waited there for him. We did not have much of a wait.

He quickly admitted his part in the fraud. He was only a pawn, of course. By midnight, we also had complete confessions from two fire-insurance solicitors, one adjuster, and an executive.

They told us how they had worked their swindle. A few weeks after a policy was issued, a fire, small and easily controlled, would be started in that home, usually in a mattress or in a closet. This justified the turning in of an alarm — so there would be a record in case anyone got nosey. The solicitor notified the agent, who called the manager. He approved the report and sent it on to the New York office, which sent back a check in full payment. The man in the New York office was not in on the swindle, and did not have to be, as the reports were written properly and would have passed anyone's examination.

In this case greed once more had tripped up the schemers. They might have gone on for years if they had not kept increasing the number of losses claimed until the senator began to suspect something was wrong. It was not until I read newspaper accounts of the arrests of those involved that I understood why the senator had seemed so upset and distressed at our first interview. The executive in the case was his campaign manager.

*

MORE than once I have been credited with great feats of detection when pure luck was responsible. One day a client from Chicago called me up. He wanted the address of a society man as quickly as I could obtain it. The only address he had was Bar Harbor, Maine, and that was two years before.

All attempts to trace the fellow, prominent though he was, had proved fruitless. My client wanted me to drop everything and go up to Bar Harbor and start the search from there. When I hung up, I thought that it could not cost more than $2 to phone the Maine summer resort. I called the postmaster, apparently a typical New Englander. He made no secret of never having heard of me.

Being a New England official, he was a stickler about the rules governing his job. "Now, Mr. Luisi," he said in a voice full of that old Down East twang, "if you are a private detective you must know that I am not permitted to give out any information over the phone, particularly when I do not know the person requesting it."

While I was coaxing him to violate his oath of office in just this one small matter, it occurred to me that it is seldom, if ever, that anyone apologizes to a small-town postmaster. So I apologized — and really laid it on. And he was tickled, judging from the change in his voice. And I guess it worked. Though he gave me no address he made a suggestion:

"Have you a *Social Register* in the office?"

"Yes, sir."

"You might look for his name there," he said, and hung up.

It was the right tip. The man's name, big as life, was there together with his New York address. I could have kicked myself for not thinking of it without the postmaster's help. I felt like kicking myself twice as hard on looking at the New York Telephone Directory. The man my Chicago client had been seeking was also in that one.

All I had to do was call the number. A servant answered, said: "Yes, sir, he is home. Just a moment, sir." I hung up, having found out everything I'd been asked to, before he could pick up the phone.

My next call was to Chicago. My client was amazed at my fast work, complimented me warmly, and still insists I am a genius. I thought it best not to explain how I found his man so rapidly. I didn't exactly whisper "My agents are everywhere!" but hoped he'd be able to figure it out for himself.

When the time came to send him a bill, I didn't know what to charge him. By that time I was getting good fees. I had always been scrupulously honest about not overcharging for my time. And on this case I had spent less than half an hour. I compromised between my conscience and my desire to be paid well by sending the client a blank bill. Let him decide. He responded handsomely with a check for $150.

An even easier case to crack was that of a man whom a lawyer had been seeking for weeks. On the hunch that the missing man might have a car, I called a friend at the city automobile-license bureau. He had a car. His correct address was on his application there. I sent a man there who served the subpoena for the harried lawyer.

A source that is often overlooked in a search for missing persons is the local board of education. If the man or woman has a child of school age, you will find the family's address and the parents' names in the board's records.

I would have welcomed any sort of lucky break in another New Jersey case I investigated, during the early days of the Great Depression, for the Peoria Life Insurance Company, of Peoria, Illinois. I was on it for months.

One day in the latter part of February, 1930, the Peoria Company mailed a $25,000 check to its branch office in Passaic, New Jersey. The check was made out to be turned over to Mrs. Aldo Marone, the widow of a fruit peddler who had died on February 1st. The Passaic office was notified at the time of his death. On February 18th the widow, Maria, had sent the necessary statement of death to the company. An illiterate, she signed this with an X, though a friend of the deceased, John Carlano, submitted a "Friend's Statement" that attested to Mr. Marone's death. This, together with the usual physician's death certificate, was also forwarded to the company.

The same afternoon that the $25,000 check went out, the head of Peoria's legal department, J. S. Wolfenberger, had a change of mind about it. He picked up his phone and called the manager of the Passaic office. "Return that check the moment you receive it," he said. "Don't let it out of your hands."

It seemed to Mr. Wolfenberger that his company recently had been sending quite a few checks to Passaic for life insurance on persons who had died quite soon after buying a policy. He looked these up. Oscar Rocco, an agent born in Italy, had sold the policies in each case and this man, Marone, had lived barely long enough to pay the first quarterly payment on his policy.

When the check was returned, Mr. Wolfenberger sent his assistant, who was also his son-in-law, Walter H. Schmidt, to Passaic to look into the matter. Schmidt, himself a lawyer, had interviewed the agent, the widow, the company doctors, and Carlano. He found nothing suspicious, and advised that payment should not be held up any longer. The agent, Oscar Rocco, was very indignant about this, he said, asserting that news that his company did not pay off promptly was making it difficult for him to get any new business from other Italians, who were his best customers.

Wolfenberger overruled him, and hired one of the country's best private detective agencies to look into the matter. They too were unable to produce proof of any fraud.

By the time I was called into the case, four months had elapsed since Marone's death.

I had conducted some life-insurance investigations, I told Mr. Wolfenberger in answer to his questions. Among them were substitution cases, so called because a healthy person is substituted at the medical examination for the insured man or woman, who may be too ill to be passed by the doctor. This was what Mr. Wolfenberger suspected.

"Do you speak Italian?" he asked.

"Yes, I was born in Italy," I told him. "But why do you ask?"

"Anyone who doesn't speak Italian isn't going to get anywhere at all with the principals in this case," he replied.

"Speaking one sort of Italian may not be enough," I said, and explained about the many different Italian dialects.

I took back to my office all the papers he had on the case, including the reports of Mr. Schmidt and the first detective agency. After reading these I agreed to take the case. It looked like a tough one, but everything about it interested me. The previous investigators had not mentioned in their reports what part of Italy the dead fruit peddler and his wife were from. My first move therefore was to send a man into their neighborhood, which was in the Italian section of the small town of Garfield, New Jersey. He had traveled all over Italy as a young man and could speak and understand many of the dialects.

He talked to many Italians there. He told them that he was searching for Pasquale Ignorate, an old friend of his boyhood days in Italy. He also was interested in buying a house in Garfield.

I did not dare send him back, of course, as he'd be recognized. But this enabled me to use one of my best men on the first phase of the job. He was Tita Cornetti, himself a Sicilian. He had been a member of my Staten Island carabinieri, was resourceful, quick-thinking, and absolutely fearless. His instructions were to seek a room as close to the Marone family as possible, in their house if it could be arranged. He was to pretend to be in the country illegally and hiding out for this reason from the Immigration authorities. Even the nosey neighbors would accept this as the explanation of why he did not leave the neighborhood, day or night, to go to work or anything else.

Cornetti, my assistant Number 171 in the office records, stayed in that neighborhood, Garfield's squalid Little Italy, more than a month. But the report he furnished gave us sound information for the other phases of the investigation.

Aldo Marone was born in Misilermi, in the province of Palermo. He was a fruit peddler.

He and his wife were married on February 10, 1907, at the Church of Our Lady of Loreto, 303 Elizabeth Street, New York City.

They had lived on Rivington Street, on New York's Lower East Side, before moving to Garfield.

He had been suffering from diabetes for four years before he died.

He was broke, and had no business or personal assets. His widow and five children were destitute.

He was a member of the Sons of Italy (Figli d'Italia) Lodge Allesandro Paternostro Number 44, and was also a member of the Mutual Benefit Society Sanguisto of Misilermi.

In other words, a more unlikely applicant for a $25,000 life-insurance policy than this penniless, diabetic Italian fruit peddler could hardly have been found. Nevertheless, he'd been accepted as a sound risk, obtained the insurance, and then died in a little more than three months.

It seemed to me likely that Marone was much older than forty-five. I asked the Italian Consul in New York to find out if there was a birth certificate for Aldo Marone in Misilermi, and, if so, to please get me a photostat showing the date. We also applied for a copy of the Marones' marriage certificate from the Church of Our Lady of Loreto.

If Marone had been a peddler in New York City, he must have had a license on which would be his signature. If he were an illiterate he would have signed his name with an X. But his application for $25,000 made in his name had been signed "Aldo Marone," in English and with a firm hand.

If he had been penniless for several years and a diabetes sufferer, he surely applied for sick benefits, his destitute widow for death benefits. That was one of the main purposes of the Italian-American societies he belonged to: to help the destitute members and their families. The dues were kept so low that even the poorest Italian could pay them. The societies had other purposes. Their rooms were meeting places for lonely Italians who were members. They held dances and outings on which they could talk to one another of their loneliness for the Old Country where the sun shone so much and there was always music, but seldom enough work or food for the bambinos.

But the officers of such societies were fanatically intent on protecting the privacy of their members. The accounts on Signor Marone's appeals for help would not be easy to obtain.

While trying to think of an intelligent approach to them, I had been making a few inquiries about Oscar Rocco, the agent who had sold the insurance. He was a likely suspect from the first. It was difficult to see how such a swindle as this appeared to be could have been arranged without at least his connivance. And it could well be that he was the architect of the whole dishonest business.

The finances of a suspect are the first matter looked into. Rocco seemed to be swimming in money troubles, and owed money to several tradespeople who regarded him as unreliable and untrustworthy. He was a small man, being only about five feet four inches tall.

His wife was working at the Colonial Insurance Company's Passaic offices. That might not mean a thing. But we started wondering about her. She was not using her married name, and had not told her boss, the branch manager, that she was married to a man who sold insurance for another company right there in Passaic.

A meticulous dresser, vain, Rocco was now twenty-nine, a good-looking young man who had been educated in Italy. He liked attractive women. We planted one in the Passaic office of the Colonial Insurance Company where his wife was employed. Assistant Number 222 had blue eyes, blond hair, was plump (the way most Italians prefer them), and pretty. Her instructions were to get friendly with Mrs. Rocco. The idea, of course, was to have Mrs. Rocco introduce her to her husband. To make that easier, Assistant 222 rented a private room close to where they lived.

The name Assistant 222 used while on this case was Sheri Ermini. Mrs. Rocco seemed to take to her on sight, particularly after Sheri told her: "I'm not Italian, but my husband is. He is in Chicago, and he is ill. That's why he doesn't come East. It's lonely for both of us this way, terribly lonely."

Mrs. Rocco, a gullible young woman, was lonely too, and was glad of making a new girl friend in the office. She did her best to help my assistant in her job of selling insurance. On hearing the newcomer had a room close to her own home, Mrs. Rocco asked her to have her meals there, with her, her mother, and husband.

So within a few days Mrs. Ermini not only met Rocco but was eating regularly in their home. It was important that the suspect and his family believe her story that she had an ailing Italian husband in Chicago who was sick with loneliness there, eager to join her but unable to do that just yet because of his poor health. We had letters written on the stationery of the Hotel La Salle in Chicago and mailed to her.

Assistant 222 gave them plenty of opportunity to check on her. She carried one or more of these letters in her bag whenever she visited or ate with his family. She left the bag in the bedroom. Each time, she observed, he went in there, stayed a minute or two, and came out. On getting her bag she could see that he had rummaged in it.

After a little while Assistant 222 asked permission of the Roccos to receive her mail at their home. When they agreed we addressed the letters from Chicago there. This gave Rocco the chance to steam open the letters and read them at his leisure, convince himself that they confirmed all she had been telling him. Then he could reseal them and hand them to "Sheri" on her next visit. The need to pick up the letters, of course, also gave her an excuse for daily visits to his home.

I also anticipated that I might want to pull Assistant 222 off her assignment abruptly before we finished the rest of the investigation. She would have an excuse if she got a telegram from Chicago saying her husband's illness had become critical. That would not alert him to her real role. Here are some facts her daily reports showed:

In the past few years Oscar Rocco had worked for ten other insurance companies, including the Colonial. He gloated over the fact that Colonial did not know that their "Miss Silvani" was his wife.

Rocco, apparently smitten with Assistant 222 on sight, suggested she go into business with him. He boasted of having $375,000 worth of business the previous year and that he met all sorts of people including "crooks, big crooks, and good ones." He also revealed that he was planning to sue Prudential for not paying him $25,000 for a life-insurance policy in which he was named beneficiary. The company, he said, was charging misrepresentation.

But the insurance salesman also was cautious about telling her about his present troubles with Peoria, something that, if repeated, might hurt him.

He also neatly sidestepped a trap we set for him through Assistant 222. One day she suggested that she had found a sixty-four-year-old woman prospect who wished to buy $20,000 worth of life insurance. He told her the $4,000-a-year premium was too high to interest anyone.

Oscar Rocco also boasted of his tie-ins with local doctors. He asserted that for a small extra fee these doctors would okay the health of even a very sick man whom he had sold a policy to.

His brother Joe was also working for Colonial under an assumed name and had been fired previously from another office of that company. Joe, who could hardly speak English, was so woman-crazy that she had to do some fast, smart sidestepping. He was not the suspect nor the one she hoped to get information from. She continued to seem interested in Oscar.

Mrs. Rocco showed her an expensive platinum wedding ring inscribed "Frank to Lily." She said it was given her by a local bootlegger who was shot to death on a Passaic street the previous winter. She had, she said, been his mistress for seven years, but had quarreled with him a month before he was killed. Her family had been terrified that the police might suspect her, but she had not been accused. A member of another mob, a brother of Margie, a girl friend of hers, had been convicted on circumstantial evidence and was doing seven years for the killing, she explained. Her husband had almost thrown her out of the house on learning of her romance with the dead gangster.

Though the information about Mrs. Rocco's love life had nothing to do with our investigation, it was typical of the startling surprises I so often encountered when we scratched below the surface of family life. Until Mrs. Rocco made her confession to Agent 222, she had seemed to our sharp-eyed investigator the most submissive and faithful of young Italian wives.

Just as Rocco was about to rent offices for his partnership deal with Assistant 222, she began to get a series of telegrams from her Chicago husband. These were buildups for one from "his physician." It read:

> HUSBAND VERY SICK COME IMMEDIATELY
> DR. SAWYER

This was sent only when I felt that she had collected about all of the information we needed about the Roccos. They liked her so very much and accepted her story completely. Mrs. Rocco for months afterward kept writing letters to "Sheri Ermini" at the La Salle Hotel. These we arranged to pick up and have answered until our investigation was closed.

In addition to everything else, Agent 222's daily reports stressed Oscar Rocco's ever-increasing nervousness. He was having stomach trouble. Several times Mrs. Rocco told Assistant 222, "Oscar can't sleep nights but he won't tell me what is bothering him."

But we knew. He was worrying about what the investigators were going to do next, how close we were coming to him. He kept wondering if anyone of the few people who knew that he had engineered the substitution of a younger, healthier man for Marone had given him away.

Part of the information we wished to show him had to be obtained from the two Italian-American mutual-benefit societies that Aldo Marone had belonged to. These, we believed, would show his real age, his signature, and the fact that he'd been a diabetic for four years before obtaining the $25,000 insurance policy. I would have wagered the societies' records would show he had been paid sick benefits and also that his wife had appealed for death benefits soon after he died.

But at the offices of the societies, as I'd feared, I ran into a brick wall. The secretaries of both flatly refused to let me look at their books, tell me anything about Marone, or any of their other members.

"I will go to the district attorney," I told them.

They laughed at me.

"I'll get a court order."

"The courts cannot order us to give up our records."

I could not convince them.

At that time the president of the Sons of Italy organization was New York State Supreme Court Justice Salvatore Cotillo, a man with whom I'd grown up on the streets of Little Italy in Harlem. Unfortunately, I was also the boyhood friend of another Supreme Court judge, Charles Freschi, who was about to run against Cotillo for the presidency of the society.

I tried to get Cotillo on the phone, to see him personally. When I failed in that I had no recourse except to get a *duces tecum* order from Assistant District Attorney Charles J. Garrison.

Out of frustration, I had thundered at the secretary of the Sons of Italy, a huge organization: "You will end up having to hire a truck to take all of your records to the district attorney's office. You will be sorry then that you would not cooperate with me."

And that is just what happened. The *duces tecum* order (which means appear and bring the documents with you) asked the secretaries to produce their membership books, books of the treasurer, minute books for that year, the books of the financial secretary from the day of organization.

The Sons of Italy did need a truck to carry all this data to the district attorney's office. The Misilermi group, being smaller, got all of theirs in a couple of taxis!

The societies' records were invaluable, and proved that for four years before his death Marone had had diabetes and had been given more than $1,000 in sick benefits. We also had his widow's pleading letter for death benefits. This stated that she and her five children were destitute.

By that time the Italian consulate in New York had the birth certificate of the fruit peddler. This proved he was born there in

1870, not 1883 as his application for life insurance stated. The license-bureau records yielded his proof of his illiteracy, for he'd signed his license there with an X.

With all this data on hand, the Peoria Company's lawyers and I decided the time had come to interrogate Rocco. We still did not have enough concrete evidence against him for a criminal prosecution. But we all agreed that we had enough material to convince him that he better do everything in his power to help us induce the widow of Marone to withdraw her claim.

The questioning of Rocco took place on October 7, 1930, in Room 1117 of the Hotel Robert Treat, in Newark. Mr. Schmidt, representing the company, another investigator, a court stenographer, and I were present. A hidden dictograph was set up with an outlet in the adjoining room so a second court stenographer could listen in there. Two records taken down by experts of the conversation, can have additional legal weight in court, we thought. But learning the room was bugged also can have a great psychological effect on a witness who gets balky or later changes his story.

Rocco proved to be not only balky but a double-talk artist. He found it impossible to explain how the poverty-stricken peddler was able to pay the first premium of $1,096, but finally said Marone had given it to him in installments. But Rocco refused to say where he kept or banked these installment payments before turning in to the company the $1,096 premium.

Rocco knew just as well as we did that the United States Supreme Court had ruled that a policy was void if any material misstatement had been made in the application. The misstatements listed by the Court included lying about one's age, concealing a serious illness during the past five years, giving a false occupation because the real one was hazardous, failing to list other life-insurance policies, or concealing the fact that other insurance had been denied or that a physician had recommended denying such insurance, or stating falsely that one is in sound health.

I kept showing this tricky little fellow more and more proof of such deception in this case. In the end, he agreed that it was a very dubious claim indeed. He was innocent, and swore that if anyone had been substituted for the dead Marone it was news to him. He agreed to try to talk the widow into withdrawing her claim. The widow and the doctors who had examined the man substituted for Marone, as far as we knew, had done nothing criminal.

Some time later the company's attorneys settled with the Widow Marone for $4,500. I think she was very wise to accept that. The evidence accumulated, I was sure, would have defeated any suit she brought for the full amount.

But attorneys for insurance companies have had cases that looked even more favorable for their side, only to lose them because the plaintiff's attorney in summing up moved the great heart of some jury with an appeal, "Look at this wealthy, powerful corporation that refuses to give this poverty-stricken widow and her half-starved children what they deserve and need so desperately. . . ."

My investigation cost the company about $5,000 more. Mr. Wolfenberger was so pleased with my work that he wrote a warm letter of commendation in which he spoke of how difficult it had been to expose "this conspiracy in which all of the conspirators' tracks were well covered."

But the company need not have paid out any of the $9,500 that settling with Marone's widow and my investigation cost them if even a routine investigation had been made *before* the policy was issued.

All the company had to go on, however, was a credit company's report on Mr. Rocco's $25,000 life-insurance prospect. The bill for this was just $2.50. That is right: *two dollars and fifty cents.*

All the credit company could do for that money was to have a phone call or two made. The persons telephoned said that Marone had been working regularly, making $5,000 a year, and was worth $15,000. He was healthy, was able to work every day, and had never had a serious illness!

Naturally, Mr. Rocco had supplied the names of those who gave this information. And if it had not been for the last-minute reservation that nagged at Mr. Wolfenberger's mind — after the $25,000 check was sent, mind you — that small fortune would have been paid out, with the crooked insurance man getting the lion's share and giving the frightened, illiterate widow whatever small share he felt like.

For years I have pleaded with officials of great insurance companies to insist on getting more thorough reports than are obtainable for a $2.50 fee before accepting risks on policies involving in some cases up to $50,000.

I was ignored.

Perhaps it would have been different if it was their companies' money that was being paid out, year after year, on claims for policies that never should have been accepted in the first place.

But it isn't their money.

It is yours and mine and the other fellow's.

Whenever the insurance companies in any particular field can prove to one of the various state insurance bureaus that their annual net profit has fallen below the long-established rate, the companies can apply for increased premiums on that insurance — and the state insurance bureau grants the increase that you and I and the rest of the public must pay.

*

THE Depression, of course, set many a man dreaming of new and better ways to cheat the insurance companies. Some of them, it is likely, in normal times might not have considered stealing. But gypping on insured personal property seems so quick, so easy. What a variety of ways there are to do this I think is demonstrated in this book, along with the even greater variety of mistakes that are made by the persons, in and out of the insurance business, who try such tricks.

Consider a racket I investigated in 1933, the peak year of the Depression. The client was the Fidelity and Guaranty Fire Corporation of Baltimore. Frank A. Gantert, president of that company, invited me to confer there one day with him, and a group of his top executives.

"We've had an epidemic of claim losses on jewels, furs, and other personal property in New York," Mr. Gantert told me. I'd noticed an increase in the reports I'd seen recently in New York, but nothing one could call an epidemic.

Mr. Gantert repeatedly had asked Harold Murphy, who handled and settled all such claims for the company in New York, for some explanation, but had obtained no satisfaction.

I knew Murphy, I told Mr. Gantert. He asked the question usually asked by executives who have become suspicious of an employee: Had I noticed or had I ever heard anything about him that seemed to indicate bad character?

The answer also was one I often had to make in those circumstances. "Nothing. But it is true that he is often seen eating and drinking with brokers in the best restaurants and speakeasies."

This is considered significant because brokers are very happy to buy meals and drinks or anything else for claim adjusters. The adjusters are the men, after all, who can help them by recommending generous settlements for the brokers' customers. The amount of business done by brokers often depends largely on their ability to obtain generous settlements of customers' claims. I would not go so far as to say that all assured persons exaggerate the amounts they lose through fire, flood, larceny or armed robbery. But I cannot recall too many who did not exaggerate when they told the insurance company the bad news. And nobody, as I remember it, ever underestimated his loss.

After the conference I returned to New York with a file of the last one hundred claims handled by Mr. Murphy. After studying these I made a chart that listed the name and address of those insured, the broker involved, the date and place of loss, amount paid, the name of the endorser of each check.

The chart, when completed, revealed a clear pattern. Many of the hundred cases for insurance had been placed with the Baltimore company by Humphrey Jones, manager of a reputable insurance broker's office. Most of the canceled checks for these claims and others had been endorsed by Jones or Murphy and cashed by the owners of the saloons they frequented.

According to the terms and conditions on all such policies, the police must be notified at the time when the insured person discovers the loss of his property. I visited the station houses in the precincts where more than twenty of the losses were supposed to have occurred. In none of these cases had the police been notified.

I next interviewed the persons who were supposed to have bought the insurance. All of them knew either Murphy or Jones. But not one of them had bought insurance from them, or remembered even discussing it with them. Furthermore, they had never owned the articles described in the applications and claims. They had never seen the checks I showed them with their names written on the back. It was in somebody else's handwriting, they said. One man whom the company had sent a check to had died two months before his application for insurance was filed.

All the papers had been notarized. But the notary publics whose stamps and seals were on these admitted that they had never seen the applicants. They had notarized the papers as a favor to Jones and Murphy without seeing them.

We had, it appeared, an open-and-shut case of forgery and also larceny against both men. The cases we had checked showed them stealing a little over $5,000.

But I thought it must amount to much more. How much more? I also wanted to find out if anyone else had worked with them. A statement from either one of them would answer both questions. I approached Murphy who seemed to me to be the weaker of the two. He was a bald man of thirty-five, with a nose curved like a scimitar.

Both he and Jones, by that time, were of course aware that I'd been interviewing the friends whose names they'd used on the policies.

When I approached Mr. Murphy he was anything but amiable. At first he refused to talk to me. And when he did he bawled me out for pestering his friends and trying to get him fired. And I had only one purpose: to get publicity for myself.

"If you have anything on me it is up to you to prove it," Murphy said. "But you better be right, Luisi. If you aren't, I'll sue you and the company from here to hell and gone."

I stopped trying to get Murphy to talk with me when he laughed in my face.

"You will stop laughing," I told him, "before our next talk. You won't like the setting, either, because it will be either a police station or the district attorney's office."

And our next meeting was at the district attorney's office. Though Murphy had stopped laughing, he still seemed confident. He and Jones were indicted by the Grand Jury and held in $1,500 bail each for trial in General Sessions Court on charges of forgery and larceny.

Both produced bail and were freed while awaiting trial. Soon afterward I heard that Jones was beginning to drink heavily, possibly a sign that he did not share Murphy's confidence that they would be cleared.

I had a rough shadow put on him. This is a shadow who purposely allows himself to be seen by the subject he is following. Wherever Jones went, he had only to look around to find his shadow on his heels. The thought of being followed everywhere made Jones drink even more. When he was not lapping up the booze, Jones was hanging around street corners. He would stare in a dazed manner at the shadow forever watching him from down the street. He also became a chain smoker, which was also something new.

After a week or so of this softening-up treatment, I approached Jones at a bar. Unlike Murphy, he seemed to bear me no resentment, and gave me a friendly hello.

"Let's go over to a table where we can talk in private," I suggested. We moved our drinks there. I began by asking for his family. I hoped that they were not too upset about the trouble he was in. "Oh, no," he said without much conviction, "and my lawyer feels I will get off, if I plead guilty, with a suspended sentence."

"I think your lawyer is wrong," I told him.

He reacted as though I'd hit him in the face. "Why do you say that?" he asked.

"I don't think the insurance company will stand for it."

"Why do you say that?" he repeated plaintively. "My lawyer should know what he's talking about, shouldn't he? Wasn't he a judge for years?"

"I can't imagine your attorney saying you could get a suspended sentence. The company won't stand for it."

Humphrey Jones did not believe me. I suggested that he call his lawyer. "Tell him that I am on the case and would be glad to discuss it with him. Because I think we can help one another, Jones."

The lawyer, it turned out, was an Italian-American who had been a friend of mine for years. He was too fine a lawyer to do anything not in his client's interest, but he was also a man whom I knew trusted me and believed I would do anything I promised to do.

The next day his lawyer called and said he and Jones would meet me in Assistant District Attorney Garrison's office. No firm promises were made to Jones at this meeting, but the lawyer told Jones:

"Go and see Luisi at his office. He'll play square with you. You'll lose nothing if you tell him everything he wants to know."

The next day Jones made a complete statement.

Murphy (Jones said in his statement) had approached him more than two years before at a speakeasy bar, and told him of his plan to make some easy money by "writing Inland Marine policies in the names of others and concocting a loss" which Mr. Murphy would pretend to investigate. Then Murphy would make up a report, adjust it, and recommend payment. A loss draft would subsequently be drawn, based upon his recommendation, and signed by one of the two men in the Baltimore company's New York office who were authorized to sign checks. Murphy would then hand the check to Jones, who would have it cashed. Later he would divide the proceeds with Murphy.

They had used the names of friends on these false policies because they felt that these men and women would be less willing to testify against them than strangers would be.

"We started with George Walters, the waiter in that bar where we first talked about it," the statement continued. "I asked Walters for his address and went to see him one night. Murphy and I cooked up a policy that Walters knew nothing about. We got the money on that first fake policy on Christmas Eve, and divided it fifty-fifty. And we went on from there."

For a while they used the names of other insurance brokers to avoid arousing the suspicions of the company in Baltimore. But it made no difference — for Mr. Murphy naturally was most careful not to let the checks get out of his hands.

The pair got away with $100,000, but neither, when brought to trial, had $10 in the world. They say crime pays, but it didn't pay them.

Humphrey Jones pleaded guilty and got the suspended sentence he was promised. But Murphy was convicted and sentenced to six months.

*

FRIENDS have often told me that a man in my line of work is apt to get oversuspicious of people. They have a point. But sometimes, when I hear anything like that, I think of the "ideal office boy" that Edward Judd, general manager of the St. Paul Fire and Marine Company, found for himself. It was 1948, and in that post-World War II time youths who would work for the kind of wages office boys are paid were almost impossible to find.

That winter as usual my wife, Lillian, and I were down in Miami for many weeks, investigating the usual annual crop of jewel robberies. I was back only a couple of days when my secretary, as she finished taking my dictation, asked if I'd noticed the new boy who brought around the mail.

"No, what about him?"

"I guess he sees too many TV shows," she remarked. I looked at her. "I say that because every single day while you were in Florida he asked me the same thing: 'When is Private Eye Luisi coming back?' "

That would have meant nothing except for one thing. The day before a Pinkerton man had told me that he'd heard a rumor about an office boy in an insurance company being arrested for burglary. He didn't know the boy's name or what company he worked for.

The next time I had a conference with General Manager Judd, I asked him about the new office boy.

"Frank Bitali?" he asked.

I nodded, and told him what the Pinkerton man had said.

He threw back his head, and laughed. "That's the best office boy we've had here in years! If you suspect him of being a burglar, I would say you spent too much time in the sun while you were in Florida."

"Just to satisfy my curiosity, I'd like to see his time card."

Mr. Judd sent for the boy's time card. Young Bitali, who was seventeen, had been there for six months. Except for one stretch of four days in March, he had never missed a day at the office.

"As you can see for yourself," said Mr. Judd, "he was at the office except for those few days. He reported ill — with a cold, I think."

"Would you mind if I questioned him?"

"Well, for heaven's sake, be careful," said Mr. Judd. "I had a devil of a time finding a decent mail boy before I hired him. He just couldn't be dishonest." Nevertheless he agreed to send for Frank Bitali.

The boy came in smiling — until he saw me. I have a good eye for thieves, and I would have bet anything after observing his reaction that he was one. "You sent for me, Mr. Judd?" he asked.

"Yes," said Judd. "Mr. Luisi wants to talk to you."

The boy turned to me. For another moment or two, I said nothing, just studied him. I imagine it seemed like hours to the youngster before I spoke. Then I asked the kind of thing he did not expect.

"Are you satisfied with your job here, Frank?"

"Yes, sir," he said, "I am."

"What work do you do here?" I asked him. "I want you to start with the very first thing from the moment you take your hat off after you arrive here in the morning."

"I start by opening the office mail."

"All of the mail?" I asked.

"Everything that isn't marked 'Personal' on the envelope."

"Does anyone in this office treat you badly?"

"No," he said, "they treat me real good here. They're swell to me." But by this time I was convinced he was the boy the Pinkerton man had heard about.

"If that's the case, why didn't you tell Mr. Judd that you were in trouble?"

He stared at me in fright.

"Why did you wait and let Mr. Judd find it out from me, from the outside. He's the man who gave you the job and who's been good to you."

I was interested less in reproaching him than in convincing him we would help him if we could. I went over to him and put my arm around the young fellow's shoulder, and told him that he would be much better off if he told his story to Mr. Judd and myself. "It will be easier than talking to the detectives down at Police Headquarters," I said. "I have two boys of my own. Mr. Judd has two boys. We wouldn't like them to be arrested, and we know how your own family will feel if you're arrested again."

He hung his head. I was sure he was going to confess.

I said quietly: "Now, Frank, if you will tell us everything you remember, starting with the first burglary you were involved in, I think the St. Paul Company will do everything within its power to help you out of this trouble."

"All right," he said, "I'll tell you everything."

The suddenness of this surprised me. But, of course, it was nothing to Mr. Judd's surprise. I called in my secretary. Mr. Judd knew too much about the way I worked to interrupt me. He just sat there looking more and more astonished as the boy told his story. The first few paragraphs must have given the staid Mr. Judd one of the great shocks of his career. And I quote:

"I started working for the St. Paul Fire and Marine Insurance Company on December 16, 1947, as a mail clerk. Beginning in January, 1948, and up to March, 1948 (when I was arrested — charged with burglary), in my position as a mail clerk I had the authority to open all mail unless it was addressed 'Personal.' In a short space of time I noticed retail credit reports coming in in connection with prospective applicants for insurance. These reports gave the name, address, property value, location of premises, number of occupants in the house, number of servants, and in some instances whether or not the house was occupied. In my position as mail clerk, in opening the mail that was not marked 'Personal,' I had occasion to note appraisals of furs and jewelry. If any of these applicants were living in Brooklyn, I would take the names and addresses with the intention of looking them over, either alone or with some friends of mine, for the purpose of committing burglary. At the present time I really do not know how many names and addresses I turned over to my friends — I would say about five or six."

I think the strange capers of Bitali's mob would give another kind of shock to readers of crime stories in which the criminals invariably are shown as brilliant fellows who case the scene, plan their jobs intelligently down to the last detail, and meet any and every emergency with quick wit and masterful ingenuity.

Different boys were in on different jobs. The whole thing was as casual as buying a pack of cigarettes. They'd move to a job on impulse, without casing it. They would not even phone in advance to make sure no one was home. They'd just look over Frank's latest list of newly insured homes and stores and go to one of them.

Their first job, based on the information the ideal office boy copied from retail credit reports in our office, was a fiasco. It was an attempt to crack the safe in the Endicott Theatre one January night. At midnight one of the boys climbed a fifty-foot-high drainpipe, got into the office floor through a window. Then he ran downstairs and let his two pals in. But they had not brought the tools they needed to open a safe. And it was too big for them to carry out. After standing there in the office for two hours arguing about how to solve their problem, they abandoned the whole idea, and went home. On most of their jobs they had no car in which to make a fast getaway. These burglars traveled to and from their work on foot, or by bus or subway, just as most honest Brooklynites do. These bunglers also had no fence. More than once they had to hide their loot overnight in an empty lot. One burglary they gave up after they arrived there because they decided that "the house was too big."

The owner was in the cellar fixing the furnace of another home they broke into. The boys took $200, three watches, and a lighter. Then they heard him coming up the stairs and ran out. Incidentally, this homeowner, who was insured by St. Paul, had claimed his loss amounted to $500 in cash and $3,000 in jewelry, including a pearl necklace which Bitali insisted he had never seen.

Of course, one of his pals might have shoved the pearls in his pocket and forgotten to mention it. They all had convenient memories. It could also be that the owner of the pearls had a convenient imagination.

When Bitali finished talking that day, I promised him he wouldn't be fired. Mr. Judd asked as soon as the boy was out of the room, "What are we going to do with him?"

"Let him continue working here for the time being," I said.

"I'm not going to feel comfortable with that boy working in the office!" he exclaimed. "Do you think I'm going to let him go on opening the mail? Hasn't he done us enough damage?"

"He has done us much more damage than he cared to mention today," I said; "at least that's what I think. Thieves very seldom indeed confess all of their crimes the first time you interrogate them."

We solved the problem simply. We kept Frank Bitali on salary for the time being. We told him that he did not have to come to the office. Frank thought that was the greatest thing that had ever happened to him — and kept telling me about more burglaries of the gang, including one big job in which these oafs had got $5,000 in cash and jewelry.

The four days he had been on sick leave covered a period between his arrest for burglary (under an alias) and quick parole granted him by a merciful judge — as a first offender. Though Frank later did not admit being in on burglaries other than the five he had described to me, he did confess that he had tipped off his friends — not always the same ones, by the way — with the reliable information he kept finding in the company's daily mail.

"Why didn't you go out yourself on these jobs?" I repeatedly asked him. He had two answers:

"I didn't feel like stealing anything that night. I had money, so I didn't have to steal." Or, "I wasn't in the mood."

Of interest to psychologists might be his girl's feeling that, unlike burglary, assault and battery was quite forgivable.

This he revealed the afternoon I asked, "Have you got a girl, Frank?"

"Yes. I'm engaged to be married to her."

"Does she know about your being arrested for burglary?"

"Well, she knows part of the story. I told her I wasn't a good boy. But I said I was arrested only for assault and battery. She says she doesn't care."

"How did you spend all that money you took, Frank?"

"I bought my girl a gold cross for Easter."

"What else?"

"I lost the rest on the ponies or in crap games."

"What else?"

"I spent it foolishly."

I had Frank kept on the payroll for several weeks. He was dropped only when I became convinced that there was nothing else he would tell us.

Though he never returned to the insurance business, he did not stop stealing. He has been arrested three times since for burglary and again in 1956 for stealing a car. He was sent to state prison for the car theft and was still behind bars when I last heard of him. The others were arrested and sent to prison later on.

*

INSURANCE men, like men in other professions, sometimes get odd ideas of what pleases their acquaintances. I recall being invited to the home of a broker for dinner one night. His wife was beautiful, but kept looking at me with increasing fear all through dinner.

I couldn't understand it. I was also a little puzzled at my host's endless praise of my feats. "Why, my dear," he told his wife, "our guest is the country's most successful private detective. He has never lost a case."

It was the sort of thing one likes to hear, even if he realizes it is a flattering exaggeration.

But I was puzzled as to why he went on that way and why his wife's fear of me increased as she listened. Many years later, I met him again, but this time he had another wife with him. He mentioned the evening when we last met, and said, "You sure saved me a lot of money that night."

"How?" I asked.

"Well, I had decided to get a divorce. I knew my wife had more than one lover, but I had been unable to trap her in a hotel with one of them. So I told her that I had hired you and that you had the goods on her. On the night you came to dinner she thought you had the incriminating evidence on you and would produce it at any moment I asked you to. That so frightened her — after the way I went on about your cleverness — that she agreed to go to Reno, waived alimony, and even paid her own counsel fees.

"You have no idea of how much money you saved me, old man."

He was utterly astonished when I told him that I despised him for having used me, a guest in his home, in that way, and also that trapping women with their lovers in hotel rooms was not one of my specialties.

I never spoke to the man again.

But the fellow who really annoyed me was a certified public accountant who had the nerve to steal from me. George Bartley had worked with me on scores of investigations, checking books. And a very capable and efficient man he was.

He went into business on his own one year, and suggested that I help him get a start as a freelance by letting him do my auditing, instead of his old firm, whenever I needed the services of a C.P.A.

I did so. One week, Ira Cass, my regular bookkeeper, became ill. I asked Bartley to take over the job until Cass recovered. He kept the payroll for me and also my employees' expense accounts. That went on for three and a half months.

Only a few days after returning to work, Cass reported some irregularities in our cashbook. Our payroll varied greatly each week because we hired men and women detectives by the day as we needed them.

What Bartley had done, Cass said, was to add $100 each week for ten weeks in a row to my payroll. Major Otto, my general manager, accustomed to my trusting Bartley, never questioned the amount of the check the substitute bookkeeper offered for his signature each week.

This happened on a Saturday, a working day for most people in those quaint days. I was in a rage, and decided to call Bartley. He was at home. "I'm at the office," I said. "I think you'd better come down here to see me."

"Oh, I'm sorry," he said, "but I'm leaving for Atlantic City with my wife and children. I'm afraid it will have to wait until I get back."

"It is too urgent for me to wait for more than an hour."

"What in the world is it?" he asked.

"I can guarantee you one thing, Bartley," I said. "If you lose any time at all coming down here, I don't think that you will be able to enjoy any vacation this weekend."

Within forty-five minutes Bartley was in the office and acting very petulant indeed. "Gee, the kids will never forgive me," he said. "I've been promising for weeks to take them to Atlantic City. We had our bags all packed."

His feelings seemed terribly hurt.

"I have a suggestion: sit down and stop talking."

When he obeyed, I asked, "How many investigations have we worked on together, Bartley?"

He thought for a moment, still maintaining his injured air. "About — well, more than a hundred, I guess," he said, finally.

I stared at him. "Well, in how many cases did you see the suspect confess?"

"In almost every one," he said. Now he was getting nervous; I thought he was ready to break, but I wanted to make sure. He was young, strong, and he knew the law from his experience with me.

"Now, Bartley," I said, "you know my tricks, how I get the truth out of people — that is, you think you do. I would say, myself, you know about half of them. And unless my memory deceives me, there is one trick you don't know."

With my right hand I pulled out my blackjack, passed it under his nose, and slapped it down so hard on the table that he jumped with nervousness.

"I'm not going to waste any time with you," I told him. "But if you deny that you pocketed $100 a week by fattening the payroll for ten weeks, I'll hit you over the head with that ugly-looking thing on the table."

"Don't hit me," he whimpered, "please!"

Actually, I would not have hit him. I have never beaten anyone in my life except in self-defense or when I was convinced I was about to be attacked.

Bartley made good on the $1,000 he had stolen within a couple of days. I don't know if he got to Atlantic City that weekend. But if he did, I doubt that he enjoyed himself very much.

THERE
IS NO THIEF
LIKE A DAME

4

RODGERS and Hammerstein made no error at all when they wrote "There's Nothing Like a Dame!" It goes triple when the ladies are crooks. No indeed, there is no thief like a dame. These Cinderellas with claws and Little Red Riding Hoods with guns in their pockets, these wide-eyed Winnies with larceny in their hearts run to all types, from the beautiful and the damned to the ugly and the ridiculous.

I begin with the case of Mrs. Blum, a divorcée who was working as a $40-a-week bookkeeper. One day she took out an insurance policy on her fur coat. She described it as mink, full length with cuffs, and worth $3,000.

Now, all that followed would have been avoided if the agent who sold that policy, or some other representative of the insurance company, had taken one look at Mrs. Blum's coat or even made a phone call to find out whether or not she had the means to buy such a luxury.

If you know an insurance broker, you need only tell him you want to insure your fur coat, and, if he's a live wire, he can call up the insurance company on the telephone, insure it for the amount requested, and give you a binder until the policy is issued. Three thousand dollars is not a large or unusual amount of insurance on a fur coat. There are times when the company asks for an appraisal, but this was not one of them.

The company began to wonder about Mrs. Blum's full-length

mink with cuffs only when the claim of loss papers came. It had disappeared, it seemed, from the checkroom of a Lower East Side dance hall. For the first time it seemed odd to a company man that a woman making $40 a week should spend $3,000 (approximately what she earned in a year and a half) for a fur coat. The doubts about Mrs. Blum grew when the company considered the place she said she had lost it. Sarah had notified the police, she said, on her claim, but they had not responded. They may have figured that no fur-bearing woman would take her coat there — unless, of course, she wished to have it disappear. It was the sort of hall that is hired by the night for Ukrainian weddings, dances of the Jolly Twelve of Delancey Street, and meetings of the Hungarian Free Thought Society.

I went to see Sarah, a dumpy, homely little woman in her late thirties at her walkup apartment.

She was alone, she told me, when she arrived that evening at the dance hall about eight o'clock. Finding no attendant in the checkroom, she herself hung her $3,000 mink coat on a hanger.

At midnight, four hours later, she decided to go home. But to her dismay her fur coat was gone. She asked the waiters who served refreshments in the place and other people if they had seen it. None of them had.

"How did you happen to go to that dance hall alone?" I asked Mrs. Blum.

"I had a date to meet my girl friend there, but she didn't show up."

"Where did you buy the coat?"

"From a peddler."

"Was he someone you knew, someone you had bought things from before?"

"No, I never saw him before in my life."

"You mean you saw this peddler of mink coats on the street and — "

"No, he came to my door with it."

"What happened when he came to the door with it?"

"He had this beautiful fur coat with him. I could see it was the bargain of a lifetime. I tried it on. It fitted me perfectly and — I bought it."

"What bank, Mrs. Blum, do you have a checking account in?"

"I have no checking account."

"What bank do you have a savings account in?"

"None. I have no savings account. I don't believe in keeping my money in banks."

"Where do you keep it?"

"I kept it at home." At my request, Mrs. Blum showed me the bureau drawer where she kept her savings.

My questions up to this point were all designed to make her realize how ridiculous her story was. A peddler came to her door with a $3,000 mink coat, this being in a two-room walkup apartment located in a near slum. The coat just fitted her, and she bought it on the spot.

Abruptly, she changed her story. She hadn't saved the money at all. A relative living in Europe had died and left her the money. When Mrs. Blum showed no inclination of changing her story, I could only tell her:

"I will investigate this. Possibly you will see me again."

I was sorry for the poor woman who lacked the sense to realize that she hadn't a chance of getting the $3,000 on so unconvincing a story.

I next went to the dance hall. It was locked but the janitor had the key. He took me upstairs after I showed him my badge. It was one flight up and over a saloon. It was in a room of about 75 by 35 feet with a cloakroom near the entrance and an orchestra stand with a piano on it at the other end. The sides of the hall were lined with chairs. I searched the place thoroughly, though I didn't expect to find anything more substantial than cobwebs and burned matches.

As he watched me, the janitor said, "What are you looking for?"

"A woman's mink coat," I said.

"Now, that's funny," he said, scratching his head. "I sleep in a room in the back of the basement. And when I got up this morning it was raining. Like I do every morning, I went to the window to look out at the yard. I saw some soaking-wet thing laying out there in the yard. I went out and got it. It turned out to be a fur coat. But I couldn't figure how it got out there."

"Was it a mink coat?"

"I never saw a mink coat," he told me, "except in the movies."

"Let's have a look at the one you found."

He took me downstairs to his kitchen where he had the coat hanging up to dry.

"You still haven't seen a mink coat," I told him.

The coat he found was a battered old muskrat that looked like it had been in a fight with another fur coat, maybe a ferocious leopard. Tufts of fur were worn off in two or three places.

"I might buy this thing," I said. "What do you figure it's worth?"

He shrugged, then said, "Oh, at most about ten bucks, I guess." I could see that he had never met any junk dealers. If he had, he wouldn't have been so optimistic.

Ten percent reward is what insurance companies usually pay for found merchandise. But in this case I decided to be generous with my employer's money, and gave him the $10.

The janitor carefully wrapped up the coat for me and I took it to the precinct station house. I showed it to the detective who had been assigned the case, and described how I found it. I wanted him to go with me to the office where Mrs. Blum worked.

"I think your being with me," I said, "might persuade her to tell the truth."

He went with me and we interviewed Mrs. Blum in her tiny office in the dress factory. I asked the bookkeeper to describe in detail once more the coat she had lost. She kept looking at the bundle I was carrying, imagining, I suppose, that we'd found some mink coat that we hoped she'd accept. She described the kind of fur, the styling, length, lining, sleeve, and collar.

When she was through I slowly opened the bundle. Her mouth dropped open and she grew pale. Without giving her a moment to think, I asked, "Is this your coat, Mrs. Blum?"

"Yes," she said, darting a frightened glance at the detective. And she signed, without argument, the release. We had no interest in arresting her, of course, but she might have shown some resistance if the police detective had not been along.

*

PATHETIC though Mrs. Blum was, she had attempted an out-and-out swindle. I felt far sorrier for a servant, Gertrude Williams, who took to crime just as stupidly, but out of terror that she might fall ill one day and not be able to support her child. Her husband had deserted her and the child some years before. Though an excellent cook, Mrs. Williams' pay was small, and the problem of providing for the little girl's future preyed on her mind.

Mrs. Williams tried to solve the problem in the most foolish way, by gradually getting into the habit of stealing articles of small value, trinkets, an old watch or ring, from her employers when she was about to quit her job.

I first heard about Mrs. Williams from a Cedarhurst, Long Island, woman, a Mrs. John Matthews, whose husband was a retired shirt manufacturer. No trinkets, but $5,000 worth of jewelry had been discovered missing from the Matthews home shortly after Mrs. Williams quit her job there.

Mrs. Matthews was very bitter about her. When she hired the cook, Mrs. Williams begged her to let her daughter live there with her, something Mrs. Matthews readily agreed to.

"She was a pretty and sweet little girl, her Lillian," Mrs. Matthews told me, "and very well mannered. Mr. Matthews and I, having no children of our own, greatly enjoyed having her around. The child, who had always lived in New York, seemed to love living with us. That is why I was so astonished when her mother suddenly announced after three weeks that she was leaving us. She asked for her pay, said she could not stand living in the country for one more moment. She did not like being so far from her friends, she said.

"On being paid she left with the little girl right away. A few nights before she left, my husband and I had gone to a reception. I wore my best jewelry that night. On coming home I put the jewelry, as usual, in a box on my bureau. This morning I opened the box on my bureau. The jewels were gone."

Mrs. Matthews had the cook's address. But before calling there I went to the employment agency that had sent her, and got a list of her former employers. The manager also gave me the address of a Park Avenue matron for whom Mrs. Williams was now working days.

My next stop was at a police station. With two detectives who were assigned to help me, I walked to the house where Mrs. Williams lived.

As we approached the house I saw a beautiful little blond child who was playing on the street with some other little girls. If I hadn't had a good notion what twelve-year-old Lillian Williams looked like, I could still have identified her. Around her neck she had a diamond-studded platinum band suspended from which was a crucifix. I had a description of that fine piece of jewelry right in my pocket. Mrs. Matthews had given it to me on the list of articles missing from her home. But she had not mentioned any gold crucifix.

"I'll know Mrs. Williams when I see her, I think," I said. "I have a good description."

But no description was necessary a few minutes later when a tired-looking woman approached, her arms full of bundles.

"Mother!" cried Lillian running to her. Mrs. Williams did not look around, but went straight into the house and upstairs. The child went back to her rope-skipping, playing with her friends. One of the detectives remained there watching the child while his partner and I followed Mrs. Williams upstairs. She put down her bundles and got out her key. As she opened the door and went in, we followed her.

We showed her our badges, and I asked her why she had quit her job in Cedarhurst. She said that the country air did not agree with her daughter and that she herself didn't like being so far from her friends. But she angrily denied ever having seen Mrs. Matthews' jewels, no less stealing them.

"Where did you buy that diamond-studded platinum band your little girl is wearing?" I asked.

Mrs. Williams burst into tears, and we did not have to ask her many more questions before she showed us where she had hidden the rest of the loot she'd picked up at Mrs. Matthews' home. Among the other pieces were a diamond sunburst with twenty-nine stones; a brooch with seventeen diamonds; a crescent pin with thirty-five more, and a solitaire diamond ring. She'd stuffed them into the toes of a pair of old shoes in the back of her clothes closet.

There was no question that her only concern was her child. "I don't care what you do to me," she kept saying, "but please, please don't let my little girl know her mother is a thief. I'll die if she finds out; I'll really die."

"Well, we'll do all we can," the detective assured her. "But you'll have to get that diamond band away from her right now."

"What will I tell her?"

"Anything you want to."

Mrs. Williams went to the window and told the child to come upstairs. She took the diamond band from around the child's neck, explaining that the gold clasp had to be repaired. She slipped off the crucifix, went to a drawer, and got out the little gold-plated chain it had been on originally, slipped the crucifix on this, and fastened it around the child's neck.

"Now, Lillian, when it gets dark I want you to go around the corner to your Aunt Jennie's house. Stay there until I come for you. I may be a little late. I have to go someplace with these gentlemen on business."

The child, scarcely giving us a glance, went happily out. I asked Mrs. Williams what she had done with the jewelry she'd taken from the other places where she had worked. It was a fairly safe guess that this was not her only theft.

"I have it all here," she said. In the next hour she pulled out all sorts of junk she had stolen — vases, old-fashioned watches, a baby spoon and other odd pieces of silver. None of it was worth much. Together the whole lot would not have brought $40 in a pawnshop.

"Didn't you every try to sell anything you stole?"

Mrs. Williams shook her head. "I just took it and kept it," she said. "I wanted to have something that would bring money for medicine and doctors that we would need in case Lillian or I got sick. I wouldn't have been able to work if she got sick. I'd worry about her too much. I'd give up whatever job I had to take care of her. And then we'd need money for our food and rent, too."

"But what about these diamonds you took from Mrs. Matthews?" the detective asked. "You were going to sell them first chance you got, weren't you?"

"No."

He kept asking her that. She admitted that she had known they were valuable, but said she had no idea that they were worth thousands of dollars. I believed her. I think the detective also believed her. But he kept questioning her to make certain that no fence or other person was involved.

Unfortunately, it was impossible to conceal from the child that her mother was a thief. After Mrs. Williams signed a confession at the station house, we sent for Mrs. Matthews. She identified the jewels and preferred charges against her former cook. At her trial Mrs. Williams pleaded guilty and was sent to the workhouse for an indefinite term. Her little blond child was turned over to the Children's Society, which then tried to find a home for her.

Mrs. Williams' real crime, of course, was loving her child too well. And there was the irony: the mother who would have died for her little girl managed by accident to find her the home, the surroundings, and quite possibly permanent security — then lost them all because of the stealing habit that was born of her fears of not being able to provide them for her little girl.

*

IN the twenties I had a much stronger case in which a mother's passionate attachment to her only child led to a weird and grisly swindling attempt. The woman was Mrs. Cortland Thomas, the wife of the millionaire corporation lawyer. Her son at the time of the melodramatic series of events was in his late twenties. He had gone straight from Yale Law School to a position in his father's law firm, and showed the utmost promise. Everyone expected him to duplicate his father's success.

For years his mother had been urging him to marry some nice girl of their own social station. Like so many middle-aged women, her greatest dream was to have grandchildren. With Mrs. Thomas it amounted to an obsession. When her son did become engaged it was to a girl of his own station. But she was one of the new breed, a flapper, the last sort of daughter-in-law his mother would have chosen.

In fact, she became so upset that just before the engagement was announced she asked me to investigate the past of Helen, her son's prospective bride.

What I found out was that Helen was no worse than the other society flappers of the day. Like so many of her friends, she was overfond of night life. She drank too much, spent too much time in speakeasies, and some of her friends were Broadway characters with rather shady reputations. But most of the men she had dated were well-bred men like Cortland, Jr.

As far as I ever learned, she was not promiscuous, had never been arrested or been in any other trouble in spite of her wild, high-kicking, hard-drinking way of life.

The older Thomases thanked me for my report. I do not think they ever mentioned to their son having hired me. He was infatuated with Helen, and I'd found out nothing that he didn't know.

Their engagement was announced and in a few months they were married. For some reason Mrs. Thomas urged the young couple to live with her and her husband. She had an idea, I think, that she would have a steadying influence on the giddy girl. But Helen continued to drink as much as ever, and rarely appeared for meals. She went out almost every night, and her infatuated husband seemed happy enough to go with her and stay out until three or four in the morning. His work and health were suffering.

The couple had been married for almost a year when Mr. and Mrs. Thomas called me in for the second time. They told me about their problems with their daughter-in-law. This served as a preface to as strange a tale as I've ever heard. Mrs. Thomas said: "I decided that there was only one thing that could possibly change my daughter-in-law's attitude and induce her to live a normal, dignified life. That was motherhood. I offered her $150,000 if she would have a baby. I said that when she became pregnant I would give her one-third of the money, the balance after the baby was born.

"A few weeks after this, Helen confided that she was pregnant. But when I urged her to go to our family doctor for an examination, she rebelled. 'I am sure,' she said, 'that he is a fine physician. But I would feel much happier in the hands of the doctor who has been treating me since I was a little girl.' I agreed quickly enough, but when I suggested that I accompany her to her family doctor's office she refused. She said she preferred to go alone, not being a child. When she came back she said that the doctor had assured her that she was indeed pregnant.

"I sat down that night and wrote out the check for $50,000 that I'd promised her."

At this point Mrs. Thomas was unable to continue, and her husband told me the rest of the story. At first impending motherhood did seem to be having the hoped-for effect on the girl. She began to stay home nights and stopped drinking, but that did not last long. Soon she resumed her practice of going out on the town with her husband. His mother pleaded with him not to endanger their unborn child in that way, but there was nothing he could do, he said.

He was still infatuated with his wife, and possibly also with the wild life she had introduced him to. I've noticed that this happens often with young men whose mothers so carefully shelter them in their early years.

Helen's mother-in-law had never stopped warning her about the danger of a miscarriage. And one day the older woman came home to find the girl in bed and apparently overwhelmed with grief at losing her baby. The maid told the story this way:

"I heard young Mrs. Thomas scream while she was in the bathroom. When I went in there the whole place was drenched with blood. 'Please, Stella,' she said, 'get the fetus for me. It's in the toilet. I want you to show it to my mother-in-law. Her heart will be broken when she finds out that I've had a miscarriage. She wanted so much to have her grandchild.' "

Stella, the maid, showed Mrs. Thomas the fetus she had recovered, and was told to dispose of it. Going into the bathroom, Mrs. Thomas could see for herself the blood Helen had lost. It was smeared all over the bathroom. There was so much blood everywhere she looked that Mrs. Thomas, feeling nauseated, left the bathroom and shut the door quickly behind her. She instructed Stella to clean up the mess as quickly as she could.

"Helen's actions immediately after that," Cortland Thomas, Sr., said in conclusion, "made us both suspicious of this whole business. When my wife suggested that a doctor be called, Helen first refused, and then, on being urged to do so for her health's sake, had an attack of wild hysterics. She would not permit my wife to call the doctor whom she said had examined her and told her she was pregnant.

"But a couple of days later Helen got out of bed without assistance and announced she would visit that doctor in his office. Again she refused to allow Mrs. Thomas to accompany her."

Both of them shook their heads. "What really saddens us most is the persistence with which she demands that she be given the $100,000. The point she makes is that this money belongs to her even though the baby wasn't born. 'It wasn't my fault I had a miscarriage,' she keeps saying."

"What is your son's attitude now about all this?"

"He's still half in love with Helen, but he's not a complete fool. In fact, it was he, Mr. Luisi, who suggested that we engage you to find out whether or not Helen was ever pregnant. He has grave doubts, you see, of that himself."

After thinking over the whole bizarre situation, I decided to undertake the investigation. My first step was to warn Mr. and Mrs. Thomas to do nothing that would cause Helen to suspect that they had hired a private detective. The Thomases had a warning for me. They said that Helen was unusually observant, and seemed to have a sixth sense that warned or alerted her when anyone was watching her, or when she thought she was in any danger.

So I dropped the usual procedure of putting a tail on her. Instead I had a talk with young Mr. Thomas. I asked him to take Helen on a brief cruise. "Treat her as though it was a second honeymoon," I told him.

But we did put a night-and-day tail on Stella, the maid. It seemed certain that if Helen had faked the miscarriage, she would have required Stella's cooperation. We waited only until the maid's day off to make a thorough search of Helen Thomas's room. My wife, an expert at this, went through everything: the young woman's trunks, bureaus, closets, and jewel boxes.

There were two interesting finds, one being a diamond pin on which we later discovered Helen had collected money from an insurance company, claiming she had lost it. Much more important were the business and other cards found in a secret cubbyhole of one of her bureaus. My wife copied down the names and addresses. I brought them to Police Headquarters, where some of the names were identified as the real names and aliases of thieves and con men.

Another of the cards, I was told, was from a clinic on West Twenty-third Street that the police had long suspected was really an abortion mill. There had been several complaints lodged against the doctor in charge of the clinic for performing illegal operations, but no action had been taken because of lack of evidence.

I lost no time in making a personal call at the clinic. It proved to be a large and apparently thriving institution. There were rooms on both sides of the corridor leading from the reception room to the office of the doctor who ran it. Adjoining his office was the examination room, which I suppose also served for the surgery. He had two other doctors and two nurses working for him, besides the receptionist. They did not like strangers there. The receptionist made that evident. She questioned me closely. Even after I explained that I was a claim adjuster for an insurance company, I had to wait for almost ten minutes to see the man who ran the clinic.

As I was ushered into the general manager's office, my heart jumped. In back of him, on a shelf, were several large bottles. Each one contained a fetus, preserved in alcohol.

Noticing me staring at them, he said, "Are you interested in these specimens?"

"Yes," I said. "How much would you charge me for one of them?"

He studied me for a moment, then said, "Fifty dollars."

"Fifty dollars!" I exclaimed. "Why, a friend of mine bought one of those embryos just a couple of weeks ago. She didn't pay anything like $50 for it."

"Did she buy it here?"

"I think she did."

"What was her name, Mr. Luisi?"

"I don't really care to say. You see, she is a young woman who was only recently married. She bought the fetus to play a joke on someone."

"Oh, I know who that was," he said. "Mrs. Cortland Thomas, Jr."

"That's correct," I said. I pulled out my shield and showed it to him. "I need not waste any time," I said, "telling you of the suspicions of the authorities concerning what goes on here. But I have some news for you. If I tell the district attorney half of what I've found out about your so-called clinic, he'll have a police squad down here within ten minutes, turning your abortion joint upside down."

He got as white as a ghost.

"What do you want of me, Mr. Luisi?"

He was so scared that I think he would have been overjoyed at the chance to buy me off. "Get out your pen and a piece of paper. I'll dictate a statement that I will ask you to read over carefully before you sign it."

This he found most disquieting, I am sure, because he hadn't an idea of what I would want in the statement. So when he discovered that all I wished was a declaration that on September 25th Mrs. Cortland Thomas, Jr., had bought from him a fetus preserved in alcohol for $50, he was vastly relieved, and happy to sign the paper, particularly when I agreed to his adding that he did not know for what purpose she had bought the fetus.

Next day I had Stella, the maid, brought to my office. I questioned her and got the other part of the story. When Mrs. Thomas, Jr., returned from her second honeymoon I was all ready for her.

She was outraged, and denied everything when I showed her the abortionist's statement. "Why, the idea!" she shrieked. "He's a liar. I never heard of the man." She kept insisting that she had been pregnant until I showed her the card we'd found in the cubbyhole of her dresser.

It was Stella's statement, though, that convinced Mrs. Cortland Thomas, Jr., that the jig was up. This said that she had given Stella $50 to help her to fake the abortion. Stella's role in the plot was to buy a large quantity of liver, squeeze the blood out of it, and to scatter the beef blood, which resembles human blood, all over the bathroom. Stella also was to back up her story when Helen's mother-in-law arrived home that day.

"If you have any doubts that Stella signed this statement," I told Helen, "I'll call her into this room so you can question her right now."

"Thank you for that privilege," Helen told me, "but please don't bother. I admit everything."

She and her husband soon after were quietly divorced.

I suppose it is useless to speculate about what would have happened to this marriage if the young couple had been permitted to work out their own problems without any interference from their elders. Right or wrong, her mother-in-law acted out of the best motives. Personally, I think that Helen, the well-bred, well-educated girl, would have gone down the wrong road regardless of anything else. Why a woman, with everything to lose and nothing to gain, gambles everything out of recklessness or boredom I've never been able to figure out. I'm happy to leave the question in the hands of the psychoanalysts.

*

ANOTHER case that I had in the twenties reminded me of poor Sarah Blum, the bookkeeper, but only because it concerned a coat thrown out of a window. This one cost $9,000 — at least that's what the claim said, and the story of how it was lost seemed as unworthy of belief as the one Sarah told me. At first glance and, I must add, at second glance also.

Jeanie Dearie, the girl involved, could not have been more different from Sarah Blum. She was young, beautiful, had sky-blue eyes and vivid red hair, and was being kept in style. A sporty shoe manufacturer, Joe Evans, had fallen in love with her on first sight. They'd met in a speakeasy, and ever since, Evans, who was about forty and very rich, after setting her up in a flashy apartment, had been filling her life with gay nights on the town. If not showering her with diamonds, he was at least sprinkling her with jewelry, furs, and all of the other fine feathers, including literally hundreds of pairs of shoes. The silver-blue mink that he had insured for $9,000 was one of these presents.

Puritans, reformers, and other straight-laced folk might disapprove of their immoral relationship, but even they would not have wondered, after seeing Jeanie, why Evans had fallen in love with her. Whenever feasible he took her along on his business trips across and around the country, while his wife and three children remained safely tucked away in Scarsdale, a fashionable suburb. He was prouder of having Jeanie Dearie than his new and exclusive numbers. It was on one of these trips that the silver-blue mink disappeared.

It happened in Chicago.

On Saturday afternoon of the weekend this happily unmarried couple spent there, Joe Evans had been invited to play poker in the showroom of another shoe manufacturer. To keep Jeanie busy and out of mischief he arranged for her and this other shoe man's sweetheart to attend a matinee at one of the Loop theaters. Jeanie wore her silver-blue.

By the time the show was over, Joe Evans assured Jeanie, the poker game would be breaking up. He suggested that the girls come to the showroom right after the theatre. From there the four of them would go out for cocktails and dinner.

But the other girl who agreed to go along was not too happy about it. As they came out of the theater she grumbled: "I know what's going to happen, Jeanie. You and I will be sitting, waiting for those old men of ours to finish their game, for hours." She complained about that all the way to the downtown building where the shoe man's place occupied the whole ninth floor. Jeanie, an impressionable young woman, was worked up to a state approaching rebellion by the time they got to the smoke-filled room where six stout, middle-aged men were solemnly playing five-dollar-limit stud poker.

"Are you ready, dear?" asked Dearie as she walked in with the other girl.

Joe Evans only grunted something about being behind $380 worth. The other girl held up her hands in an "I told you so," gesture. Jeanie, feeling like a fool because she had been sure that Joe would not keep her waiting, thereupon threw her purse, hat, and silver-blue mink on a table. At this point that is what she probably intended. But the table was against a window and the window was open, and all three went sailing out.

"Oh, my God, Joe! My coat's gone out the window." The screech she uttered stopped the game.

Mr. Evans dropped his hand, raced to the window, glanced out, saw the coat, purse, and hat lying on the street. Too impatient to wait for the elevator, he, with the ladies and the other card players following, raced down the stairs and out to the street in record time — but too late. The hat and girl's purse were still lying there, but someone had made off with the $9,000 coat.

I went to Chicago to investigate this. Each of the poker players confirmed the facts. Evans advertised, offering a reward, in the Chicago newspapers — and got no answers.

When I got back to New York I went to see the furrier from whom Mr. Evans had bought the coat, and asked him to authenticate the purchase price. I knew this man well and expected him to show me his books.

He laughed at me.

"What are you laughing at, Jake?" I asked. "I showed you the bill of sale Mr. Evans' friend got. Isn't it yours?"

"It's a $9,000 sale on that piece of paper. But the coat cost him only $6,000."

"You mean you gave it to him wholesale?"

"No," Jake replied. "That was the retail price, $6,000, and that's what he paid for it."

"Why did you give him a bill saying $9,000?"

"Should I interfere if he wants to look like $3,000 more of a sport to her? After all, what I write on a piece of paper is not what I ring up on the cash register. I wish it was. This town is full of wives and girl friends who believe that they have coats that cost more than their friends' coats. And when the friends doubt it they just show them the price tag. It brings me business and keeps them happy. Is that bad?"

Not wanting him to laugh at me, I did not say that it was bad — for the insurance company, at any rate.

But in this case the last laugh was on Joe Evans and the furrier. Joe was embarrassed and also furious at the furrier for telling me the right price. It was not the $3,000 cash difference but the fact that Jeanie would know that he had lied to her about paying so much for her mink, and put him in the doghouse.

This she did, claiming that he had humiliated her and made her look like a phony to all her girl friends. Tearfully, she complained that everyone could tell a $9,000 mink from a $6,000 number, and had laughed at her behind her back.

The result was that the unhappy shoe manufacturer, after listening to about all of this that he cared to, offered to buy her a $9,000 coat if she would only forget the terrible thing he'd done to her.

"This time I'll buy it myself — without you making advance arrangements with the furrier. I'll go and pick it out all by myself — and if you don't like the $9,000 mink coat I select, you can just go and buy me another one that you do like."

With many a groan, Joe Evans sat down and wrote the lady a check for $9,000. There was another turn to the joke when Jeanie called me in about the insurance.

"This time I want no trouble if the coat is lost or stolen," she said, "so I'm just insuring it for $3,800, but don't tell Joe." I didn't, and he will know about it only now if he reads it here.

*

As an insurance detective I was often an involuntary witness to domestic dramas. Also comedies.

One of the latter revolved around the mysterious disappearance of a $10,000 diamond ring from the jewel box of pretty, vivacious Miriam Wilson. The ring, along with her other jewelry, was, of course, fully insured. The other jewels had not been touched by whoever caused the ring to disappear. Mrs. Wilson's story was that she had put the ring in the box with all her jewels one night. In the morning — *presto!* — it was gone.

I talked to her husband (another furrier, incidentally) about this. I had checked his finances and his credit rating. Both were in fine shape. And his business was big enough to make it seem, on the face of it, anyway, to be a ridiculous idea that he would have any interest in picking up a fast $10,000 by faking the loss of a diamond ring. Ninety-eight times out of a hundred substantial businessmen turn to such flimflam only when facing bankruptcy or needing money in a hurry. And I got the impression that he was honestly bewildered by the ring's disappearance. He had done all the right things promptly, including notifying the police and his insurance broker.

"I would like to talk to Mrs. Wilson about this as soon as convenient," I told him.

This seemed to trouble Mr. Wilson. "I sure would appreciate it if you waited until she returned from the country before interviewing her."

I said nothing. "You see," he explained, "losing that ring upset her dreadfully. She carried on like a baby about it. It had sentimental value for both of us, that ring. You see, when we were married I wasn't doing too well. I had not been able to buy her an engagement ring. Then a couple of years later the breaks started coming. I bought her that beautiful ring on our third anniversary — as an engagement present.

"So it was a terrible blow to both of us. When I saw how hard she was taking it, I got her to go to Hunter. She's always loved the Hinsdale Hotel there — because that's where we spent our honeymoon.

"And I'm telling you all this so you'll give her a chance to recover a bit. She hates to think about losing that ring, no less talk about it. So, I'd consider it a great favor if you waited until she got over the shock before questioning her."

I believed he was animated only by concern for his wife's sensibilities. I nodded and gave a noncommittal shrug. I worked for the insurance company, and wasn't paid to do favors for men whose wives lost $10,000 rings that were fully insured.

I was able to catch a train for Hunter that same day, and checked into the Hinsdale Hotel, as Jerry Louis, by four o'clock. I gave one of the hotel's bellboys a dollar to point out Mrs. Wilson to me. She was enjoying herself thoroughly, talking to friends on the porch, and if she was touched by grief over the loss of her belated engagement ring she gave no sign of it.

There was no place vacant at her table, but I hoped to meet her after dinner, for that evening they were holding a "get acquainted" dance at the hotel. I did ask her for a dance, and while we were still on the floor I told her, "You have beautiful hands." She looked down at the hand I was holding in mine, and thanked me for the compliment. I said quietly, "Hands like yours were made to wear beautiful jewels."

Her face grew sad. I asked her why.

She told me she had lost a beautiful diamond ring only a few days before. She had noticed that it was missing while she was bathing at Long Beach, the ocean resort near New York. She had forgotten to take off the engagement ring, and felt terrible about it. "I still don't know whether I lost it in the sand or the water."

"Did you spend much time looking for it?" I asked.

"I sure did. I even went to the Long Beach Police Station before I left. I told the man in charge that I would pay a substantial reward to anyone who found it."

"Your husband must have been very angry about the ring."

She laughed. "Thank God, he wasn't with me at the beach that day, or we would have been there yet digging in the sand and looking for it. And that night he didn't notice it was missing. So I had a lot of time to think up a story. In the morning I just told him that it was missing from my jewel box. I insisted I'd put it in the box just before I went to bed."

When the music stopped I escorted her to a corner of the room where no one else was sitting. I think something about my manner may have worried her; possibly it may have occurred to her that after all I was a complete stranger and she'd been foolish to blurt out the story.

"Mr. Louis," she said, "you have not told me what business you are in," she said somewhat nervously.

"No, I haven't," I said, "but I happen to be a private investigator of the insurance company that insured your ring for $10,000."

She gasped, and stared at me. "That policy, though you may not be aware of it," I went on, "covers only losses of jewelry in your home."

"But — but — "

"All you have to do, Mrs. Wilson, is to sign a statement telling how you really lost the ring. I think we can do that very quietly right now in the writing room."

She was too petrified to argue, but wrote out the statement and signed it. "I'll take the first train back to New York," I said. "And I imagine you would prefer telling your husband the truth yourself. I'll hold the matter in abeyance for a while. All that is necessary is for him to advise the company he is withdrawing the claim." Now this woman wasn't a cheat or a thief. If she hadn't been so apprehensive of her husband's wrath, it would never have occurred to her to claim she'd put the ring in the jewel box that night.

*

I HAD other cases in which couples seemed to think that the fact that they were away from home put them beyond the reach of the company's investigators.

For example in 1929 when my own vacation in the Adirondacks with my family was interrupted by a request from the New York office of the St. Paul Fire and Guaranty Company. A claim had just been received for $20,000 worth of jewels and clothing lost in a cabin fire at Speculator. This is the small town in upper New York that briefly became famous as the place where Gene Tunney trained for the 1926 fight in which he won the world heavyweight championship from Jack Dempsey.

I drove to Speculator with my older son, George, whom I hoped was going to follow in my footsteps and become an investigator when he left college. I had with me a description of the jewels reported lost in the fire by the insured, Mr. and Mrs. Smithson, of New York.

The ruins of the cabin, which had burned to the ground, were there, but not the Smithsons. Nobody seemed to know where they had gone, including the man who had rented the cabin to them for the summer. As far as he knew, the New York couple had been out on the lake, fishing, when fire broke out, destroying the jewels and all the clothes except their fishing outfits. There was no doubt that Mrs. Smithson had brought her jewelry with her. She had worn the three pieces, and their beauty was much admired by some of the town people. Before leaving town, the Smithsons had asked him to sift the ashes, when they cooled sufficiently, to make sure there was nothing of value left. Mr. Smithson said that if he found anything he was to mail it to their New York address. The couple then had driven away in their car, not saying if they were going directly home or to another resort for the rest of their vacation. By the time we arrived, the man who owned the cabin had almost finished the sifting job, and had found nothing. My car had broken a spring on the way, so we stayed in Speculator overnight. In the morning I dropped in at the post office. It was just possible, I thought, that the Smithsons who had left town so hurriedly after the fire might have left a forwarding address with the postmaster.

I've had a lot of luck with post-office officials, though strictly speaking they are not supposed to give out any addresses. My approach to small-town postmasters was very simple. I just went in, asked for the postmaster, and smiled as he came up to the window.

If he didn't smile back I would make some casual remark, walk out, and try my luck with the sheriff or the chief of police.

This one smiled back. I showed him my credentials.

"Why, yes," he told me, "those summer people did leave another forwarding address — Saratoga Springs, I think." He looked it up, and nodded. "Yes, that's right, the Hotel Gideon Putnam there. If I remember correctly, Mrs. Smithson mentioned that her daughter was sending some clothes to her. She'd need them at the Springs, she said." As soon as our car was repaired, George and I headed for the Springs. On getting there we checked in at the Gideon Putnam. When I asked the maître d'hôtel whether Mr. and Mrs. Smithson had arrived he pointed out to me a middle-aged, sedate-looking couple who were sitting at a table for four. The other two seats were empty.

I told my son to go in and sit down at the table. I followed him. Mrs. Smithson was wearing jewels that looked exactly like the ones described to me in the long-distance call. They were beauties.

I am afraid I was guilty of staring rather rudely at them, and they seemed to be all there: diamond ring, earrings, brooch, pearl necklace. I did not wonder that Mrs. Smithson flushed deeply and covered her throat with a hand as I sat down.

I wasted no time on the amenities. I displayed my shield. "You are Mrs. Smithson, I believe," I said. "I am a special investigator of the St. Paul Fire and Marine Insurance Company."

Her husband just glared at me. When she found her voice she said, weakly, "Yes, I am Mrs. Smithson."

Seeing that I had her dead to rights, I saw no reason not to make it easy for her to give me what I wanted. I said, "I wish to be the first to congratulate you, madam, on recovering the jewels you believed you had lost in that fire at Speculator."

This helped her get over her fear, but not her embarrassment. Embarrassed or not, she was able to explain that much to her relief she had found the jewels shortly after sending in the report of their loss. "They weren't in the cabin, at all," she explained. "I'd put them in a little chamois bag I had pinned to my brassiere. In the excitement of seeing everything else go up in the fire, I forgot that. So did my husband. We were going to wire your company the good news right after dinner."

"So you must be glad to see me," I said, "for I can save you that trouble, Mrs. Smithson. All you need do is sign a statement saying that you have recovered the jewels and withdraw the claim for them. Whatever clothes you actually lost in the fire you can put in a claim for." I took out a sheet of paper and wrote out the statement of withdrawal for her, and she signed it right then and there at the table.

All of this time Mr. Smithson was glaring at me.

"Who told you we were in Saratoga Springs?" asked her husband.

"You are in the clothing business, Mr. Smithson?" I asked.

He nodded.

"You have no difficulty knowing good-quality cloth from bad, have you?"

"No-o."

"Well, I am a detective, and have no trouble learning where people have gone and even at what hotel they are stopping. That's part of my job."

I summoned the maître d'hôtel, and asked him to assign us to another table. "You'll excuse us, I'm sure," I said to the Smithsons. "My son and I have some things to talk over."

We enjoyed our dinner better at another table than we could have with both the Smithsons glowering at us. I imagine the move improved their digestion too. When the Smithsons sent in the claim for the clothing they lost in the fire, the charges were so reasonable that I okayed it at once.

A strange thing about such women as Mrs. Smithson is that even after they'd tried such a fraud and been caught they go blithely on in the delusion that they are honest and respectable. Sometimes, when dealing with such women, I've had the feeling that they thought I was the dishonorable one for catching them.

*

MRS. Helen Heatherstone, a fat, middle-aged Brooklyn housewife, was another to puzzle the psychiatrists. On April 25, 1945, she reported that she had lost a diamond and ruby pin she had insured for $2,500. My wife, Lillian, drove me out to her home to interview her. With her husband, who was in the brass business, Mrs. Heatherstone lived in a neat-looking two-story brick home, one in a row on a quiet, tree-lined street. It was a surprise, on going inside, to discover how poorly furnished it was.

Mrs. Heatherstone told us this story:

On the evening she lost the pin she was dining with her husband in a French restaurant in midtown Manhattan. The pin was quite distinctive, being shaped like a dancing doll. It was made of fourteen-karat gold covered with seventeen Oriental rubies and thirty-five round diamonds. But one of the diamonds and a ruby had fallen out. She had never had them replaced.

Before leaving home, she took the pin out of her jewel box and pinned it on her dress. In the restaurant, she was certain, she was still wearing it. After the meal she and her husband drove to the home of a relative in the Bronx, a rabbi. They did not stay there long, for they started home at about 8:30 P.M. Now, it is a drive of more than twenty-five miles from the Bronx to the part of Brooklyn where Mrs. Heatherstone lived, and they stopped several times so her husband could make business calls on customers. I interrupted her at this point to ask, "What sort of establishments remain open for business calls that late at night?"

"I don't know," said Mrs. Heatherstone. "I did not get out of the car. All I know is that because of these calls we did not get home until between twelve-thirty and one in the morning."

"You remained, sitting in the car, each time while Mr. Heatherstone got out and talked to these customers of his?"

"That is correct," said Mrs. Heatherstone, bobbing her head.

She did not recall taking the pin off her dress on retiring that night.

"What did you do with the dress?"

"I put it on a hanger and hung it in the closet."

She did not think again of the dancing-doll pin until a few days later. But when she looked for it, the pin was no longer on her dress. A painstaking search of the closet, its floor, her bedroom, and other rooms had been made but with no success. She lost no time in notifying the police and the insurance company of her loss.

With Mrs. Heatherstone's permission we searched the house, starting with the closet where she had last seen the dancing-doll pin. We had no better luck than Mrs. Heatherstone. She and her husband were alone there most of the time. She had two children, a married daughter and a son who was away at college and came home only for weekends. She had no maid or other domestic help, she said. No friends had visited her between the night she last saw the pin and the day she discovered it was missing. In fact no one except her and her husband, so far as she knew, had been in the house during that time. She did not think it was a burglary. (Neither did we.) Mrs. Heatherstone owned several other more expensive jewels and a luxurious wardrobe that no thief would have overlooked.

As we drove away, Lil commented on the striking contrast between Mrs. Heatherstone's elegant wardrobe and jewelry and the shabbiness of her furniture. But this was not too unusual in our experience. We had found that the woman who wants to be a peacock often can be parsimonious about everything else.

We next called on Mr. Heatherstone at his place of business. Like his wife, he turned out to have a convenient memory. He did recall the name of the restaurant — the Chalet Suisse, which was on West Fifty-second Street, not Fiftieth, and of course is Swiss, not French. He said he had noticed the dancing-doll pin on his wife's dress while they were at the home of their Bronx relative, the rabbi. But that was the last time he could recall seeing it.

Our next visit was to the jeweler who had sold the pin to the Heatherstones. His memory was not too good, either, though after fending off repeated questions he told us the Heatherstones had paid him $2,500 cash for the pin.

"But, even so, you would have made a record of that cash transaction, wouldn't you?" I asked.

"Yes."

"Would you let me see the notation you made of it for your records?"

"I do not consider that necessary," the jeweler replied. Nothing I could say changed his mind. We now made a second visit to Mr. Heatherstone's place of business.

"Did you pay for the dancing-doll pin with a check or cash?" I asked him.

"What has that got to do with it?" he wanted to know.

The terms and conditions of his policy, I pointed out, required him to cooperate with me and give me any information I asked him for. And all I wanted now was some proof that he had paid $2,500 for the pin. But he was stubborn. Only after a long argument did he admit he'd paid him in cash.

"Where did you get the cash? Did you take it out of your drawing account as a salesman?"

He refused to tell me that, or where he had kept the cash. All I could get out of him was the names and addresses of the customers he had stopped to see on the night his wife's pin was last seen. We already had the name and address of the Bronx rabbi, and started there. Then we followed the Heatherstones' path on the long ride home, talking to everyone whose name he had given us.

We did not expect to find a trace of the pin, but I like to do a thorough job. I have found that much of what is called luck comes when one covers every possibility, touches all the bases, as they say in baseball. One of the persons he said he called on that night, I thought, might give some information I could use in getting the brass-fixtures salesman to tell me what really happened to the pin.

I found, heard, saw nothing. Nevertheless, I did not believe the couple's fishy tale, and said so in my report to the St. Paul Company. Nevertheless, they settled for the full amount. There were several reasons. The broker who had sold the Heatherstones the insurance was urging a full settlement. He gave the company a great deal of business each year, and the company was eager to retain his goodwill. The Heatherstones were threatening to sue, and the amount involved was less than defending the suit would cost.

In the next two or three years I investigated thousands of other cases, including quite a few in the Heatherstones' neighborhood. One of these concerned the loss of a $5,200 diamond ring. This weighed five carats, and had two tapering baguette diamonds.

Mr. Judd, the general manager of St. Paul, had intended to look into the case himself. But at the last moment urgent business came up that had to be attended to at once, and he asked me to interview the woman with whom he had made the appointment.

This home was also a neat two-story brick dwelling, but the furniture was new; so were the drapes and the wall-to-wall carpeting. The house seemed vaguely familiar to me, and as I began questioning the woman who opened the door for us I noticed she seemed worried, but she managed to tell her story.

She had last seen the missing ring at 1:30 A.M. on January 17, 1948. At 6:00 P.M. on the day before that, her jeweler, whose name she gave me, had driven her to her married daughter's home. Her husband and son-in-law joined them there for dinner and the four of them spent a pleasant evening playing bridge. They left at one and arrived home at about one-thirty.

During the evening she had no reason to take off the diamond ring, which she wore on the third finger of her left hand just above her wedding band. Besides these two rings, she was wearing on that night a diamond cocktail ring, a cocktail watch, and a pair of diamond earrings. As she answered my questions I noticed that Lillian was signaling me that we'd been here before. But I could not recall the occasion nor the circumstances. The woman became more and more nervous during our interview. That could mean nothing, but it was something to bear in mind.

She was tired on getting home, and went immediately to bed. Usually she removed all her jewelry, except her wedding ring, and put it into a large leather-covered jewel box that she kept in the bottom bureau drawer. On this there was no lock, she said. And on evenings like this one, when she was very tired, she did not bother getting out the jewel box until morning, but put the jewelry on top of the bureau.

On waking up next morning she put away her five-carat diamond ring and the smaller cocktail ring. She wore the earrings and watch every day, so she left them out. I asked her at this point about the cocktail watch, which she did not have on. She explained that it was at the jeweler's, being repaired.

In answer to questions, she said that between January 17th and 29th, she had hired no help and given no parties. Her only house guests had been her daughter and son-in-law. They had come for a weekend visit on Friday, January 23rd, and left on Sunday evening, January 25th. Her other child, a boy, was a student at Yale, and unmarried. He had not come down from New Haven that weekend. However he had arrived on Tuesday, January 27th, and left on Thursday, January 29th. The 29th was, of course, the day on which she had noticed that her five-carat ring was missing.

"Did you open the jewel box for any reason between the morning you last saw the missing ring, and January 29th?"

"Oh, yes," she told me, "several times — to take out my other jewelry."

And now, that she thought it over, she did recall one thing that might be of help to us. On Sunday, January 18, the day after her visit to her daughter, she and her husband went out to a funeral. As they were leaving her husband asked her to make sure that the back door was locked. Meanwhile he checked the windows. The back door was locked. She was positive of that. She told him that then, just as she was now telling it to me.

It snowed so heavily that day that by the time they got home, about two hours later, so much snow covered the walk that her husband decided to go around to the back to avoid tracking water through the front rooms.

To their surprise the back door was unlocked. But there was no sign of any intruder having been there. Her husband, in the know-it-all manner husbands have, insisted that she had never tried the door at all and that it had been open all of the time. I asked her if she had not gone upstairs to see if her jewels were still there.

"No, I didn't," she said. "Nothing in the house looked disturbed."

In the end, her husband had convinced her that the door must have been unlocked all the time. She now realized she could not really have tried it.

But even after that she had not thought of going upstairs that day to see if anything was missing from her jewel box.

"Is it your theory now," I asked, "that some thief came in that day, went upstairs, leaving no trace of snow, and took one piece of jewelry out of your jewel box? Just that, the one five-carat diamond ring? Then, not stealing anything else, he carefully put the jewel box back in the drawer, and closed the drawer. Why wouldn't he have taken your other jewels?"

She bit her lip, thought for a moment, then said, "I have nothing else of much value."

"Thieves are usually in a hurry," I told her. "They do not waste any time in a house, unless they are sure the family is away and the house is in some isolated place. So they seldom examine the jewelry and pick out the best things. They snatch up everything in sight and get out as fast as possible. Above all, why would a thief waste the time to put back the jewel box and close the drawer?"

Now we asked her permission to go upstairs to examine her jewel box. Our hostess hesitated, and said: "Well, if you want to. But my other jewels are hardly worth looking at."

Of course, we did not expect to be interested in her other jewels.

There were three bedrooms and a bath on the upstairs floor. The Heatherstones' bedroom was in the front. The next largest bedroom was in the rear, and was the one which her married daughter had used when she lived with them. The smallest of the three rooms was the one her son used whenever he was home from college. The weekend her daughter and son-in-law spent there, the daughter slept in her old room, and the son-in-law used the studio couch downstairs, in the living room.

There was a double bed with a night table on each side in the room in which she and her husband slept, and a double dresser. In the left side were her husband's things, in the right, hers.

"Now we would like to see your jewel box, if you please." She got it out and at my request opened it up.

The jewel box was made of leather and was quite large. It was lined with chamois. It had a little pocket at each end, and it was in the one on the left side, she explained, that she had kept her five-carat diamond ring with the tapering baguettes. There were many pieces of jewelry in the box, including several rings and pins that looked expensive to me.

I was studying the woman's face when my wife suddenly leaned forward and picked out a gold pin covered with diamonds and rubies. It was the dancing-doll pin. No wonder our hostess, who was of course Mrs. Heatherstone, was so upset when she opened the door and saw us standing there, instead of Mr. Judd, whom her broker had promised would come out to see about this new loss, instead of us, that nosey, troublesome husband-and-wife team.

There was no doubt about its being the same pin. My wife was holding it in such a way that I could see that one small diamond chip and one ruby were missing.

I took the pin from Lil, and turned it slowly in my hand.

"I think, Mrs. Heatherstone," I said, "you will recall one question among the many I asked you downstairs. It was whether you had ever lost any other jewelry that you had insured. You possibly also remember your answer." I waited, but she seemed unable to speak.

"You told me — correct me if I am mistaken — that a fob watch that belonged to your daughter was the only jewelry a member of your family had ever lost. You also said that you never had collected money from an insurance company for any lost or stolen jewelry.

"But, Mrs. Heatherstone, can't you recall now having lost this very pin less than three years ago, and reporting the disappearance to the St. Paul Fire Insurance Company and getting paid $2,500 for it?"

"Yes, yes, I lost a pin, one exactly like that one in fact," she stammered on finding her voice. "But I used the money to buy this one, which is exactly like it. In fact, I ordered it from Sam

Valligny, the very same man from whom I got the first dancing-doll pin."

"Look at the pin, Mrs. Heatherstone," I suggested. "Were you so fond of the one that you lost that you asked Mr. Valligny to make sure that a diamond and ruby were missing from this one?"

She didn't answer.

I asked her whether her husband had paid with cash or by check for this second dancing-doll pin. "I don't know," she said, angrily, "you will have to see my husband about that."

But the time for shadowboxing was over. "I don't think it will be necessary for me to see your husband," I told her. "I do suggest that you may find it to your advantage to make another intensive search of this house for the missing ring. I do not think it was stolen. It seems to me that you must have misplaced it.

"But let me tell you this: I wish you no harm and I sincerely hope that you find your five-carat ring within the next forty-eight hours. If you don't, I shall have to take up the matter with the police. I shall also submit the facts to the district attorney's office."

Before I left I gave her the telephone number of my office and also my home number. The next day her insurance broker called up and said he had good news for me. Mrs. Heatherstone asked him to notify me that she had found the $5,200 ring and was withdrawing her claim of loss.

That night Lillian and I had a long talk about the case. She recalled complimenting Mrs. Heatherstone on the handsome decor and furnishings.

"Oh, wait till next year," she had said. "I've spent only $2,000 on it. But I intend to add a new room in the spring and I'm having the house painted. I have the estimate. These improvements will cost $3,500 more, almost twice as much as all of the decorating I've done so far."

I don't know whether she ever carried out this plan. If so, the St. Paul Company did not finance this second set of improvements. But I suspect it paid for Mrs. Heatherstone's new furniture, drapes, and wall-to-wall carpeting.

I recommended that her policy be canceled, which was done.

At the worst, Mrs. Heatherstone suffered only humiliation. She was lucky compared to Mrs. Fritzi Heller, a young matron who reported that her jewels had been stolen for another reason entirely.

A great many persons would have said that Fritzi, young, good-looking, and wealthy, had everything in the world to make her happy: an adoring (if ugly) husband, three charming little children, and a governess to take care of them, a luxurious home. But —

On the morning of the day that the jewelry disappeared, Mrs. Heller told me she had been alone in the house. The woman who did the housework was ill and had phoned she would be unable to come to work. The three children, whose ages were then five, three, and one and a half, had been taken to the park by the governess.

She herself had an appointment at the hairdresser's. She distinctly remembered, she said, locking the door and fastening the latch on the kitchen window outside which was the fire escape. Her apartment was on the eighth floor, which made it unlikely that a thief in daytime could have got in that way.

On thinking it over, Mrs. Heller, who had a bewitching smile, said she was not so sure that she locked the kitchen window. During the hours she was out of the apartment, she thought, he must somehow have got in that way. I looked over the fire escape and became convinced she was mistaken. Pigeon dung, encrusted on the sill and on the fire-escape stairs apparently for months, showed no sign of being disturbed.

Later, while I was talking about the missing jewels to her husband, I asked his permission to take pictures of the sill and the fire escape. When he gave it I asked him not to mention the matter to anyone. The pictures were made next day, though I arranged things so Mrs. Heller did not know it.

Meanwhile I had a man trying to check on how Mrs. Heller usually spent her time when not in the house. Antoine, the owner of the beauty parlor where she'd gone that day, confirmed her story of having been there for three hours. He showed me the appointment book with her name down for a hairwash, marcel, and manicure.

There was something proprietary in the way he talked about Mrs. Heller. Or so I thought. He looked to me like a gigolo. Just on a hunch I had his finances checked. The report showed that he had been about to go into bankruptcy. But a day or two after Mrs. Heller's jewels disappeared, he surprised his creditors by paying them several thousand dollars.

By that time the shadow man I'd put on Mrs. Heller reported that she had lunched with Antoine in a café. They seemed to be enjoying a distinctly intimate relationship. And they met for lunch at the same café the next day.

On last seeing Mrs. Heller I had told her I would call for an appointment. Instead I decided to surprise her. I went to the house and had the telephone operator in the lobby tell her I was downstairs. Mrs. Heller seemed undisturbed, said I was to come right up, and greeted me with one of her most melting smiles.

When we were seated in the living room I hinted that I had found out who had the jewelry. I asked her, "Would you prefer charges, Mrs. Heller, against the person who has your jewelry?"

The trick in such situations, of course, is to let the person you are questioning believe you know a great deal more than you do. It worked with little Mrs. Heller. She had difficulty pulling herself together, and for a few minutes could not even speak. On regaining some degree of composure, she demanded: "What did you mean by that question? Do you really know who has the jewels?"

Instead of replying, I showed her the photographs of the fire escape and the sill outside her kitchen window, with the marks of old pigeon dust clearly shown. I explained what it meant. "And you know yourself that no burglar could get in through the front door without being noticed by the doorman, the telephone operator, or the elevator man. You must have thought of that yourself, Mrs. Heller, when you suggested that it was a burglar and he had come in from the fire escape."

It took just about half an hour for her to break down. She sobbed as though her heart would break. "How could you know that I gave Antoine the jewelry?"

For once it served my purpose to explain. "We found out," I said, "how terribly worried about money he was. The poor fellow was facing bankruptcy, was looking around for an offer for his shop. He would have sold it for almost anything.

"But all of that changed. Before your husband even had a chance to notify us, Antoine turned into the happiest and gayest of men. But he never smiled so much or seemed so full of joy as he did while he was having lunch with you, Mrs. Heller."

"All right," she suddenly cried, "I'll admit everything. I had to help Antoine. I gave him the jewels myself on the morning the burglary was supposed to have happened."

She put her head in her hands and cried like a child of kindergarten age. I was sorry for her, and I told her so.

"I only did it to help Antoine out," she kept saying over and over.

"But now you will have to help me out," I said. "I simply must have a signed statement from your husband withdrawing the claim."

"Give me twenty-four hours. And above all, do not see Antoine."

I stared at her. What was there about this effeminate gigolo that inspired such love in her? She had possibly wrecked her marriage and put herself in a position where she might lose her children. But the one thing that seemed to concern her was a hairdresser who seemed to me a grimacing, hip-swinging little half-man.

"My advice to you," I said, "is to tell your husband the whole story. You cannot stop it from coming out, no matter what you do."

Her only response to this was to sigh, "Poor Antoine!"

That night little Mrs. Heller jumped off the second-story fire escape. Apparently, while talking to her husband, she climbed out of the window and ran down the fire escape with him in pursuit. Fearing he would catch up with her, she apparently jumped to the street on getting to the second-floor fire escape, breaking both legs and sustaining severe internal injuries.

In the morning her husband, looking like a man who was living through a nightmare, came to my office. His physical appearance suggested one good reason why Mrs. Heller had chosen a lover.

Sigmund Heller was almost twenty years older than his wife. He looked almost like a gorilla, being short and stocky, with long arms, low forehead, and lips almost as thick as a Ubangi's. He had the release in his hand.

"How is your wife?" I asked.

He shook his head. "To be honest, I don't care any more whether she lives or dies. I don't care about losing the $12,000 worth of jewels, either.

"Last night she told me she had given those jewels to her lover. It was terrible hearing that from that sweet-faced little thing. I grabbed her and shook her. I wanted to know one thing: that was about the children. Are those kids mine or this other guy's?

"But she wouldn't tell me his name. I wanted to see him to find out whether my babies look more like him than me. When I kept insisting she jumped out on the fire escape, and started down. I kept gaining on her and — well, she jumped when she got to the second floor. But now I don't care whether she lives or dies."

In his anguish he told me the story of their marriage. She had been in love, when Heller first saw her, with a young law student. Her father worked in one of Heller's garment factories. Her parents were very poor, and lived with their beautiful daughter in a two-room tenement flat on the Lower East Side.

The old man was overjoyed when his boss told him he wanted to marry Fritzi. "If it comes off," Heller promised him, "you'll never have to work again for the rest of your life."

Fritzi's parents talked her into the marriage that would end the poverty they'd known all their lives. That day in the office Heller kept saying over and over, "Nothing else would matter if I could only be sure about the children."

"I saw your three kids several times," I told him. "You can stop worrying, my friend. They are yours, all right. Each of them is a living image of you."

He seemed to believe it, and when he went out he appeared greatly relieved. I hoped that he could eventually find it possible to forgive his wife — for the children's sake. But, shortly after she recovered and came out of the hospital, they were divorced.

BLACKMAIL
IS A DIRTY WORD
IN
ANY LANGUAGE

5

LATE one afternoon in 1928 I got a telephone call from a corporation lawyer for whom I'd done a great deal of work. He asked if I could come right over to the office. One of his clients was there, he said, and needed my advice. I happened to be very busy, and suggested an appointment later in the week.

"This gentlemen is not only one of my best clients," the attorney said, "he's also a very close friend. I'd consider it a personal favor if you could come now. It's a delicate matter, believe me."

His office was only a couple of blocks away from mine. I was able to get over there in a very few minutes. The client proved to be the biggest one in his very large practice: F. T. Reginald, the president of one of the country's richest banks and a director of a dozen great corporations. The bank and the corporations between them had enough working capital and reserve funds to take a mortgage on half of the Balkan Peninsula.

Mr. Reginald was then about fifty, a tall, slim, aristocratic-looking man who stood straight as a solider and looked through you with piercing blue eyes.

But this day the blue eyes appeared to be full of trouble. Even after I arrived, his attorney had to plead with him to tell me his story. "I vouch for Mr. Luisi's discretion," he said. "As I have told you, I've trusted him again and again with the most confidential sort of investigation. He's never failed to justify my faith, F.T."

But Mr. Reginald continued to look as though he would enjoy nothing better than jumping out of the window. When he was induced to talk he began by explaining that his wife, two sons, his daughter, and her fiancé were traveling in Europe. In the fall his daughter and her young man were to be married in a formal wedding.

He had planned to tour Europe with his family and future son-in-law, but at the last moment the boom in the stock market and a delay in the merger of two huge corporations had prevented him from leaving.

Mr. Reginald hesitated at this point. Then he took a deep breath, and with an effort, continued.

"Since the family left," he went on, "I've been spending most of my nights in town. I find it lonely in our big house out at Sands Point with neither Mrs. Reginald nor the children there. So most of the time I've remained in town, staying over at my club.

"But one can become bored, as you know, with talking everlastingly about the market and playing bridge. I should also explain, Mr. Luisi, that I am a man who enjoys drinking in moderation. I have always been able to hold my liquor. That is what so mystifies me about what happened on this particular evening. I went alone to a Broadway show that night, but left after the first act. I dropped into a speakeasy on West Fifty-second Street, hoping to meet someone I knew. Then I visited two or three others. I saw no one I knew in any of these places. I recalled later on that I spoke to an attractive young lady who was sitting alone at the bar in the last of these places. But that is about all I remembered when I woke up next morning. My first impression was that I had either been drugged or served poisoned whiskey. Never in my life, I must say, have I suffered from such a monstrous and ghastly hangover.

"I was astonished to find myself in my own bedroom at Sands Point, for I could not recall leaving New York. But it was when I looked at the other bed that I got the shock of my life. Lying there in my wife's bed was the good-looking young woman with red hair. She was sleeping blissfully. She had not a stitch on. Neither had I. I hastily slipped into pajamas and a dressing gown, then woke her up. I wanted only one thing: to get her out of the house."

At this point Mr. Reginald seemed to find it impossible to continue his story. After a moment or two his attorney responded to his silent appeal by going on with it. Here is the substance of what he said.

The young woman was sleeping so soundly that he had to shake her by the shoulder three or four times before he could wake her up. When she opened her eyes she smiled happily at him, and held out her arms. Even more alarming to Mr. Reginald was what she had to say.

"Imagine, darling," she told him rapturously, "this is our wedding day. And yesterday we did not even know one another! It's like a wonderful dream come true, isn't it, dear?"

"Young lady," said Mr. Reginald, "please stop talking nonsense. I do not even know who you are, and I ask only one thing: that you get dressed and leave this house immediately."

At first she pretended to be amused, acted as though she thought he was joking. But when he continued to urge her to dress and leave, she burst into a flood of tears.

"What am I going to tell my mother?" she wailed. "What can I tell her? You wouldn't even let me phone her last night. She would have believed a story, any story at all then. But you wouldn't let me phone her. You kept begging and pleading so hard that I gave in, finally. 'What does it matter, darling?' That's what you kept on saying. 'I told you I am a widower. Don't you trust me? Why can't you trust me just this one night? Don't you believe that we'll get the license the first thing in the morning?' "

Mr. Reginald could not recall in all his life saying such things and behaving that way. But it occurred to him that, no matter how distressing, it might be wise to get her version of what had happened. The girl told him that they had not met at a speakeasy, as he thought, but at a restaurant. He had flirted with her, she said. He was a charming-looking man and looked so lonely that she smiled back at him. He insisted on paying her dinner check and then she went with him to a speakeasy. She did not remember the name of the place or the street it was on, she said, because she was a stranger in New York, having moved there from Washington just recently. He told her he was a widower, and at his insistence they had taken a taxicab from the speakeasy to his home in Sands Point. Yes, she said, the butler had let them in. And once he got her alone in this room he was like a wild man, she said. He insisted on undressing her himself. She showed him the panties he had torn in his frenzied eagerness to disrobe her completely.

Mr. Reginald stopped her at this point. He explained that he was a married man with three grown children, and had not the slightest intention of getting a divorce. This brought on another flood of tears. Unable to think of any better way of getting rid of her, he asked if money would help her forget.

The young lady finally accepted $3,500, which happened to be all the cash he had in the house. As she accepted the money she complained that he'd robbed her of her virginity, something no amount of money could compensate her for. She also kept moaning, "And what explanation do I give my mother?"

But in the end he got her into a taxicab and she started for New York. Only after she left did it occur to Mr. Reginald that he had neglected to ask her her name.

On going back into the house he had a reassuring talk with his butler. Yes, he had let them in, the servant said.

"Did I seem drunk?" asked Mr. Reginald.

"You looked more dazed, sir, than anything else. I wanted very much to assist you to your room, but the young lady said she would take care of you. As you made no objection, I did not interfere."

"What did I say?"

"Nothing, sir."

"What about the other servants — do they know?"

"Yes, Mr. Reginald, I regret to say they do. But I do not think you have to be concerned about us. You and Mrs. Reginald have been far too kind down through the years for any of us ever to do or say anything that might cause you embarrassment."

Mr. Reginald's peace of mind lasted just three weeks. Or until the afternoon that the bank's switchboard operator buzzed him, and said that a Miss Hooper was on the wire and refused to talk to anyone but him. She refused to say what about.

Assuming she must be a depositor with a complaint to make, he picked up the phone. "You have got me into a fine mess," shrieked Miss Hooper. "I'm pregnant!"

Fearing that the operator might be listening in, he agreed to meet her within an hour. He found her waiting for him. Her eyes were red and she burst into a fit of wild sobbing on seeing him. When she quieted down she told him she must have some money right away.

"What did you do with the money I gave you?" he asked.

"I left it in the cab. The closer I came to home, the more hysterical I became at the thought of facing my mother. We got to my door and I just went in, thinking only of that. By the time I noticed I didn't have my purse with me, the cab was gone. So I lost all of my own money, along with the money you gave me."

After raining more recriminations at the banker whom she said had raped her, she made a deal with him. At least, he thought of it as a deal. He would give her $5,000 as payment in full for all and any obligation to her. He got her to promise solemnly not to bother him for money again. She told him she was going down to Washington and beg for help of her family physician.

"What's his name?" asked Mr. Reginald.

"It would not be right to tell you that," she exclaimed, "any more than it would be fair to give him your name if he asked who the father was. Why, the poor man could lose his license to practice if I gave him away. Now, I know how worried you will be, Mr. Reginald, until you hear that it's all over. I'll phone you that I'm all right the first chance I get."

"Don't call me at the bank or at home," he said. "Somebody, at either place, may be listening in."

"But how will I get in touch with you?"

He gave her his private phone number.

She phoned him at the private number within another week — with disappointing news. The doctor had given her medication, with no result. The doctor then advised her to have the baby. She would prefer that herself, but for the obligation she felt for him, Mr. Reginald. What worried her, she said, was the possibility that news that he was the father might leak out. On the other hand she dreaded an abortion, and was afraid she might die while under the knife. But she had heard of a very expensive place in Westchester County that did such work — and took proper precaution. It was expensive, though, very expensive indeed.

This time Mr. Reginald gave her $20,000.

Incredible as it may sound, he believed her. And, of course, $3,500, $5,000, or $20,000 meant very little to him. He sometimes made far more than $20,000 in a day speculating in stocks.

It was only when Miss Hooper came back once again and asked for more money that the banker realized that she would never quit until she had bled him white. This time she needed $25,000.

He forced himself to meet her again. He also managed to listen politely to what she had to say. If she died as a result of the abortion, she said, her mother would be left penniless, and she was the old woman's only support. But the $25,000 would take care of her mother for the rest of her days no matter what happened.

"I'm afraid it may take me several days to get that much money together," the banker told her apologetically. "But why don't you give me your number so that I can call you when I do have it?"

And Miss Hooper wrote her name and phone number for him on a small piece of white paper. That was this afternoon, and on leaving her Mr. Reginald had gone directly to his lawyer's office, and told his story. Unquestionably the girl had made a fool of him. Anyone could understand why he did not care to repeat his story to me, a stranger. It must have been an ordeal listening to it being repeated. But once it was over he unhesitatingly answered the many questions I put to him. I was convinced, after two hours of questions and answers, that the banker had been drugged.

I got him to give me the list of the midtown speakeasies and nightclubs he'd been in. By a process of elimination we came to the conclusion that the sucker trap where the girl had met him was the Club Hi-de-Ho. That was on West Fifty-second Street, had a floor show of sorts, and employed hostesses, so-called. I did not believe they'd met in a restaurant. In my opinion she'd made that up, possibly because being picked up in a restaurant sounded a little more respectable.

That evening the lawyer and I drove out to Mr. Reginald's estate on Long Island. I wanted to look over the place and question the servants. But I learned nothing new. What the butler told me confirmed my theory that he had been drugged.

The lady had made only one mistake: giving Mr. Reginald her telephone number. Just knowing the number enabled me to learn (through a connection in the New York Telephone Company) that her real name might be Finch, Jewel Finch. For that was the name on the application for the phone. She lived in a five-room apartment on the ground floor of a well-kept apartment house a half-block from the Hudson River.

She gave as her last residence an address in Washington, D.C. I instructed my man there to find out what he could about the Finch family. Jewel and one of her sisters had worked for a time as typists in the Department of the Interior. They'd been indifferent employees, and had resigned to come to New York.

The family, mother, four daughters, and a son, had come to

Washington from Grand Rapids, Michigan. My contact there did a fast check and found out that the family had run a small dry-goods store in Grand Rapids. Jewel, her sisters, and the brother had gone through high school there. Two of the girls, both of whom were now married, had attended small Midwestern colleges and become grade-school teachers. They had sold the business and left Grand Rapids after Solomon Finch, Jewel's father, died. As far as could be learned, no member of the family had been in trouble or had a police record.

By the time we had this background information, we had our investigation well launched. The first thing I wanted to find out was whether the woman had anybody working with her. I sent Lillian, my wife, Assistant 115 in our office records, to rent an apartment, on the first floor, if possible, in the house where Miss Finch lived. She was to get acquainted with the girl, if she could, and do a roping job on her. This consists of establishing direct contact with the subject and getting from her whatever information the roper can.

At the same time I sent out a team of undercover men into the nightclub belt. I instructed them to find and talk to the taxi driver who had taken the blackmailer and the banker to his home that night. I also wanted them to learn whether the Finch woman worked as a hostess in the Hi-de-Ho. If so, it was a lead-pipe cinch that she had at least one co-worker. She'd have to have one, at least one other employee, the manager, the bartender, or a waiter.

In some places these girls doubled as waitresses or worked in the show. Regardless of that, their real job was inducing their amorous companions to drink more and faster. They got a cut on everything the men drank and also on the water colored to look like whiskey which they themselves kept putting away. The sucker traps' big money-maker, of course, was their fake champagne, made of cheap sauterne spiked with seltzer water to make it fizz, at $20 a bottle. The hostess got a much bigger percentage for getting the sucker to buy bottles of their phony champagne.

Hostesses in these joints were forbidden to leave with a customer or meet him outside. The theory was that the man whose girl disappeared just before closing time usually came back to get an explanation from her. Those who went home with the hostesses almost never did. Jewel Finch and her sister Nettie, the undercover men learned, had been hostesses, at times, in other spots. But in the Hi-de-Ho Jewel Finch had just been another girl on the make who came in, sat at the bar either alone or with her sister, and hoped that Mr. Right, or even Mr. Wrong, would come along and take care of the check.

Apparently the staff had paid little attention when Mr. Reginald picked her up.

"Why should we? All we ask of broads on the make like her is that they don't start no trouble in the joint," the manager explained. "They can be teasers, whores, pushovers who'll roll over for a pair of stockings, a square meal, or maybe just a room for the night. It makes no difference on my scorecard.

"The hostesses don't like them because they're competition. But those bar-broads keep my hostesses on their toes, if you ask me. But there's hundreds of dames like that one around Broadway, who have nothing to do all night but sit at a bar. They come and go. And as I say, if they make no trouble, they're welcome."

Nobody around the night places seemed hep to the fact that Miss Jewel Finch was a blackmailer. So she might be working alone. The shake on Reginald could even well be the first she'd ever tried.

We also found the cabdriver. This was through the club's doorman. I had figured he'd know which driver had taken the couple on that long ride out to Sands Point. But I hadn't known whether he'd care to admit it. The doorman of each speakeasy spot got a kickback from the drivers he let park in front of or near the entrance.

Not that the driver added much to the story. Mr. Reginald had slept all the way to Sands Point, he said, and the girl had said little. When they got near the door she went through Mr. Reginald's pockets and got out his wallet. She took the money for the fare and a $10 tip, then put back the wallet. The banker was able to walk once they woke him up. She helped him up the steps. The butler opened the door. He wanted to help but she waved him aside.

For a day or two the fact that neither Jewel nor her sister showed up at their favorite hangouts had me worried. Had someone tipped her off that we were on her trail? But I got over that idea when she had the audacity to throw a new kind of fast one at the bank president. I'd advised him to play it cute, keep stalling her and saying he hoped to have the $25,000 for her in just a few more days. But she'd quickly run out of patience. She had a lawyer serve papers on him for $50,000 damages. The papers charged assault and battery but gave no details.

Fortunately for his peace of mind, we'd meanwhile been enjoying extraordinary luck in the roping job my wife had started in the apartment house. On that first day as she was asking the superintendent about a vacancy, a young woman came out of apartment 1-C. My wife imagined it was Jewel Finch because she had red hair. As the redhead walked past, she overheard the conversation. In a moment she came back and asked Lillian if she'd care to look at her place, which she was thinking of subletting for the summer.

Lillian could not have been more eager, of course. She was shown the five-room apartment, which was both filthy and in complete disorder, and introduced to Jewel's older, homely sister, Nettie.

"I may take it," she said, "but I'd like to bring my sister tomorrow to see it. She's going to live with me."

On getting back to the office my wife, who is blond, soft-spoken, and sweet-faced, and the last human being you'd believe was a private detective, suggested I pull her off the case. That was why she'd abruptly invented the sister.

"I just can't talk those people's language," she said. "They're night people. All they talk about is nightclubs, speakeasies, and the various quick ways to make a man spend his money."

Talking "the language" of the persons you're roping or trying to get information from is, as can be imagined, the very first requirement for success. What we had to do here was ease the "sister" in and Lillian out of the picture, but as gently as possible.

I hoped Joan Lanigan, my Assistant 152, and the most versatile woman roper who ever worked for me, was available. Joan was a stage actress who'd had a chance only at bits and walk-on parts on Broadway. But she'd played almost everything but Juliet's nurse for me. She was quick-witted, missed nothing going on, and had plenty of moxie. I had seen her on different jobs convince very suspicious persons, some of them dangerous to fool around with, that she was a whore, a shoplifter, a gold digger, gangster's moll, chorus girl, stenographer, department-store salesgirl, a debutante. She was mistress of the Broadway and underworld lingo, and had also mastered the southern accent, the midwestern nasal drawl, the Irish brogue, Brooklynese, cockney, and many another.

I was introduced to her at a party by her escort, a lawyer I'd worked with often. "This is the fellow I told you about, Joan," he said. "He's the smartest private detective in New York."

She smiled and said something about having always wanted to try that sort of work. I'd heard that often before, and replied with my stock answer — one that invariably cured the woman's ambition quickly and permanently.

"I may be able to use you," I said, "if you're not afraid of some-body cutting your ear off or sticking a knife in your eye."

But this cute little blond thing seemed undisturbed. She said, "I wouldn't be afraid of anything like that."

"You might even have to live with some bum to get information," I told her.

"That wouldn't stop me," she said. Surprised, I turned to her escort, the lawyer.

"It would be all right with me," he said, "if she wants to try it."

I'd been using Joan ever since on cases involving larceny, dis-honest servants, and blackmail. Her closest shave, incidentally, had come at the Hotel Gotham on a blackmail job. In that case another private detective was involved in the shakedown, and I think it was he who first suspected Joan and alerted the other thieves.

Fortunately, she became aware of the danger before they had made up their minds, and managed to call me. "Get into a taxi as quickly as you can," she said. "Keep it parked near the hotel until I come out. If — " Then she hung up. It was possible, but not likely, that she'd been interrupted.

But I didn't intend to wait outside for very long before going up to the suite she was in. The thieves she was with were rude, rough, tough, and nasty. However, she got away just as I arrived.

Joan got off to a fast start on the Finch job. Here is my wife's (Assistant 115's) report covering the day she brought her "sister" to see the woman's apartment:

Assistants were received by Miss Nettie and saw the Subject Jewel in the kitchen in negligée. When she passed through the hall to go to her bedroom, Assistant 115 introduced her to As-sistant 152.

Subject became very friendly with Assistant 152 and during the conversation Assistant learned in substance the following:

That Jewel, the Subject, goes under so many names that she

cannot keep track of them. When she meets a man and is not sure whether she wishes to continue her friendship with him, she gives him an assumed name. She recognizes these men by the name they call her when they telephone. She volunteered the fact that she goes under the name of "Collins" professionally. She is going to start taking vocal lessons.

When the conversation turned to alimony and divorce, she stated that it was wonderful the way a girl recently got $100,000 from a wealthy man for Breach of Promise. She further stated that the most a girl can get out of a man these days is $5,000.

Subject states she is leaving for Toronto on Sunday or Monday to see an old man sweetheart of hers, who is fifty-eight years old, married and separated from his wife, and also "broke," to spend a few days with him. She stated this man loves her and she feels sorry for him. That she thinks if this man were "free" she would marry him whether he had a nickel or not. The station she gets off at on the way is Sunnyside, the first station this side of Toronto.

Assistant 152 immediately seized on this bit of news and stated she was motoring up to Montreal the beginning of the week with two men and would love to have Jewel accompany her as she would like to have another woman along. This was agreed upon, and Assistant 152 promised to get in touch with her boy friends and let Jewel know the results by 5:00 P.M.

At 5:30 P.M. Assistant 152 called Subject and made an appointment with her for 7:30 P.M. at her home, at which time she expected the boys to call.

Subject stated she expected a call at 6:30 P.M. from a man from Southampton who was coming in especially to see her. Subject also stated that the place for girls (preferably two girls together) to go was Newport or Southampton to get the proper contact with men.

In the conversation regarding the trip to Toronto, Subject was anxious to know whether she could get a silver fox out of the trip. Assistant 152 assured her they would positively come back with a silver fox each. Subject was anxious to know whether the men were very wealthy.

Subject also spoke of her girl friend, whom she did not refer to by name but described as a blonde of the doll type and spoke of her ways with men. Subject stated she has been going around with this girl since last Tuesday and had just come back from Connecticut with her. This girl friend lives on Park Avenue and travels about with her personal maid.

During the conversation with Miss Nettie, Assistant learned

they have a home in Miami, Fla. Nettie also spoke of her girl friend "Alice" whose photograph she showed Assistants and stated her name prior to her marriage was MacLain. She is now married to a man in the Stock Exchange by the name of Henderson. This girl worked with Nettie in Washington, D.C.

Jewel stated she could handle fat old men nicely. That she did not care for foreigners and was afraid of Italians. She also expressed a preference for diamond bracelets in the way of gifts from men.

Assistants then left the home of Subject with the promise that Assistant 152 would call at 5:00 P.M. and let Jewel know about the trip to Toronto.

The next day the "sisters" came around to put a $50 deposit down on the apartment. Both of them had been supplied with luxurious clothes, and 152 also had a fat roll of one hundred dollar and fifty dollar bills to flash when paying the deposit.

A room at the Hotel Roosevelt was rented for Lillian in the name of Mrs. Helen Smith. But now Lillian announced she was moving from there and would "camp out" for a few days with friends in Providence, Rhode Island, until the apartment was made available to them. Besides getting her out of the picture, this enabled the sisters to ask permission to have a wardrobe trunk of theirs sent there. Later, 152 went to the apartment to get something from the trunk and left the trunk keys there. This gave the Finch sisters a chance to open the trunk at their leisure and see what splendid clothes Mrs. Smith and her sister had acquired.

The purpose at this point was to convince Jewel that 152 was a gold digger worth teaming up with. Meanwhile an evening date was arranged for a foursome at a $300-a-month furnished apartment. We had to rent it for two months just to get it for that one evening.

The men were the same two hot-spending good-time Charlies who were taking 152 on the trip to Canada. They were Pennsylvania coal barons, rough-and-ready, simple-hearted fellows, Miss Finch was told. "But the richest one, Spike, is mine. Keep your hands off him. Your guy is Dick Osborne, the vice president of Spike's company. Dick isn't as rich as Spike, but you can get that silver fox you want from him with no trouble."

Meanwhile it did not go unnoticed that through all the day-by-day exchange of such girlish confidences, Jewel said not one word about her big operation on Mr. F. T. Reginald.

The night the foursome had their party, I was Spike Devlin, the coal baron who was keeping 152, and Major Otto, my chief assistant and office manager, was Dick Osborne.

I have said I enjoyed every minute of my work. But I seldom have enjoyed it so much as on that evening. As we were enjoying our first Martini, Joan sat on my lap, teased and tickled me, roughed up my hair. "What lut-tle present," she said in baby talk, "is my sugar daddy bringing his lonely lut-tle doll baby this time?"

I let her plead and tease for a moment or two more, then pulled a $3,000 diamond bracelet from my pocket and put it on her wrist. While 152 kissed me and then danced around the room in pure joy, Jewel apparently made up her mind that mine was the bankroll she wanted. The bracelet, and the other jewels that made 152 sparkle and rattle each time she moved, had been obtained by the way on memo from a friendly jeweler. Her fine feathers had been rented from a theatrical costumer.

The four of us dined that night at the Cascades Roof of the Hotel Biltmore. All was gaiety, all was joy. We had a first-rate meal and drank the champagne we had brought along for the management to ice in buckets. Jewel Finch, we noticed, drank almost nothing, and at twelve o'clock she announced she had to leave.

"I have to see some old friends from out of town," she said. "They're at the Commodore. But I'll be back in half an hour." She looked at me. "Would you get my coat for me, Spike?" She bade the other two a cordial good night. We then went out to the cloakroom where I got her coat and helped her into it. As we were shaking hands, she slipped me a piece of paper she had folded into a tiny square.

"I'd like to see you again, Spike, but next time I hope we'll be alone. You seem like a wonderful, wonderful man to me."

"Don't worry, you beautiful thing," I told her, "you'll see me alone next time. Just leave it to me."

She had written her name and phone number on the paper; when I had a chance to compare the writing with that on the paper Miss Hooper had given Mr. Reginald, they proved identical.

It was easy to anticipate her next two moves.

Having done everything possible to interest the man she thought had the bigger bankroll, she did not rejoin the party. However, we waited at the Cascades Roof for her until one-thirty.

At two o'clock she telephoned 152 at the apartment we'd rented, apologized for not rejoining us. She was effusive about "that wonderful Dick Osborne," and thanked 152 for getting her the chance to meet him. This, of course, was to find out whether I'd told the other girl that she'd given me her phone number.

We'd put a shadow on her. He followed her from her home to our furnished apartment, from there to the Biltmore and now he tailed her from there. She had gone straight home from the Biltmore, which also figured. What did take us by surprise was Jewel's next move after that.

Number 152 had explained that the boys had to run down to Washington on business but would be back in two or three days. The trip to Canada was all set and there would be no trouble about getting the silver fox from Dick Osborne. My being out of town, of course, explained why I hadn't phoned Jewel for a date.

The morning before we were supposed to leave, Jewel called up 152 to say that she'd be unable to come along with us. She was going to Toronto the following morning but had to rush up by train to see the middle-aged man she was in love with. The woman detective was able, however, to get from her the phone number in Canada at which she could be reached. "After all, you can easily sweet-talk Dick out of the silver fox you want if you can come back with us," 152 told her.

"Ask for Mrs. Stack when you call," said Jewel. "I'll be with that middle-aged man I told you about. He may be there when you call, so be careful of what you say."

Jewel took the train that night. That was where having a round-the-clock tail on her paid off. He followed her to Grand Central Station, watched her buy her ticket and a lower berth, and even got the number of the car. He was able to phone me just in time for me to tell him to get two berths in the same car. I sent another man to join him. He got to the gate two minutes before the train pulled out.

On the train Jewel acted like a woman who was drunk. I had a man in Toronto who met the train. With my two New York detectives he followed Jewel to a dingy little hotel. There was no Stack registered there. Number 152 had not quite caught the name right. It was "Black."

I went up to Toronto myself the next day. By that time the men there had a good description of Jewel Finch's middle-aged lover.

After reading their reports I went to the immigration authorities, and displayed my credentials. "I want to question a woman named Jewel Finch whom I am investigating. It's a blackmailing case." I gave the name of the hotel. "She is registered there with a man she isn't married to as Mr. and Mrs. J. R. Black." Such false registration is against the law in Canada. Our conversation went about like this:

"Have you a warrant for this woman?"

"No."

"Have you a warrant for the man?"

"No."

"Have you any evidence that either of them entered Canada under a false name?"

"No."

"Has either the man or the woman been indicted?"

"Not to my knowledge."

"Sorry, sir, but I can do nothing for you."

A second good reason for wanting to have Miss Finch arrested was that she'd be given a physical examination by a doctor. This would show whether she was pregnant. And it would be official proof of her fraud.

I went back to my hotel room, and brooded. After a while it occurred to me that it was possible that New York might want J. R. Black, even if Toronto didn't. So I sent this query to New York Headquarters:

DO YOU WANT J. R. BLACK? HE IS GERMAN OR JEWISH FIVE FEET ELEVEN AND A HALF INCHES GRAY TINGED HAIR WEARS PINCE NEZ EYEGLASSES STOPPING AT RARITAN HOTEL TORONTO

G. LUISI

The answer came back:

NEW YORK POLICE CASE SIXTEEN THIRTY EIGHT DASH NINETEEN TWENTY EIGHT J. B. BLACK DESCRIPTION FIFTY TO FIFTY FIVE SIX FEET TWO HUNDRED POUNDS GRAY HAIR RUDDY COMPLEXION GOOD DRESSER CHARGE GRAND LARCENY STOP NINETIETH SQUAD WEST FORTY SEVENTH STREET WANTS HIM STOP NO POLICE RECORD OF J. R. BLACK OF GIVEN ADDRESSES

I'd had one of his initials wrong.

All I needed to do then was show the wire to the Toronto police. The pair was arrested on the charge of false registration.

I was waiting at the customs office where they were brought first to be questioned about whether they'd entered the country illegally.

What happened when Jewel Finch saw me there was pitiful. I was almost sorry for her. She believed that somehow her admirer, Spike Devlin, the millionaire coal baron, had heard that she was in trouble and rushed in to offer his aid.

But I had to disillusion her with the truth. When I got the chance to question her, she readily confessed that she had not been assaulted nor had she had sexual relations with Reginald on the night she'd slept in his home. She'd met him in the speakeasy and gone home with him solely for the purpose of blackmailing him. But she denied that she'd put any drug in his drink that night.

When two New York police detectives arrived, the full story about her lover came out. J. B. Black was a crook, but no ordinary one. He was a society jeweler and lived with his wife and two children on an estate in Southold, Long Island, which was then one of New York's more fashionable suburbs.

He had been Jewel's lover for more than a year. But it was reverses in the stock market that caused him to turn thief, abscond with $75,000 worth of jewels he had obtained on memorandum, and head for Canada. Abandoning his family, his business, and many debts, Mr. Black had taken Jewel with him to Canada. She knew he was married. But they'd stopped at Niagara Falls for a few days — just like honeymooners. "This is the man I love and want to marry," she kept telling the authorities.

Someone could make a romantic story of their affair. But it will not be I. However, as far as I ever learned, her expert clipping of Mr. Reginald *was* her first attempt at crime. There was no question that she'd turned to blackmailing in order to raise money enough for Black to get a divorce, marry her, and make a fresh start in life together.

The pair could have been prosecuted for a variety of offenses, including the charge of entering the country illegally. But they were tried only for illegal registration, and sentenced to ten days in jail or $100 fine. Despite the fortune in jewels he'd stolen and her $28,500 blackmail haul, neither could pay the fine. Jewel's sister Nettie came up after a few days and got her out of jail by paying the fine. But J. B. Black did his ten days and then was taken to New York to face larceny charges. These were dropped when his wife and other members of his family made full restitution for him.

The examination of Jewel Finch in Toronto proved, as I thought it would, that she was not pregnant. But it did prove something else.

She had syphilis.

All Mr. Reginald wanted from Jewel Finch was that she leave him alone. However, the idea of a girl suffering from a social disease sleeping in his wife's bed all but unhinged him.

Though the stock market was still booming, he rushed off to Europe. He stayed there for a long time, resting his nerves.

Two months later I interrogated a shapely, beautiful young blonde. While returning from Europe aboard the S.S. *Berengaria,* she said, $12,000 worth of jewelry had disappeared from her cabin. She had noticed the loss on the night before the liner arrived in New York. She had notified the purser, but the jewels had not been recovered. The night before a ship puts into port after a transatlantic voyage is a very good time to lose jewelry. The crew, busy getting the passengers and baggage ready, have very little time to make a thorough search or ask any embarrassing questions.

The lovely young blonde said she had no other jewels. The missing ones had been purchased in Paris, but she could not recollect the name of the shop.

"Did you buy them yourself, miss?" I asked.

She bit her lip. "Must I answer that question?"

"I cannot recommend settlement unless you do."

"No. I did not buy them myself. A man I met in Paris, an American gentleman, bought them for me."

"And his name?"

She hesitated, but only for a moment, and then said:

"F. T. Reginald."

*

By an odd coincidence it was Mr. Reginald's lawyer who called me in on another strange blackmailing case. In this one there were no less than twelve millionaires — all scared to death of the same man. He was the liveried chauffeur of one of the dozen wealthy men. This time I was asked to come to the Gramercy Park home of the attorney. The millionaires preferred seeing me there. They thought they would have more privacy there. I must say that the dozen millionaires greeted me as though I were the United States Marines, but with much more generous pay offers. The group included bankers, Wall Street brokers, and industrialists. The oldest was seventy, the youngest forty-five.

"If you can get me out of this terrible jam," yelled one of the brokers, "I will give you $5,000."

"I'll make that $10,000, and pay all your expenses," said the man next to him.

I waited for someone to explain how I was to earn these large fees. But the lawyer shouted, "Please restrain yourselves, gentlemen. Mr. Luisi, I assure you, will do whatever he can for his regular fee — that's if he takes the case at all."

"He *must* take the case," one of the others said. "If he doesn't we're all sunk."

The lawyer waited a moment for them to calm down, then told me: "I think you know Mr. Dwight Huntington, Luisi. You've done some confidential work for his bank. He tells me you also know his chauffeur, Jameson."

I nodded. Mr. Huntington had allowed me to use his car while I was on an investigation for his bank. Jameson had driven me around town several times.

"What was your impression of Jameson?" asked the lawyer.

"Oh, I thought he was a good man, as most private chauffeurs are, loyal to his boss. In fact, now that you ask me, I recall his telling me that Mr. and Mrs. Dwight had been so good to his family that he would be grateful to them for the rest of his life."

"Maybe he said that two years ago," commented Mr. Huntington, shaking his head, "but he hasn't acted lately like a man bursting with gratitude."

It turned out that by "lately" Mr. Huntington meant that morning. "I stayed over all night last night at my little friend's apartment," he explained. "I had meant to go home by one or two at the latest. But she said she was lonely, and I let her talk me into staying over. As usual, I had Jameson wait downstairs for me.

"His job does call for a long day's work. I'd noticed that he seemed somewhat annoyed on previous occasions when I kept him out all night. But he never lost his temper as he did *this* morning. He drove me to the office, muttering all of the way. And from the back seat I could see his neck getting more and more red.

"But I said nothing until I got out of the car. If I'd been feeling less benevolent, I would simply have ignored his display of temper. As I was getting out I took out a ten-dollar bill and handed it to him.

"To my astonishment, that caused him to explode. 'I don't want your money. All I want is to get my regular sleep,' he said. 'I'm fed up with waiting for you all night on the street while you're loving it up with your young floosie.'

"Luisi, I could hardly believe my ears. I'd never expected Jameson to be so disrespectful, to say nothing about turning on me like that. And he wasn't finished! 'I have a good mind to tell Mrs. Huntington about what you really do nights when she thinks you're working late,' he said. 'I think you should be ashamed of yourself, Mr. Huntington! All those rich friends of yours, too. While I'm at it maybe I'll tell *their* wives too about *their* love nests!'

" 'That's quite enough, Jameson,' I managed to say.

" 'Enough is right,' he replied, and got out of the car. 'I'm fed up with your lousy job, anyway,' he yelled, and with that he walked off."

That was at eight-thirty that morning. By noon Mr. Huntington had alerted those friends of his whose secret love lives Jameson might expose. They were shocked to hear of his outburst. A few of them, not trusting their own chauffeurs, had occasionally borrowed Jameson's services for a few hours, sometimes to drive their own girl friends on shopping excursions or to and from a matinee. With their mistresses they had been in the car after parties. Jameson knew where all of their girls lived, and much else about them. The least the twelve millionaires expected was a bit of blackmail. They would gladly have settled for that then and there.

"Don't Jameson and his family live in a cottage on your Long Island estate?" I asked Mr. Huntington.

He nodded, gloomily.

"Have you tried to phone him there?"

"What! And take the chance of having my wife or some other member of the family pick up the phone and hear me pleading with him for mercy? And suppose he's sleeping. If I woke him . . ."

"So you don't really know whether he's still there or not?"

"No, and I'm afraid to call up the house to ask my wife about it. If he's told her a tenth of what he threatened, I am not going to enjoy her comments."

There was only one way to begin the job. That was to drive out to Mr. Huntington's estate. If Jameson was there, I could talk to him. If he'd already left with his family — he had three children, if my memory was not misleading me — the other servants might know where I could find him.

However Jameson had not left.

The chauffeur's wife did a little light housekeeping work for Mrs. Huntington, and the couple's salary was $200 a month and the use of the cottage. They also grew in their own garden most of the vegetables they needed. That was a good setup in 1928.

In five minutes the whole investigation was over.

"I'm sorry I made that threat, Mr. Luisi," Jameson said, "and I certainly have no intention of doing what I said, either to my boss or his friends. But I just got fed up waiting all night for him. I only hope he isn't going to fire me."

"I'm sure he won't," I said.

Mr. Huntington did not fire Jameson, but he never used him for night-life duty again, nor did any of his friends. Despite my assurances, none of these aging Romeos relaxed for quite a while, but on the other hand none of them gave up maintaining love nests for their women at addresses unknown to Jameson.

*

JUST as odd was a case in which blackmail of a sort played a part. Dr. George Stuart, whom the newspapers, though not other surgeons, described as the "eminent surgeon," was the central actor in this minor drama.

Dr. Stuart, a man fonder of money than men of science usually are, rented a cottage on his sprawling landed estate in Connecticut, to a divorcée for $4,000. He and Mrs. Stuart gloated over this achievement because they'd never been able to get more than $1,500 a year for the cottage.

But they abruptly stopped gloating and shaking hands with themselves when their free-handed tenant's rent checks bounced. They were also displeased to discover that the lady herself had moved into their big house, with her child and some of her possessions. A claim for loss was filed with the doctor's insurance broker when they discovered a shotgun, much liquor, fishing equipment, and some of their other possessions were missing.

When I was asked to look into this situation, I was told that it was "a delicate matter" and that I should assist Dr. Stuart. The reason was one I heard often: his broker gave the insurance company considerable business and the claim was for a small amount.

I was living in Connecticut myself at that time. Before going to see Dr. Stuart in New York, I drove over to look over the estate. It was a beautiful house set in the center of many green rolling acres. I also saw the divorcée — but from a distance. But I got a distinct impression that she was quite a worldly person.

When I went in to see Dr. Stuart, he got uneasy when I asked certain questions about the woman. I finally said, "Doctor, you cannot cure a patient if he does not answer your questions frankly and truthfully. It is the same way with me, a doctor of crime."

"I am a married man, a grandfather," he replied, "and I don't wish to be put in an embarrassing position."

"Embarrassing you is the last thing I want to do, doctor." He must have believed me because in answer to subsequent questions he admitted that he liked his woman tenant personally, had taken her out to dinner, and had visited her without taking his wife along.

He had permitted her to occupy the cottage, then move into the main house without her signing a lease or making any payment. He had also sold a car to her for $850. The check she gave him for this also had bounced.

After our talk, I interviewed the Connecticut State Troopers to find out whether they knew anything about the woman. They showed me a newspaper clipping that told a part of the story that the doctor had not mentioned. He'd had her arrested for giving him a check that was returned by the bank and marked "insufficient funds." A local taxidriver was charging that a $55 check the lady had given him had also bounced. And they had discontinued their investigation.

"We do not think a larceny was committed," I was told. "We think that all the insured articles were given her by the doctor."

The insurance company, however, instructed me to continue working on the case and to learn what I could about her. I soon found out that she had been arrested twice in New York for grand larceny.

She had previously pulled the same trick — moving into a Connecticut house, having an affair with the owner, then threatening him with a lawsuit if he tried to have her evicted. Each time the man had made a small settlement to avoid publicity.

I also found most of the items that she had taken from the doctor's summer home. Yet neither the doctor nor his wife would sign a complaint against her, charging larceny. In view of this I recommended that the insurance company refuse to pay the doctor for the articles I'd been unable to recover.

This woman blackmailer did not do too badly. The other charge of larceny, based on one check that bounced, was dismissed in court. She then turned around and sued the doctor for false arrest. On orders from the company I turned over to Dr. Stuart my information about her record and her other illegal acts. Nevertheless, this woman thief forced him to pay off with a small sum. As a company official remarked, on hearing of this:

"He may be a surgeon, but that woman performed this operation."

But the doctor had almost as much nerve as she.

He must have known that the woman with whom he was having an affair had stolen the insured articles. He had her arrested on the bad-check charge, but would not prosecute for the articles insured, thinking his insurance company would pony up the money for them.

*

AT the beginning of the twenties one of the most beautiful women in the world was gripped by the fear of blackmail. The woman was the lush brunette silent movie star Estelle Taylor. She was in love with Jack Dempsey, world heavyweight champion, who was in training for his title fight with Georges Carpentier. That fight, of course, turned out to be the first sports event ever to draw a million-dollar gate.

Jack Kearns, Dempsey's manager, was at this time doing everything in his power to stop his champion from marrying Miss Taylor. He thought that once Estelle became Mrs. Dempsey she would become Jack's real manager, and perhaps even demand an accounting from him of the millions of dollars Dempsey had earned with his fists, in personal appearances with a circus, and in vaudeville and movies.

Miss Taylor, a shrewd and witty woman, knew that the crafty, tricky Kearns was a genius at holding on to everything he wanted, and considered Dempsey his personal property.

This was a good reason for her getting into a panic when she received the following letter at the Fox Studios in New York where

she was a contract star. Though the letter was addressed to "Miss
Estelle Taylor," it read:

Dear Lola,
I have been looking for you for the past five years and I would
suggest that you communicate with me at once, or I will be
forced to come to New York City and prove by law who you are,
and what relation I am to you.
Wishing you continued success and awaiting an early reply,
I am,

Sincerely yours,
Grosvenor F. Collins

She had never seen or met or heard of anyone by that name.

Letters from nuts, cranks, and crackpots are no novelty to movie
stars. But it occurred to the beautiful star that someone might be
trying to frame her by discrediting her in Dempsey's eyes. She had
been married before, and it could be her ex-husband playing a
cruel joke on her, she thought.

But she did not decide to do anything about the letter until
a week or two later, when she got a phone call from Grosvenor F.
Collins, or someone who said he was Collins.

"You must come back to me, Lola," he pleaded over the phone.
"After all, we are still married. I can't live without you, my darling.
I will forgive everything you have done if only you will come back
and live with me."

In a turmoil of worry and confusion, Miss Taylor asked the help
of her lawyer, Henry Herzbrun, who later became one of the
men who ran Paramount Pictures Corporation. Herzbrun arranged
for me to meet her in his office.

I read the letter from Collins, heard her description of the crazy
phone conversation. "Are you sure you never met this man Collins?"
I asked.

She was emphatic about that. But she explained: "I mean, I never
had a personal relationship of any kind with anyone named Collins. As a star, of course, I meet hundreds of people at parties and
receptions wherever I travel. I may have met him under such circumstances. But if so, he did not make enough of an impression on
me for me to remember him."

The letter was postmarked Philadelphia and the return address
on it was a number on Walnut Street. I went there and was told
that Collins had a furnished room there, was a short-order cook, and

at the moment was out of town. I had to return to New York on
pressing business. There I found a message from Miss Taylor saying that she wanted to see me. I asked her to come to my office. She
had another letter from Collins that mystified her more than the
first one. It also was postmarked Philadelphia, was dated May 14th,.
and said:

My name is Grosvenor F. Collins. I reside at 1033 Walnut
Street in this city (Philadelphia). I have lived here for two years.
On January 1, 1910 or 1911, I do not recall which year, I was
married to Lola M. Beach (now appearing in the Fox Films as
Estelle Taylor) at St. Joseph's Roman Catholic Church, 2nd
and C Streets, N.E., Washington, D.C.

Her mother was dead and her father was a wanderer. I never
saw him. At that time Lola was living with her grandmother,
Mrs. Ostrander. She had two aunts — Mrs. Lucy Jones and Mrs.
Lydia (or Lida) Rosten, Washington, D.C. The latter is the wife
of the Police Officer John Rosten, Washington, D.C. He owns
the house at 518–22 Street, N.W., and lived there at that time.

Mrs. Collins was a very extravagant lady and was never con-
tented. Less than a year after she married me she went away.
Later she sent to me for money to come home on. I sent the
money and she returned. But she remained with me for only
two or three months, and then once more went again. This time
she wrote for money which I sent her, and she came home,
stayed a while and left again. But she never came back to me.
That broke up our home. I was always kind to her and I guess
I petted her too much.

I searched everywhere for her. I wrote her Aunt Lydia, or
Lida, and told her all about it. I received a sweet letter back,
this was in 1914 — but her aunt could give me no information
as to my wife's whereabouts, I never ceased to search for her.

Some weeks ago I went to the Victoria Theatre in this city
and in the screen production "While New York Sleeps" I recognized in the character "Estelle Taylor" my wife.

From *Photoplay*, April, 1921, issue, on page 68 I learned my
wife's address. The birthplace as given was correct, but the age
has been lowered, she is between 27–28. The same issue contained pictures of my legal wife, Lola M. Collins, page 52 in
"Blind Wives" and page 17 as "Estelle Taylor."

Grosvenor F. Collins

I made another trip to Philadelphia. This time I was lucky
enough to catch him at home. He was a tall, serious-looking man

who was then about thirty-five. Mild, earnest, he looked and appeared to be harmless. But there was no questioning the strength of his conviction that the woman, Lola M. Beach, he had married ten or eleven years before had become Estelle Taylor, the glamorous film star.

If he was a tool of men eager to wreck her marriage to Jack Dempsey, he must be an unconscious one, I thought. I asked him who his lawyer was. He told me readily enough, but the lawyer, Lewis M. Hyndman, proved to be out of town. I left a request at his office that he get in touch with me. I also got a promise from Grosvenor F. Collins that he would not attempt to communicate with Estelle Taylor until I had a chance to talk to Mr. Hyndman.

Once again I had to go back to New York. But not long afterward, Mr. Hyndman came there on business and we had a talk in my office.

"I don't know if Collins actually was her husband," he said, "or just imagined the whole thing. But there is only one way to find out: that would be by bringing them face to face."

Mr. Enrico Caruso once told me that I would have made a success as an actor. This time I tried my hand at staging a little real-life drama. Instead of one Estelle Taylor for Mr. Collins to see, I produced seven with the aid of a casting director. He found me six brunettes about her height, weight, and build, who looked like her. We then brought Collins into the room.

"Well, Mr. Collins," I said, "which one of these ladies is your wife?"

He walked from one to another, studying the face of each one. In the end he shook his head.

"She isn't here, my Lola," he said, disconsolately, then added, "Which one is Miss Taylor?"

"Why do you want to know?" I asked.

"I wish to apologize to her for causing her all this trouble."

I looked at Mr. Herzbrun, who nodded. I pointed to the actress, and, wishing to nail it down, "Is she your wife?"

He said, "No," apologized to her, and held out his hand. She took it.

She was married shortly afterward to the champion. I felt, when I read of that, like an assistant cupid.

*

I HAD cases in the twenties with other celebrated performers. Even by then the faking of jewel robberies to get actresses publicity had been used too often to fool newspaper editors. One of the last of these fakes to make the headlines was the invention of Mme. Olga Petrova's press agent. The great Polish beauty was playing in vaudeville when she sued a bird act appearing on the same bill for the loss of the diamond in one of her rings. Petrova's complaint alleged that the star of this bird act, a parrot named Finnegan, had flown out at her in the wings, bitten off the diamond, and swallowed it before her very eyes.

Petrova may have got the idea from Chicago May, a handsome woman thief who lured men into the nearest hallway. While the man was hugging her, Chicago May would lean over and bite the diamond out of his stickpin.

By the twenties stories that the jewelry of stars had been stolen got only sneers and laughs from Broadway reporters. This may have been one of the reasons that Billie Burke, wife of Florenz Ziegfeld, Jr., insisted that news of the loss of some of her jewelry be kept out of the newspapers. I don't know what her husband, the Great Glorifier and most publicized showman since Barnum, said when she told him that. And she may have had another reason for not wanting any news items published about her loss. Though the watch and bracelet had disappeared mysteriously from her dressing room while she was onstage, she had notified neither the police nor her insurance broker. It was through Henry Herzbrun, who was also her lawyer, that she got in touch with me.

She was playing in Booth Tarkington's *The Intimate Strangers* and Herzbrun and I had dinner with her at the Hunting Room of the Hotel Astor before her evening performance. Miss Burke was about thirty-five then, but looked no more than twenty. To me, the big surprise was how shrewd and observant this lovely little creature was. I thought of that often later when I saw her playing bird-brain roles on the stage and the screen.

Her dressing-room maid was ill on the evening her jewelry disappeared. Miss Burke was told of that too late to get a substitute. So no attendant was in the room while she was onstage.

While dressing, she took off her watch and bracelet as usual and put them in the unlocked drawer of her dressing table. Besides, other women often dropped into her dressing room when they were not onstage to wait for her to come off. That was also true of several actresses who were close friends of hers. In fact, on coming off after one scene in the second act, she met one of these women walking out of her dressing room.

"Oh," said this actress, looking at her watch, "I guess I'm slow. I thought you would be off, so I popped in for a minute to see you." She went back into the dressing room, chatted, and smoked a cigarette until the star went out again.

"Did you mention the disappearance of your jewelry to your friends and to the other actresses who are appearing with you?"

"Of course," said Miss Burke. "I asked them if they'd noticed that I was wearing the watch and bracelet when I arrived. Two of them said they'd noticed the bracelet; the others had not noticed either piece."

"Can you have all those girls, the ones in your show and also your friends, in your dressing room after tonight's show?"

"I think so," she said.

"We'll be there too. You might mention that, but say nothing to any of them about our little talk."

After dropping Miss Burke at the stage door I went down to my office with Herzbrun. I picked up a fingerprinting outfit there, and a card with two fingerprints already on it.

There were eight girls crowded into the star's dressing room when we got there, all pretty, all young. I looked for a moment at each of them, as we were introduced. One, a shy-looking girl of about twenty, seemed quite nervous. I glanced her way a couple of times. I found her watching me with a worried expression. But on seeing me look at her, she'd drop her eyes.

"This afternoon," I announced, "I came here to the dressing room to take photographs of every square inch of the drawer where Miss Burke keeps her jewelry."

"Mr. Luisi!" exclaimed Miss Burke, "Why I — "

I cut her short. "Please, Miss Burke, I am conducting this investigation. I'd appreciate it if you save any comment you care to make until I have finished." The famous Billie Burke twinkle reappeared in her eyes. She nodded, and said, "Pardon me."

I turned to one of the girls, "Did you at any time during last night's performance open the dresser drawer in which Miss Burke keeps her diamond watch and bracelet?"

"No," she said.

As she replied, I started taking out my fingerprinting kit. I carefully laid down the little slab of glass, inked it, and spread it with the roller.

"You can go," I told the girl.

I turned to the second girl. "What about you, miss? Did you have occasion last night to touch this drawer?"

"No," she said, "oh, no."

I told her she could go. I saved the nervous girl, who by this time was tearing her handkerchief in her anxiety, until all of the others had answered "No" to my question, and been dismissed. As a final touch I took out the fingerprint card from my pocket and examined it carefully.

Then I turned to the nervous actress, and asked her, "Did you, last night, happen to touch the inside of this drawer with your fingers?"

She took a deep breath, then said, hesitantly, "No-o-o."

I shook my head, and said, "I'm sorry, but I'll have to take your fingerprints now, and compare them with those on the card."

At this she burst into tears, ran over to Miss Burke, and sobbed, "I'll tell the truth, Miss Burke, the whole story."

Miss Burke put her arms around her as an understanding mother might. The other actress then explained, between convulsive sobs: "I had a date last night with a man I'm wild about. I wanted so much to impress him, Miss Burke. So I borrowed your jewelry. I was sure, crazy as it sounds, that I'd be able to return it tonight. But I never did get that chance."

"Where is the jewelry now?"

"In my dressing room," she said. "I will get it."

"Just a minute," I said, stopping her and opening the door. The other girls were all waiting outside, curious to find out what was going on.

"Why don't all you girls get dressed?" I said. "Miss Burke wants to take us all out for a little midnight supper. She wants you to help her celebrate because the jewelry has been found. She misplaced it."

That of course gave the guilty actress a chance to get the jewelry and hand it to Miss Burke. And Mrs. Florenz Ziegfeld, Jr., did take us out for a midnight dinner. I enjoyed it so much that, as she and I said good night, I refused her suggestion that I send her a bill.

"I've already been more than paid for this slight service," I told her, "by the pleasure of spending an evening in your company."

*

ON coming home after such an experience with a Broadway star, I always expected my two sons, who were then at the impressionable pre-teen age, to be impressed. They disappointed me — except on one occasion: the day I got the job of finding the jewels of Pearl White, dauntless queen of the movie serials, the woman of their young dreams and the girl both of them wished to marry when they grew up.

Miss White had lost her jewels at a party given by Peggy Hopkins Joyce, whose husbands and many other admirers had made her the most decorated woman in America. The jewels were worth about $15,000, and included two diamond rings, a bracelet, and a diamond brooch. I saw Miss White at about six o'clock on the evening after the party. She was a lovely-looking creature, a true blonde with an exquisite complexion, flashing blue eyes, and a merry disposition. But of course she was not very merry this day.

"I think I was still wearing my jewels when I left that party. My escort left me at the door. I had had plenty to drink, and cannot remember taking off those jewels before going to sleep."

On waking up about noon, she had called Peggy Joyce to say she couldn't find her diamonds. "I had my apartment searched," she said, "but with no luck." Miss Joyce had her servants search her home, with no better result.

There was no sign of anyone having entered the serial queen's apartment during the night. Her escort had been a steel millionaire and among the other guests there was nobody one would suspect of being a jewel thief.

I searched Pearl White's house. I believed we'd find the diamonds there. When I didn't, I tried again the next night, looking everywhere in the apartment all over again. Still no luck. I was thoroughly exasperated. But on the way home it dawned on me that there was one place I had neglected. I went back for the third time.

"Where are the slippers you wore that night?" I asked Miss White. She had them on one of the racks in her bedroom closet. I picked up one of the shoes, and shook it. There was a rattle! She had hidden the jewels there. I never heard a woman laugh with such wholehearted hilarity.

The most gratifying thing about my success in finding Pearl White's jewels was that I had a chance to ask her for two autographed photos for my sons. When she heard that they were ardent fans of hers, she invited them to visit her. They said later that they had never tasted such ice cream, cookies, and candy as the movie girl of their dreams served them that day.

*

I DID miss a really comic scene involving jewels and Peggy Joyce, whose names were almost synonymous in the twenties. She admired some she had looked at at Cartier's just before going to the Poconos for the summer. Fearing someone else would buy them, she called up the store one morning and asked that they send them up.

She was at the station when Cartier's man arrived, and greeted him like an old friend. As they started off in her limousine, she exclaimed; "All right, show them to me. I've been dreaming every night about the damn things."

"If you don't mind," he told her, "I'd prefer waiting, Miss Joyce, until we get to your home."

"The hell with waiting," said Peggy, a woman accustomed to getting her own way.

"Please bear with me, Miss Joyce. You'll appreciate them even more when you're relaxed. I do not like to show a client such beautiful diamonds in a moving car."

Peggy fell silent, but was getting angrier and more impatient by the minute. After a little while, she told her chauffeur,

"Stop the car!"

When he had done so, she said, "Okay, kid! Let's see those diamonds!"

"Won't you please wait until we arrive at your home?" he pleaded.

"*Now* what's your excuse?" she demanded. When he shook his head: "If you don't show me those jewels without any more delay, I won't buy them. Not only that: I'll never go into Cartier's again, neither in New York nor Paris. And if they open any more stores, I'll boycott them too."

"This is most embarrassing," murmured the jewel salesman. "Would you please turn your head away for a moment?"

Though Peggy pretended to, she peeked. She saw the salesman shyly unbutton his fly and reach inside. He had put a jockstrap on and pinned the jewels to the inside of that.

Miss Joyce whooped with amusement. She bought all of the diamonds he'd brought to show her. She also told the story at all the parties she went to for weeks afterward. Bill Fallon even gave a title to the anecdote. He called it "The Mystery of the Diamond-Loaded Jockstrap."

*

My own greatest thrill was meeting Enrico Caruso, whose golden voice has been called the greatest in musical history. I met and talked with the tenor when $400,000 worth of jewels he had given his wife were stolen from their summer home at Easthampton, Long Island. I was brought into the case months later by a company which had insured some of the jewels for $45,000.

The singer had been on tour when a sneak thief got into the house and carried off a lightweight miniature safe — it was two by two feet. The chauffeur chased him, firing two or three shots. But the thief managed to open the little safe as he ran, scooped out the jewels, and threw it into the bushes. He got away.

The local police and investigators for all the insurance companies involved had worked on the case for months. For a time, the chauffeur was suspected because years before he had been arrested in connection with the theft of a car. But he was freed in that case and it seemed certain that he had no part in this great jewel robbery either. But he was fired when Caruso came home.

All sorts of mysteries and oddities featured this case. The servants had played with the safe when their employers were away. It had a sort of built-in alarm which went off if anyone tried to move or open it. Usually this alarm could be heard all over the big house. But it had not gone off this evening. Mrs. Caruso was the daughter of Park Benjamin, the New York financier. That evening she was sitting downstairs, sewing. With her was her sister-in-law, Mrs. Park Benjamin, Jr. They told police they heard heavy footsteps upstairs and then the commotion and shots outside.

Mrs. Caruso had questioned the servants herself before notifying the authorities or the insurance companies. None of them except the chauffeur had ever been in trouble with the police. She seemed interested only in whether any of them — there were ten servants in her employ — had been able to see anything but the thief's back.

It took me two whole evenings to read and digest the many reports on the case. The investigators had made a thorough investigation of the servants and other potential suspects — with one exception.

I was greeted very cordially by Caruso when I went to Easthampton, but not by his wife. She seemed displeased when he hailed me as *"paesano."* Before I started asking questions, the singer offered me a demitasse of Italian coffee and anisette. Italians consider this a wonderful morning pickup, by the way, and many of my countrymen have it instead of breakfast.

After we'd enjoyed this drink I asked to see the safe. The alarm had been broken when it fell in the bushes. "Until then it rang loud enough to be heard downstairs by the servants," Mrs. Caruso said.

"Who knows about this alarm?"

"Only my personal maid."

"Was the alarm on the morning of the robbery?"

"I usually put it on before I go out, switch it off when I'm home. It must have been on that day for the chauffeur heard it as he was chasing the thief."

I asked her for a list of all the persons who might have seen or known about her jewel box. This appeared to disturb Mrs. Caruso, and she explained that she preferred not to put her friends to any inconvenience. At this point her husband urged her to give me any information I asked for.

"That's the only way you'll ever be able to get your jewelry back, Dorothy," he said.

She gave me a list of fourteen persons, but with some reluctance. None of them were Italians, I noticed, though it was no secret that her husband had no close friends who weren't Italian. I also observed that her brother, whom the reports said often stayed overnight at the house, was not on the list. I asked about some of the persons on the list, and also about her brother.

"He is very well fixed," she said.

I sneaked a look at Caruso. He said *"Così, così!"* which is Italian for "So so." I had dinner at their home that evening, the feature being chicken with Tetrazzini sauce. Mrs. Caruso seemed disinclined to leave me alone with her husband during or after the meal.

Next morning I put tails on her brother and several other of Mrs. Caruso's list of overnight guests. Shortly afterward, Mrs. Caruso protested.

"Why are you having my brother and my friends followed? Why are you having their finances looked into?"

"That is routine, Mrs. Caruso, in a case of this sort," I told her.

"Routine or not, I will not stand for it."

A couple of days later Caruso's insurance broker arranged an appointment with me. He came with the singer, who greeted me again with "Hello, *paesano!*" and that wonderful boyish smile of his.

When they were seated, Caruso asked: "Luisi, are you going to recommend that the claim be paid or not? The attorney for the insurance company said, 'We are still investigating, and have hopes of recovering the jewelry.' "

The singer turned to me, "Do you suspect somebody, Luisi?"

"I've eliminated everyone except one man. He is someone who is very familiar with your Easthampton home and also the grounds around it." I could have added that this one man had no means of supporting himself but had been spending money wildly on Broadway since the robbery.

To my surprise, Caruso did not ask who he was, but said: "I do not think you will find the jewelry. I will either put the matter in the hands of my lawyer, or I will drop the whole thing."

He got up to go, and it was then that he said to me, "Luisi, you would have made a good actor."

The next day I was instructed to discontinue my investigation. The man who had been spending money so wildly on Broadway was Mrs. Caruso's brother, Park Benjamin, Jr.

WHERE TO FIND THE LOOT 6

THIEVES sometimes display extraordinary ingenuity in hiding loot. Gerard Graham Dennis, the Canadian second-story man, hid a fortune in diamonds in holes he bored into the bottom of a dressing table, then plugged up. The police would never have found these gems if his girl friend had not tipped them off.

Whole generations of crooks before him have secreted jewels in their mouths, up their nostrils, behind their ears, and in their private parts, front and rear. Others in attempting to avoid arrest have swallowed jewels, counting on recovering them later from their excrement.

Some old-time thieves must have been moved by nostalgia when Jackie Kennedy made stylish her bouffant hairdo. In the old days the moll's bun was a handy hiding place for hot gems, and before that the bustle. We've found jewels in every unlikely place around houses, in all kinds of hollowed-out places, behind gas meters, the kid's piggy bank, and Mom's sanitary belt. The water tank over the chain-pull toilet was a favored hiding place for jewels up to the time such toilets became almost as rare as old-fashioned women.

Many times when I had the job of finding loot in such strange places I remembered the old story about the village fool who found a farmer's horse that had been missing for three days. Asked how he did it, the fool replied: "I just figured out where I would go if I was a horse. And so I went there, and there he was."

It is possible, I suppose, to find loot in the same way — by imagining where you would hide it if you were the thief. But that system certainly would not have worked the day I drew the job of figuring what had happened to one hundred large commercial fans. By an odd coincidence, they had disappeared shortly before a fire burned out the New Jersey plant that manufactured them. Arson was suspected.

No genius was required to figure out that the big fans either had been carted away on several large trucks or on one that made several trips. But where in the world could crooks hide a hundred bulky machines? What I did finally was to have a house-to-house canvass made of the neighborhood. And sure enough we found a woman who had seen a truck repeatedly going in and coming out of the plant on the morning of the fire. She also had noticed that the name of a local junkman was on the truck.

I went to this man's yard and told him what I knew. He may have thought I knew a great deal more than that. He showed me where the one hundred commercial fans were hidden: in the middle of the yard, buried under a mountain of junk.

*

BUT the find I am proudest of making had nothing to do with loot. A jeweler with offices in New York's Radio City reported that a $5,000 diamond ring had disappeared overnight from his safe. He'd had it made to order by an expert craftsman for a good customer.

The ring had arrived at his place by messenger the previous day, just before he closed his office. It came wrapped in tissue paper. With it was an assortment of loose diamonds, also wrapped in several layers of tissue paper. The firm's five traveling salesman and his secretary were with him in his office for the regular monthly conference. "Wait till you see this odd one," he said, and passed the ring around so they could all admire it.

It *was* an odd one, and had been made to the customer's specifications. The center stone was a large diamond which had been colored green by applying radium. It was surrounded by eighteen baguette and thirty round diamonds, two half-moon diamonds, and two pieces of carved jade. The setting was platinum.

The jeweler's story, confirmed by the five salesmen and his secretary, was that after showing them the ring he had put it and the loose diamonds into his safe. The secretary added that on this afternoon, as was her habit, she had looked all over the store and on the floor for scraps of tissue paper. She'd found more than one piece of jewelry in discarded wrappings down through the years. But she'd found no scraps of paper on this day.

A brief check cleared the employees. I became convinced that the ring must have accidentally been dropped in a wastepaper basket, or swept out. The superintendent, on being consulted, said that a firm of professional office-building cleaners had a contract with Radio City. He thought that they baled together the waste, then sold it to some paper mill.

This proved to be the case.

The mill was in Pennsylvania. Luckily, the shipment had not arrived there yet. I wired the mill's superintendent a request to hold the waste until we could have it searched. It was a whopping shipment of eleven bales weighing about 1,100 pounds each, or a little over six tons!

Word came back that the shipment could not be held. The custom was to process waste as it arrived. In the end I offered to buy the lot. It cost several hundred dollars, with the shipping and handling charges thrown in. I had the eleven bales of waste sent to a salvage company.

Some of my associates at the insurance company told me I had lost my mind. But I trusted my instinct. I had an X-ray company send a technician to the salvage company. I hoped he would find the ring with a fluoroscope. But he quit the job after using the fluoroscope on the first bale. There were too many other solid objects — clips, discarded typewriter ribbons, ink bottles, and the like, to locate so small an object with that instrument.

I next hired two cleaning women to go through the eleven bales of waste. We paid them their regular wages but promised a reward of $500 if they found the ring. They were at the job for ten days and going through the fifth bale when one of the old girls picked up the ring.

She fainted with joy.

The whole cost of the investigation, including their pay, the reward, and the cost of the eleven bales of waste, was $970. The insurance company saved more than $4,000, and the jeweler was able to deliver the beautiful and unusual ring he'd had made to order for his customer — without the delay or the expense or having another made to replace it.

*

LIKE show business and the other spectacular professions, the jewel trade seems to attract both very fine men and also some of the shiftiest scoundrels alive. The honest ones, I am sure, outnumber by far the thieves. One reads all of the time about jewel salesmen and jewelers who will chance getting stabbed, shot, or beaten to protect property belonging to their employers. There are many, many more we do not hear about.

The crooks who go into that business are master hands at making gems disappear. I have often estimated that at least one-fourth of all robberies, burglaries, and disappearances of jewelry reported by jewelers and their traveling salesmen are fakes. In a recent year insurance companies paid out more than $3,000,000 for such losses, actual and alleged.

Critics of police efficiency might consider once in a while how many "crimes" reported in the ever-rising crime statistics never happened.

The insurance companies, of course, cannot escape their share of the blame. If they obtained better reports on the finances of businessmen before issuing to them policies representing fortunes, they could cut such losses sharply. But most of them will take the chance of issuing policies for as much as $50,000 after reading a $2.50 credit-company report. And there is no end to the reasons they can find to settle claims in which frauds are all too obvious.

In my opinion, the insurance companies have always been too liberal in settling these cases, thus encouraging carelessness or dishonesty, whichever you wish to call it. They have even settled cases in which salesmen have had more than one loss in such absurd circumstances. If the salesman is fired, he seldom has much trouble getting another job in his line.

The jewelers are protected by what is called the Jewelers' Block Policy. This benevolent policy insures the jeweler for every sort of personal property, property of others for which they may become liable, for the property of others for which they agree to provide insurance, or assume responsibility to restore, replace, or pay others for. There are few exclusions except against dishonest employees, or conversion by contractors or possessors, natural disasters, and the like. They get another policy usually to protect themselves against dishonesty by their employees.

To take a recent year, 1956, insurance companies paid out about $3,000,000 in losses in the jewel trade. One robbery accounted for

$300,000, or one-tenth of this. A few of the salesmen who stole, either directly or indirectly, went to jail.

There is always too little manpower in the law-enforcement agencies. But the insurance companies could cut down the losses if they had more investigators to devote all of their time exclusively to these claims. Perhaps there would then be fewer salesmen trying to get away with a fortune in jewels.

On the other hand, insurance companies are not law-enforcement agencies. And if they cause somebody's arrest and, innocent or guilty, he is acquitted for lack of evidence or any other reason, the arrested person can turn around and sue the insurance people for false arrest, slander, etc. (see your lawyer for the full list).

The generosity of juries in awarding enormous verdicts against insurance companies, public utilities, and other giant corporations is another ever-present fact to consider. For many decades now, in New York and other states, judges throw out cases between individuals if anyone even mentions that the defendant is insured. The jurymen feel they are striking a blow for the little man, but far too often the little man is a crook.

Because insurance companies are considered such fair game, their investigators and other representatives have to be careful of what they do, of how they handle persons suspected of exaggerating the claims or inventing crimes. And, as I've mentioned, brokers who can give them a large volume of business wish them to settle quickly and generously the claims of their clients. If they don't, the broker gives his business to some other insurance company.

The men who handle such matters feel that their first obligation is to their stockholders. And I have never met a stockholder yet who was more interested in seeing the proper thing done than in collecting dividends. As I've said, the ethics of the insurance business are those of businessmen everywhere.

But let us look at a few dubious claims of jewelers on which thousands of dollars were paid. We will begin with the case of one Gregory Aronowitz, a New York jewel dealer who claimed to have been robbed by two masked men. That morning he had just opened the office. As always, he closed and locked the door behind him on entering. He wanted to look around and put his stock on display before opening for business. But he had hardly opened the safe, when two masked men came in through the front door. Both were armed and they made him lie on the floor. They did not bind or gag him, just warned him to be quiet, and turned their backs on him. They then scooped up $110,000 in jewels from the safe. The thieves selected only his finest gems, and left behind those of less value.

There were holes in his story:

No signs on the door, which he said was locked, indicating forced entry. The office was on the ninth floor of a building in the heart of New York's Midtown diamond district, but neither the elevator man nor anyone else saw the thieves come in or leave. If there was a robbery I doubted that they'd walked up nine flights of stairs, even though they might have run down them on their way out.

Aronowitz took lie-detector tests that proved inconclusive. These merely showed increased tension when crucial questions were asked. Reports from Amsterdam where he had been a partner in a jewel business showed that he was trusted there, had always paid his bills, and enjoyed a good moral reputation. For that matter, he had a good reputation here both in the trade and with the banks he had accounts in.

Nevertheless, I felt sure that Aronowitz had faked the crime. I could not believe that thieves, as stupid as I've found some of them to be, would fail to search somebody for weapons and turn their backs on them. Mr. Aronowitz threatened to sue the company that eventually settled his $110,000 claim for $25,000. The company's legal department said it would cost $15,000 to defend the suit if the jeweler brought the matter into the courts. The risk of losing the case and possibly having to pay Aronowitz $110,000 besides seemed bad business.

*

But it is the traveling salesmen who are the undisputed champs in the jewel trade when it comes to losing precious stones, retail and wholesale. If you really want to lose something valuable, give it to one of these absentminded knights of the road. And nothing embarrasses them, including admitting they were careless beyond belief. Here are some stories salesmen told me with a straight face.

One checked a sample case containing $40,000 worth of jewelry at a railroad station, then managed to lose the ticket. On returning to the checkroom he found that whoever found the ticket had already exchanged it for the sample case.

Another just left his sample case outside the door of a bus terminal when he went in to buy a ticket. That too was gone. The third salesman lost $100,000 worth of jewels belonging to his company while he was eating a filet mignon in the diner. He left them safely locked in a sample case on his coach seat. But he at least brought home the empty sample case. The thoughtful crook had discarded the case in the men's washroom.

A fourth traveling man took no chances while washing in the public lavatory of a railway station. He kept his little treasure box on the floor, between his feet, while he scrubbed his hands. On finishing, he realized he had no towel, and stepped away just long enough to get one from the porter. In the minute it took to dry his hands and face, the case full of jewels vanished forever. A fifth guy lost his firm's $100,000 worth of jewels in the New York subway. He put the case they were in between his feet, then forgot to take it with him when he arrived at the station.

"Thank God you didn't trip over the case when you got up," I told this Baron Munchausen on listening to that cock-and-bull story.

But let's examine in some detail a few of the stories told me by other jewel salesmen and merchants to explain such losses. We'll start with Henry Eliscu, who claimed he had just such an expensive misadventure one sunny day in Minneapolis. He left his employer's jewels, which had cost his boss slightly less than $75,000, in his car while he went into a hotel to ask if there was a room available. There was, so he registered and then went out to discover that some sneak thief had made off with the jewels.

The Pinkertons, a reputable firm of adjusters, and the Minneapolis police all investigated this tale. None of them believed Eliscu's story. You wouldn't either if you'd listened to it. But at the same time they couldn't disprove it or get him to admit he had dreamed the whole thing up. By the time I was called in, Mr. E. was heartily sick of answering questions. I interviewed him in my office, not once, but twice.

He was then thirty-nine years old, a dark, wiry man of average height who told me he worked on a straight commission and had earned $10,000 during the previous year. He was married, had three children, and was living in a four-and-a-half-room cooperative apartment that he and his wife had bought four years before for $2,550. He paid a modest rent, and when I sent men out to check his statements, they discovered nothing to indicate that he was gambling, had a sweetheart, or was living above his income.

But Eliscu, for a man not yet forty, had changed jobs a little too frequently. After leaving New York University he had been in the food business, selling butter, eggs, and frozen foods. Then he had worked in several restaurants, including a couple on Broadway. He had been in the Army for three years and two months during World War II. He finished as a private and had an honorable discharge. It was his father-in-law, a manufacturing jeweler, who at first interested him in his present business. Since his father-in-law's death five years before, he had been working for one jeweler after another.

We checked on him with every employer he'd ever had since leaving college. They all agreed that his honesty was above question. Nevertheless, one of them — and he was the only ex-boss who disliked Eliscu personally — said he would not believe his former salesman under oath.

This man said: "His wife was going to have a baby while he was traveling. So I asked him: 'What do you want me to do in case of an emergency? Is everything taken care of, all the arrangements made? Does she know just what town you will be in each day — in case she wants to call you?'

"His answer to all of these questions was a curt 'Yes.' But he lied about that. A few days after he started on the trip, his wife called me up. She was in the hospital, had had her baby, and wanted to know where he was. He had not called her or given her a schedule.

"The terrible thing was that I couldn't tell her where he was. Against all company rules this S.O.B. had not communicated with us for a week. And he did not communicate with Mrs. Eliscu either until he got home over a month later. He did not even know while he was away that his son had been born. He had not cared enough about his wife or the child to call up the hospital.

"I did not want so cruel and callous a man working for me, so I fired him. The excuse was breaking the company rules by not making daily reports to the New York office for a whole week. But the way he treated his wife was my real reason. Yet I must repeat: he was a scrupulously honest employee."

Naturally, this proof of how poor a husband Eliscu was did not help our investigation.

There were two or three things about Eliscu's account of the trip on which he'd lost a fortune of jewels so stupidly that did arouse my interest. He had one of those convenient memories that enabled him to recall only what he wished to. He replied to questions "I don't know" and "I don't recall" entirely too many times. That is not usually the way with an honest man who is as intelligent and quick with words as Eliscu. The fellow who has nothing to hide keeps contributing helpful little details. Eliscu's answers were all cryptic, restricted to "Yes" and "No" when possible.

I made him account for every moment of the trip, which had lasted two months. He had stopped at thirty-one towns and called on seventy-three dealers. He had run into two other jewel salesmen whose reputations were on the gamey side. One of these men had reported three years before that he'd been held up and robbed of almost $100,000 in jewels. The police of Cincinnati, where it happened, had not believed his story either.

But none of this proved Eliscu was a crook.

Now, here is what made me suspicious of Eliscu's story, besides his convenient memory and his failure to volunteer any information.

Minneapolis had not been on his route at all, and he could not give a convincing reason why he had stopped there. On checking the hotels where he stopped, I observed that he made no telephone calls from his room. Asked about this, he said he preferred to get change and make the calls from a coin telephone in the lobby. But Mr. Eliscu did not seem to me that economical a man, the type that would go to all that trouble to save the few cents the hotel tacked onto the telephone charges.

He carried two sample cases. One weighed twenty-five pounds, the other, thirty-five. He kept them at his side in the front seat. He told a strange story about seeing outside Minneapolis a car with two men in it that appeared to be following him. The first thing a man carrying $75,000 worth of jewelry in his car would do under such circumstances would be to head for the nearest police station to report the matter. It seemed to me certain that he would not have left the fortune in diamonds behind in his car.

In Minneapolis I interviewed and obtained affidavits from the doorman and the bellman who'd come out with the jewelry salesman to get his luggage. The doorman had seen Eliscu lock only the left front door of the car. They both agreed that, on seeing the sample cases were missing, Eliscu had exclaimed: "Who has been in my car? I've been robbed! Somebody has taken a couple of bags from the front seat!"

The doorman's affidavit explained that the driver of a yellow cab who was parked behind Eliscu's car called him, the doorman, over and asked what was going on. When told, the cab driver, a colored man who worked part time for the post office, said: "The man's crazy. No one has been near his car. I've been parked here ever since he pulled in. If he lost them, he lost them someplace else."

There were other minor discrepancies in Eliscu's story and other evidence.

A lie-detector test was made of Eliscu in Minneapolis. This cleared him, but I observed that the expert who made it had had only three months' experience at that work. Eliscu had no objection to my having him photographed and fingerprinted. He did not mind taking another lie-detector test in New York, but the seasoned expert, Fabian L. Rouke, who made this second test, told me afterward that he could learn nothing from the test. It was his opinion that this was due to the fact that the subject was close to a nervous breakdown.

After I turned in my report, the insurance company denied liability. Eliscu's employers brought suit. In the salesman's pretrial examination by the company's attorney, Henry Eliscu for the first time said that he had not noticed being followed by another car as he neared Minneapolis. This contradicted the sworn statement he had made in four separate affidavits.

The company decided to let it go to trial. But on the day the proceedings were scheduled to start, the company authorized the attorney to settle for anything up to $55,000. It was settled for $52,000. They did not have a clean-cut case against Henry Eliscu, and there was the fear that the jury would be against the company if the plaintiff's counsel did the usual routine about his client "being just a little man denied his rights by a soulless corporation."

*

THE next case I cite is a perfect illustration of why insurance companies could save a fortune each year by making more detailed investigations of jewel dealers, jewelers and their salesmen *before* granting block policies.

Mike Korowski, a dealer, lost $35,000 in jewels, he said, but it was in a place where he should not have taken them. His story was that he had gone with a friend to see a movie in a Pittsburgh theater. Mr. Korowski, a refugee not long out of Poland, said a lady was in the seat to his left (he had the jewels in pockets on that side) when they came in. He did not feel her feeling around in his pockets. She left a half-hour before he and his friend, who had the seat to Mike's right, got up to go. The jeweler then discovered that his two wallets were gone. One had been in his hip pocket (which had a flap that buttoned down); the other was in his side trousers pocket.

The story was ridiculous. The Pittsburgh police did not believe it, and told Korowski he was a liar. We went to the theater in Pittsburgh with the detective who'd had the case. He weighed 165, about what Korowski did. I had him sit down in the jewel dealer's chair with wallets slightly smaller than had been lost by Korowski. I tried to get them out of the detective's pockets, and couldn't.

"A man couldn't ignore that," he said, "any more than he would having someone trying to pull his hat off his head."

In his application for the insurance the dealer claimed an inventory of $53,395. An investigation of Korowski would have shown that he kept no books or records, that he was getting jewels on memorandum, and then hocking them to keep going. When one of these jewelers wanted his gems back, Mr. Korowski would get some more loose diamonds on memorandum and get the other lot out. And he was doing this Ponzi-like business at the very time he got out the insurance policy. He also had time and again issued checks that came back stamped "Insufficient funds." And I forced him to admit that he had hocked $50,000 worth of jewels belonging to other people in the past two years!

It was the old story. The credit company had just made one or two calls to friends whose names the dealer had given them. A very brief investigation of Korowski would have cost only a fraction of the expenses and fee paid me for my work *after* the jewels went thataway.

During this investigation Korowski said he would reduce his claim from $35,000 to $25,000. But the St. Paul Company authorized me to deny liability and pay him nothing.

I thought that would end the matter. But later this jeweler hired one of the best lawyers in the field. He called me up to find out why I had denied liability.

"The loss did not come within the terms and conditions of the policy." That told him nothing, of course. Because the terms and conditions covered everything, I could mean anything, and was telling him nothing. He knew me well enough to know I'd give him no information, but, being a good lawyer, he was taking nothing for granted.

The jeweler's lawyer had several conferences with lawyers representing the St. Paul Company. When the former agreed to settle for $2,500, I recommended that we accept. With a good lawyer on the other side, the old saying "No one can tell what a jury will do" goes double.

*

But if you can't win them all, you can win some, a few by a stroke of luck. Sidney Erbstein, a man who had been in the jewelry trade for years, put in a claim during the forties for a twelve-carat diamond he claimed his wife had lost while at a roadhouse on Long Island. At least, that's the last place anyone saw it on her finger.

I tried to make a date with Mrs. Erbstein through her husband. But he suggested I see him first. While I was interviewing him, he asked, "When are you going to see Mrs. Erbstein?"

"As soon as I finish with you," I told him.

"I'm afraid you'll get her excited," he said. "She is a very nervous woman, and losing her ring is something she's taking very hard."

"The last thing I want to do is get the people excited when I'm asking them questions. I'm interested only in getting them to tell everything they recall about the loss."

"I'd better go with you," he said.

"That's unnecessary," I told him. But he persisted, and called up his chauffeur to bring his car from the garage. He next phoned his wife to announce he was bringing out the insurance investigator. In ten minutes we were on our way to the Erbstein home, far out on Long Island. He insisted on stopping for lunch at a lavish restaurant. There he pressed first cocktails, then wine on me. After he had a couple of drinks he told me what a regular guy and a square shooter he was. He never forgot a favor, he added, took care of all his friends. I could depend on him to sell me jewelry at wholesale prices. The same went for my relatives and friends.

There is only one way, of course, to respond to this approach. This is by telling the man who is trying to win you over that you too are a regular guy, a square shooter, a prince of a chap who never forgot a favor.

"Don't get nervous about me," I said; "just tell me your story."

When we arrived Erbstein repeated to his wife what I said. Nevertheless it took her three hours to tell me how she had lost her ring. They'd met friends at the roadhouse where it had disappeared. It was a regular crowd that got together once each week. They were on their way home when they discovered the ring was no longer on her finger. They stopped, and searched the car on their hands and knees. No ring. They went back to the roadhouse. The ring had not been turned in, the manager said. They sent for the police, who questioned the help, and searched the roadhouse very efficiently.

After hearing her story, I questioned the Erbstein's colored chauffeur. I talked to the friends of the couple who had been at the weekly dine-and-dance affair, and I talked to the police. The chauffeur had been working for the Erbsteins for only a week. He said that he had seen the ring the night it was lost. His employers, it would seem, had wanted to make certain of that. In fact, while the chauffeur was helping Mrs. Erbstein out of the car she had almost hit him in the eye with it. Their friends had also seen the ring on the lady's finger that night. One of them had noticed the ring on the finger of the jeweler's wife fifteen minutes before the party broke up. The police records said that the ring had been lost at the roadhouse. But that, they explained, was because of lack of evidence to the contrary.

When I returned to talk to Mr. Erbstein, he regarded me with an offended air. "Questioning all my friends, even my chauffeur. I'm beginning to think that you doubt our story."

I just looked at him — and waited.

"The next thing I hear is that you are investigating my finances, even my wife's reputation."

"That's right," I told him, "and I have news for you: my investigation is just starting."

"And I suppose you want me to help you?"

"You have no choice," I said. "A condition of your policy stipulates that you must cooperate. If you don't, I will have to recommend that our liability be denied."

He made a show of helping after that. But it was not too good a show. Though he told me the name of the jeweler who appraised the ring for him (this man turned out to be a relative of his), who the fellow was from whom he'd bought the twelve-carat ring for $25,000 had completely slipped his mind.

He seemed reluctant to tell me the name of his bank. I could hardly blame him after I'd talked to officials there. He was in financial trouble. It was the same story at two other banks where he'd done business previously. But does this prove that the Erbsteins had faked the loss?

Indeed not.

However, as with newspapermen, connections are a private detective's most valuable asset. And being a friend of the chief clerk of the New York County Clerk's office was the accident that helped me on this case.

While on the Erbstein case I had another matter to check in his building. I often dropped in to see him when in the neighborhood. And that's what I did this day.

"What are you working on?" he asked.

I mentioned a couple of cases, including the Erbsteins' claim. "That one is a phony in my opinion," I said, "come on out to lunch."

He said he ate lunch in his office, and we sent out for sandwiches and coffee. While we were eating, he said in a hurt voice, "Did you come in here to see if there is any other judgment against those people?"

"No," I said, "if I had I would have said that right away. I hadn't given it a thought. Because they live in another county, I guess. But now that you mention it I — "

"What's their name?" he said. I wrote it down for him, and he asked a clerk to look it up in the file. The clerk came back with the interesting information that Mrs. Erbstein had three judgments listed against her. One was for $18,000, another for $9,000, the third for $3,000 — a total of $30,000.

I grinned. "I'd like to look at the papers in those cases."

One affidavit that Mrs. Erbstein had signed could put her in jail for perjury. It stated that she owned no property, stock, or jewelry, and had no bank account. Judgment in all three cases was obtained by her creditors by default. She hadn't paid any of them a cent.

Armed with photostatic copies of the judgments, I made an appointment at my office with the couple. I also asked their broker and an official of the insurance company to be there.

The company official had urged me to push the investigation. The broker gave his company a great deal of business, and would be pleased if the matter could be settled quickly, Mr. Erbstein being a good client of his.

When the four were gathered in my office, I began by congratulating the Erbsteins on having a broker with such a fine reputation for integrity. I'd never heard one thing against him in all my years as an investigator.

"Luisi," asked the astonished broker, "what in the world are you getting at?"

I handed him the affidavit Mrs. Erbstein had signed for me. He said he could see nothing wrong with it. I then handed him the three she had signed for the attorneys of the persons who had sued her.

When he'd read them, I said: "Note that the date of each of these precedes the date when she filed the claim loss for the ring. Please also note that in each of the three Mrs. Erbstein declares that she owned no jewelry. She makes no mention of the ring that she says on the claim loss her husband gave her and that she has owned for six years."

The broker said nothing at all as he put down the papers I'd asked him to read. I turned to Mr. Erbstein, and said: "I'm afraid that your wife has committed perjury. Possibly when she signed the affidavit for me. Possibly it was when she signed the three affidavits I have just asked your broker to read.

"But if you maintain that the company must pay you for the $25,000 ring you lost, it is my duty, as you can see, to notify the attorneys to whom she swore under oath that she owned no jewelry."

The broker, the company official, and I left them alone in my private office to discuss the matter. And in a few minutes they sent for us. They had decided to withdraw the claim against the insurance company and sign a release. This done, Mr. Erbstein said something that indicated that he had been through this sort of ordeal before. If not, he knew that the man whose loss claim is rejected can demand the return of the premium he paid for the period covering the loss for which his claim was rejected.

"What about the premium I paid?" he demanded. "When do I get my money back?"

"I will order a check drawn tomorrow," said the company official. He felt he was getting off very reasonably. Instead of his company paying out $25,000 for the lost ring, he merely had to return to Erbstein the last premium and pay my bill which amounted to $2,650. Returning the premium for the period covered is, incidentally, the rule when a claim is rejected.

*

To me it is often pitiful to observe the painstaking care a crook will take to build up a story that can withstand scrutiny. Because the thief who creates such a fiction always overlooks at least one small detail. And the more elaborate his tale, the more mistakes and omissions he will make.

Sol Wayne, a cocky, tough-minded jewel dealer, was such a fellow. Sol really was convinced that he'd overlooked nothing when he faked a $20,000 jewel robbery.

The plot called for him to take his wife and mother to Atlantic City for a weekend. That was the start, the first act. He had the jewels with him there to show various shopowners along the Boardwalk. He was unable to make a sale. Some of the pieces belonged to him, some to another jewel dealer named Godfrey Gelb in whose Broadway office Mr. Wayne had a desk. He also kept his sparkling merchandise in Gelb's safe, but paid no rent.

On Sunday night Sol decided to come home alone. The women wished to stay in Atlantic City for a day or two longer. He had the jewels with him except for a piece or two that he left for the women to wear. From Atlantic City Mr. Wayne took a train to Philadelphia. He changed to a New York-bound train at the North Philadelphia Station. On this he obtained a parlor-car seat and later managed to remember both the car number and the seat number.

Sol Wayne arrived at Pennsylvania Station at 12:10 A.M., went upstairs to the street, and got a cup of coffee and a cruller in an all-night cafeteria. Coming out of the cafeteria he hailed a Yellow

Taxicab. He gave the driver, a Negro, his Washington Heights address. This is about seven miles north of the station, and is reached by going straight up Broadway or one of the other avenues on the west side.

But they had proceeded for only a half-a-dozen blocks when the driver, while stopped by a red light, called out a greeting to a white man with red hair who was standing on the corner.

"Going home, Red?" the driver asked. "If you are, I'm going your way and can drop you off."

The red-haired man walked over and hopped into the front seat next to the driver. The cab continued north for most of the way, then suddenly turned right. Imagining that the driver had got the address wrong, Mr. Wayne tapped on the window and cried, "Hey, you're going the wrong way!"

This was on a dark street. The cab stopped. Red got out of the front seat, drew a gun, and jumped into the back with the passenger.

"Shut your big mouth," he said, "or I'll blow your brains out."

The cab proceeded east into the Bronx. On an even darker street it stopped. Sol was ordered out of the cab at gun's point. The two men walked him deep into an empty lot where they gagged him, bound his hands, and took $20,000 worth of jewels and also $100 in cash that Sol had on him. Then they slugged him across the face, knocking him down and leaving him stunned. Later, on recovering full consciousness, Sol managed to get to his feet and walk to the street. A cab came along, and the driver and another passerby freed Sol from his bonds and the gag. These Good Samaritans took him to the nearest police station where he told his story to Detective Joseph J. Murphy. The two other men confirmed his account of how they'd found and released him.

The $20,000 worth of jewelry was covered by two policies. One was a Jewelers' Block Policy issued by Lloyd's of London; the other was a personal holdup policy issued by the National Surety Company. Both companies engaged me to investigate the holdup.

Sol Wayne again told his story of the weekend at Atlantic City, this time to me, and later it checked out perfectly, possibly a little too perfectly. Only a man with either perfect recall or who expects to be questioned on the matter later on would readily be able to account for each moment he'd spent at the resort. Also, why should he remember the parlor-car number and the number of the seat he'd occupied unless he thought that might prove helpful later on?

It was his description of what happened when he got into New York that really aroused my suspicions. My interrogation was conducted in the presence of Mr. Wayne's lawyer, and at this point proceeded in this manner:

Q. When you got to New York what happened?

A. I got out at Penn Station, went up to the Thirty-third Street exit, and went into the Hanover lunchroom.

Q. Did you have a bag with you?

A. No.

Q. You didn't take a bag?

A. No, I only intended to stay a few days and took just a little stuff, which I left with my wife and mother.

Q. Why did you pick out Eighth Avenue?

A. For no special reason; the exit I came out on was the nearest to the corner.

Q. If I were getting out at Penn Station I would walk through the station until I got to the subway entrance.

A. That may be, but what has that to do with —

Q. I am just trying to figure how your mind worked; I want to picture this thing in my own mind. Have you ever been in that lunchroom before, Mr. Wayne?

A. Not that I recall, but I may have been.

Q. Now surely, Mr. Wayne, you know whether you have ever been in that restaurant or not.

A. No, I don't remember just now whether I had ever been in there before. As I came up the steps I saw the cafeteria sign facing me and just walked over in that direction because I felt like having something to eat.

Q. How would you have gone home in case you were not hungry?

A. I don't know, according to the mood I was in. That night I felt I wanted to go home that way.

Q. What did you order in the cafeteria?

A. Just a cup of coffee and a cruller.

Q. A cup of coffee and a cruller; and after you satisfied your great hunger, what did you do?

A. As I came out of the restaurant there was a taxi standing there and I called the chauffeur.

The second mistake that Sol Wayne made was saying that a second man — "Red" as he called him — got into the cab. At that time there happened to be a New York City ordinance against taxicab drivers permitting anyone else to ride with them in the front part of the cab. Every cabdriver knew this, and every cop. Any traffic policeman or other officer would have halted the cab on seeing "Red."

There were several other oddities. For example, it was impossible to find the two men who had brought him in to the station house. That cabdriver had been a Negro, the other man, white.

They may have been the men who tied and gagged the jewel dealer, it seemed to me. Otherwise, why should they have given Detective Murphy addresses that proved to be phony? It looked to me as though Sol Wayne had got himself punched in the face by his own request, to make the holdup look good. Here is his description of what happened following the robbery and the assault:

Q. Where did you fall?

A. In some weeds or whatever you call it.

Q. And then what happened?

A. I lay there a few minutes; I was lying frontwards this way, on my face.

Q. How did you happen to lie on your face?

A. I was lying there trying to work the handkerchief down off my face by rubbing my chin on the grass; it was not tied too tight.

Q. After you came to, you saw you had fallen down on your face?

A. I presume I fell on my face, but I found myself rolling. I tried to get up, but my legs were shaking so I thought if I lay quietly and started to scream it might bring some help. I hollered at the top of my voice, and when my nerves quieted down I thought I'd try to walk. I got up and tried to run but could not; I staggered from side to side as if I were intoxicated.

Q. Were your arms tied then?

A. Yes. I got to the corner and saw the lights of Mott Avenue and kept hollering until I got to the hill and I saw a taxi and I hollered "Stop" at the top of my voice, but the taxi kept going; it wouldn't stop. Then a colored chauffeur came along, and he was going to pass me too, but I hollered, "For God's sake stop and take me to the nearest officer!" He didn't want

to stop either; he said they might have thought he did it. Then
he took me to Mott Avenue and 149th Street, but there was
no officer in sight. Then another taxi came along and another,
and someone said "Why don't you untie that fellow?" and the
colored fellow said he didn't want the police to think he did
it. Then they opened the ropes.

Q. What sort of rope was it?

A. It looked like window-sash rope.

From the time the first reports on Wayne's business background
and general reputation began coming in, it was obvious that here
was another man who should never have been considered a good
property-insurance risk.

From the time he'd left school Wayne had jumped from job to
job, never holding one for more than a year or a year and a half.
He left the jewelry business to buy a liquor store. He then sold
the liquor store to buy a movie theater, and quickly went bankrupt.
Wherever he'd worked for others there had been trouble, disputes,
lawsuits.

Few of his old employers spoke well of him. He owed money
all over the place, had accounts at three banks, a safe-deposit box
in a fourth — and almost no money in any of the accounts. A year
before, he had a mysterious loss in his home on which he claimed
$800 and had been paid $600.

But he'd had no trouble getting a $10,000 policy from Lloyd's
of London on jewelry which he may never have owned, and now
he was demanding over $6,000 on that policy. In the middle of my
investigation the National Surety Company, for reasons of its own,
settled Gelb's claim. But Lloyd's authorized me to refuse to settle.

On hearing this, Sol Wayne threatened to sue Lloyd's of London
and me for $1,000,000. I am proud of my record for abstaining from
violence, but that was one time I wanted to let myself go and
punch a man in the nose.

Along with Sol Wayne I investigated Joshua Wayne, his older
brother, whose reputation was even more unsavory. Josh had
formerly had a partner who had a Cadillac, driven by a Negro
chauffeur named Dan Sidney. Josh and Sol had often borrowed
the limousine and been driven around town in it. The brother
and the chauffeur were obvious suspects. But I never got the chance

to question Joshua Wayne because he died abruptly while we were shadowing him.

I hired a Negro detective to shadow the chauffeur, Dan Sidney, in Harlem, but shortly after the shadowing began Sidney dropped mysteriously from sight.

Weeks later my Harlem man tipped me off that he'd learned the whereabouts of the missing chauffeur. He was in the Tombs, held in $10,000 bail for the larceny of a car. With the help of Charles J. Garrison, the same assistant district attorney I'd worked with so many times, I had Sidney brought from the Tombs to the prosecutor's office. The Negro, a big, ignorant fellow, didn't ask who I was; he just took it for granted that I was a police detective. We saw no reason to enlighten him. I looked at Mr. Sidney appraisingly. I kept looking at him, and shaking my head in silence, for five minutes or so, or long enough to make him apprehensive.

"I have bad news for you, Dan," I told him then in a solemn voice. "Very bad news. Poor Sol Wayne has just passed away from that terrible wallop you gave him that night in the Bronx."

The poor fellow looked as though he were going to faint. "My God!" he moaned. His eyes rolled around and around. They protruded as though about to pop out of his head. And he went on, "But — no, no, *sir! I couldn't* have killed him. I just didn't hit him that hard."

It took very little urging for him to tell what he knew of the story. It was only on the insistence of Joshua Wayne that he had socked Sol. He'd not been paid for it, either — not one cent. He had not known what it was all about. He did not know even now that he'd played a role in a fake holdup. The Waynes had told him they wanted him to tie up and gag Sol Wayne as part of a joke they were playing on a friend. The poor, ignorant giant was appalled when Sol asked him to hit him on the jaw hard. But he'd done it — and been scared ever since.

Once I obtained a written confession from the chauffeur, I lost no time in assuring him that Sol was not dead. He fell on his knees, clasped his hands together, and thanked God.

Next day I had him retell the story in the presence of Sol Wayne. The jeweler then confessed. He and his brother had cooked up the whole intricate plot, including the carefully planned trip to Atlantic City. They thought that leaving two pieces of jewelry with Sol's wife and mother would convince investigators that the holdup was no fake.

("For what crook, arranging to be robbed, would think of a trick like that?" the brothers asked each other. The real answer, of course, is "Almost any thief on your mental level would have thought of that very trick.")

By prearrangement Sol had met his brother Josh and the chauffeur outside the Pennsylvania Station. They'd gone into the cafeteria and sent Dan out to find a cab. Then Sol gave his brother the jewelry. This was worth much less, of course, than he reported on his insurance claim. They'd gone first to Central Park, then over to Riverside Park, which borders the Hudson, but could find no spot dark and lonely enough until they went to the Bronx. Dan, the Negro dupe, had brought along the rope.

That day I asked Dan Sidney, in Sol Wayne's presence, "Was anything said, when you got to this place in the Bronx, about tying him up?"

"After we walked over there to the center of the lot," said Dan, "he asked me if I had a rope. I said 'Yes.' He had a couple of clean handkerchiefs, and I took one and tied his mouth, and he wanted his hands and feet tied. The place was so dark and lonely I said, 'If you are tied, nobody would find you.'" So he had tied only Sol's hands, not his feet.

Josh had held the jewelry for Sol for ten days, then gave it back to him. Sol said he had sold some of it, and hocked some of the jewelry. He sold one of the pawn tickets, and had a couple more at home. One $675 ring he had dismounted, then remounted in another sort of setting and sold it to his brother for $500. Being in the jewel business, he had been able to arrange much more profitable deals than the ordinary thief who must peddle his hot ice to a fence. But even so, he had to turn over practically every cent to pay off loans from banks.

Of course, the money he'd expected to get from the insurance companies would have given him adequate capital to make another fresh start for himself.

Instead he was arrested for grand larceny. But, on the joint recommendation of the two companies and myself, the charges against Sol Wayne were dropped. His family had agreed to make restitution, not only to Lloyd's but to National, though it already had settled the claim.

I couldn't help feeling sorry for Wayne — once he confessed. He'd been so cocky until then, but now he was just one more crushed little creature who had overestimated his ability to fool the world, and stripped himself of dignity and honor and, most irreplaceable of all, his self-respect.

*

THE trapping machine all thieves challenge is a very big one. When they lose out, they discover it has ten thousand eyes and ten thousand hands that touch everything, overlook nothing.

The great Fifth Avenue house of Van Cleef and Arpels carries more than a million dollars' worth of gems in stock. Some years ago several pieces of jewelry, worth about $10,000, disappeared from its vaults. The embarrassing thing about this to the management was that some of these pieces had been left there by old customers.

The annual inventory in March, 1944, had revealed that the pieces were lost, strayed, or stolen. In the next few weeks the police, the Pinkertons, and investigators for two insurance companies had vainly tried to solve the mystery.

The St. Paul Fire and Marine Company had insured the company under a Jewelers' Block Policy against every sort of loss except thefts by employees. The twenty-five men and women who worked for Van Cleef and Arpels were bonded by the second company.

I was called into the case by George Coward, manager of the St. Paul Company. That was late in April.

"Why waste your money on more investigations?" I asked. "Settle it."

He was agreeable to my trying to do that, but he said that the other company insisted St. Paul pay the whole loss. After going over the files I called upon the manager of the company that had bonded the employees.

"Why not get this over with?" I asked. "Pay half the loss, and I'll ask St. Paul to pay the rest."

He laughed, and replied: "I challenge you to prove an employee is responsible. I'll bet you a $20 hat you can't."

I took the challenge. I suspect that the reason he was so cocky was that the employees had all taken lie-detector tests, and passed them.

On being interviewed, Julius Arpels, president of the firm, said he was delighted to have the investigation reopened. Mr. Arpels was a businessman in a thousand. He was far more interested in knowing who robbed him than in getting recompensed for his missing property. But he asked me not to subject his people to any more lie-detector tests.

"It upsets my whole staff for weeks afterward."

The company's personnel manager turned over to me all the data on his employees. I sent out undercover people to check on them. They brought back exactly the same reports previous investigators had. Not one of the twenty-five was living over his income; none of them gambled, drank to excess, had questionable friends, or lived unconventional lives. We went on to their relationships with one another.

Miss Syd Cancell, the bookkeeper, and one of the company's designers we learned were friends. The latter told us that Miss Cancell had cancer and was being treated by a Dr. Emerson Gilbert, who had a big apartment on Riverside Drive. A perfunctory check on him revealed the curious fact that he also conducted seances twice a week attended by the usual group of forlorn widows and old maids. I had my wife, Assistant 115, attend one of these. She reported that the usual hocus-pocus went on, with the pathetic circle of visitors being fooled into believing they were communicating with the spirits of their dear departed ones.

Even more interesting was the information given us by the elevator man in Gilbert's apartment house. The spiritualist-doctor formerly had two effeminate young men living with him, as well as an elderly woman believed to be his aunt. At that time the elevator man had once overheard one of the young men saying that he had a job in a Fifth Avenue jewelry store.

I next interviewed Miss Cancell, the bookkeeper. She told me that she had first met Dr. Gilbert at a seance in Philadelphia and that he had been her doctor ever since. She explained that he was living in Haverford, Pennsylvania, when they first met. Gilbert had introduced her to many people.

"One of them was a nice young fellow named Jack Moran," she said. "At Dr. Gilbert's suggestion I got him a job in the store as a messenger."

"He isn't working there now, is he?"

"Oh, no," she said. "Jack started with us last year, in March, and quit in October. I was told he had got a better job."

I thanked Miss Cancell and went to see the personnel manager. I wanted to look over Moran's work record and the application he had filled out when he got the job. There was no such paper. I was told that Moran had not been asked to fill one out because he was recommended by an old and trusted employee. But he'd been considered a good worker. His personality did puzzle some of his fellow workers. A few of them thought he might be a homosexual. "He said he was a writer," one of them told me, "but I never could make up my mind whether he was a phony or not. And then he seemed to spend more money than any fellow making only a messenger's salary should."

From the cashier I obtained a letter that Moran, who was in his late twenties, had sent her after he quit the job without notice:

Inclosed you will find my identification card and keys. I have secured employ — more desirable.

Why I left you should know — at least, I talked about the condition several times to you without accomplishing anything. In my new work I am sure of cooperation.

If you will send a check to and made out in Dr. Gilbert's name for what I have coming in salary and war bonds I would greatly appreciate it.

Sincerely,
Jack Moran

This was dated October, 1943.

The cashier also recalled that Moran had a middle name that she'd made a note of, but she couldn't find the memo. She allowed us to search her office for this, and my wife succeeded in turning it up. The middle name was "Patrick." A Jack Moran or a Patrick Moran would be harder to find than a Jack Patrick Moran.

The note established enough of a connection with the physician-spiritualist for me to interview him. I had been having undercover work done on other recent ex-employees of the jewelry house, but Moran seemed the only likely suspect.

Dr. Gilbert proved to be a big, fleshy man. He was forty-three, almost six feet tall, and weighed 210. He had red hair and a ruddy complexion. He also proved to be adroit at verbal sparring and evading questions. He did say that Moran had lived with him. In fact, he had been quite worried about the lad after Moran quit his job. The young man had moved out of the apartment without taking his clothes. He'd known Moran for some years. They'd met in the West. But that is about all he did tell me. He insisted he did not know where his young friend was.

I had hardly left his apartment when I was informed that Miss Cancell, the bookkeeper whom he had been treating for cancer, was now in a hospital and apparently dying. It was time, I thought, that the police looked up Emerson Gilbert's credentials as a medical man.

A visit to Headquarters revealed that they'd done just that nine years before. On March 21, 1935, Dr. Gilbert was convicted for violation of the New York State Medical Law. He was fined $50 and sentenced to four months, but sentence was suspended. He was also arrested for fortune-telling but got off for lack of evidence. He also seemingly posed at times as a clergyman, for his aliases were listed as "Rev. Dr. Gilbert" and "Dr. Gilbert." The record on him also showed a conviction in 1940 for practicing "drugless therapy" in Ardmore, Pennsylvania. He'd served six months there. There was nothing at Headquarters on Moran.

I decided that a visit to Ardmore might possibly give me information on Moran's present whereabouts. He and the spiritualist apparently had known each other there. But before I could leave, I heard that since quitting his job Jack Patrick Moran had gone to live with another effeminate young man in a boardinghouse at East Orange, New Jersey. I went there first. Both had flown that coop. The landlady did not know where they'd gone. But she did tell me that Dr. Gilbert had phoned Moran there. When I went back to New York to confront Dr. Gilbert with proof that he had known where Moran moved, he glibly said: "Oh, yes, I guess I must have phoned Jack there. I just forgot about it."

But what the interrogator is up against when questioning such a man as Gilbert is shown in the report I got when I visited the authorities at Ardmore Township to inquire about him. They really had to squeeze the truth out of this gentleman by backing him down, step by step.

The interrogation took place at Gilbert's Haverford home and was conducted by two very smart law officials, Captain William E. Shaffer, Lower Merion Police, and Thomas P. Long, a Pennsylvania

State official. In answer to their first questions Dr. Gilbert explained that he was married, but lived alone now except for a maid:

Q. You give seances here?
A. We have meetings, yes.
Q. Do you also practice medicine?
A. No, sir.
Q. Have you ever been in difficulty for this sort of thing?
A. No, sir.
Q. Not here or anywhere?
A. I have never had any trouble for practicing medicine of any kind, because I don't.
Q. How about the charge over in New York?
A. That was fortune-telling and readings.
Q. What was the charge?
A. Fortune-telling.
Q. Nothing about practicing medicine?
A. It wasn't mentioned. I just give faith healing.
Q. You reincarnate Dr. Walker?
A. Yes.
Q. Do you do any massaging of the hands?
A. No.
Q. Who does that? Dr. Walker?
A. Yes.
Q. He does that through spiritual means of bringing him to the patient?
A. Yes.
Q. And through that medium there is a method of massage or treatment?
A. No.
Q. Haven't you ever, through Dr. Walker or yourself, massaged the stomach of any patient who has been here seeking assistance from you?
A. No.
Q. These statements are being taken for the record; it may be of value to you to state the facts as we know they already exist.
A. I know.
Q. Do you still want to state that you do no drugless therapy work on the body?

A. Nothing; only the laying on of hands.

Q. You have done that? Haven't you done that to remove tumors and other ailments?

A. Yes.

Q. You have done that yourself?

A. No. Never.

Q. You have done it through the reincarnation of Dr. Walker?

A. Yes.

Q. You did that for a financial consideration?

A. For a donation.

Q. Well, Dr. Walker, as a reincarnation, would hardly be interested in anything of so material a nature as money?

A. It's for my existence. It is a donation; not a charge.

Q. However, your livelihood depends on the fees you make through the reincarnation of Dr. Walker and the good he does your patients, is that right?

A. That is correct.

There was an alarm out for Jack Patrick Moran, and two weeks later he was picked up in Oklahoma City where he was working in — you guessed it — another jewelry store. He was questioned there, and did not fight against coming to New York.

He blamed the thefts on the "hypnotic influence" of Emerson Gilbert, whom he had originally met in Chicago. His main duty as a messenger for Van Cleef and Arpels was to pick up and deliver jewelry customers wanted repaired.

Like many of the other employees, he had access to the safe in which they were kept. On impulse one day, he explained, he picked up a couple of these packages and walked out with them. One was a Hawaiian tribal ring worth $700, the other a $2,100 pair of diamond earclips. They had been left in a discarded box by a careless co-worker. Gilbert had the habit of going downtown to lunch with him once or twice a week. This was one of those days.

He showed the jewelry to Gilbert, who urged him to steal more jewels, saying, "I'll sell them for you." Once, the older man complained, "Can't you find something better than this junk in that wonderful store?"

Moran was almost as agile-tongued a liar as the fake doctor and clergyman who acted as his fence. But the truth was finally also squeezed out of him. Altogether he stole $10,000 worth of merchandise, including a $4,500 diamond bracelet. Among the other valuable loot were nine loose diamonds each weighing more than a carat.

Gilbert, a lover of fine jewelry, broke the pieces up, reset many of them, and sold these to dealers he knew at bargain prices. The arrangement was that he and Moran would split the proceeds. Moran got $800 for his end, but held out one or two pieces. But Emerson Gilbert held out much more on the money the dealers paid. One ring that he remade he sent to his daughter, then nineteen, who lived with her mother in California. He made enough to furnish his apartment with modernistic furniture.

There was no honor between these two thieves. Emerson Gilbert was tried for grand larceny and sentenced to a term of years in state prison. Jack Patrick Moran was sent to the psychopathic ward at Bellevue. He, too, had a police record, but only for misdemeanors. He had been arrested twice, once in Chicago for vagrancy, once in Atlantic City for failure to carry a draft registration card.

Only a very small amount of the stolen jewelry was recovered, though Gilbert guided the police to the stores of the dealers to whom he had sold the loot. Besides my fee I won a $20 hat from the official of the bonding company. They got no more business from Van Cleef and Arpels. He told his broker to get a blanket fidelity bond from another company. He said:

"I can't afford to do business with a company that is so short-sighted. It could have settled for half and saved us all a great deal of time and trouble. Thanks to its stupidity and stubbornness, it ends up paying the full bill."

WHO ROBS MILLIONAIRES?   7

I WONDER how many people you would have to stop on the street today before you found one who had ever heard of Joshua Cosden. But during the twenties, the early twenties particularly, he was among the flashiest and most fabulous of all Wall Street plungers. Cosden was a pale, slightly built loose-jointed man with a wide jaw and piercing black eyes.

He spent money like a madman.

As a gambler he had the questionable distinction of being about the juiciest sucker that ever fell into Arnold Rothstein's soft and greedy hands.

And sucker is the proper word. Leo Katcher, Rothstein's gifted biographer, tells in *The Big Bankroll* how Cosden lost half a million dollars in two nights of gambling at Rothstein's Brook Club at Saratoga. On the third night the oil man won $20,000, and boasted about it for weeks afterward.

Cosden, a West Virginian, came up the hard way. As a young man he sold insurance, hats, shoes, and was a trolley-car conductor. He went to the Oklahoma oil fields, where he worked as a teamster, handyman, and rigger's helper. But that's where he struck it rich — in the oil fields. He made millions, lost them, made more millions. He came back so often after going broke that he acquired the nickname of the "rubber ball of the oil industry." I did not know his first wife. But his second wife was a warm, smiling, gracious woman, a lady and a charmer.

They had money to burn, and they burned it.

When the couple came to New York in 1918, they accomplished the impossible: they crashed society, and were accepted. They bought The Cedars, a 322-acre estate at Sands Point on Long Island. It adjoined Vincent Astor's place, and Cosden spent $300,000 improving it. He bought a Palm Beach home that he reportedly embellished with gold faucets and other gaudy equipment. He also had a yacht, a private railway car that cost $350,000, and Mrs. Cosden owned a $600,000 string of pearls.

Diamond Jim Brady once told an interviewer, "It's fun to be a sucker — if you can afford it." Cosden, it appeared, could afford it. He had suffered a terrific financial setback in the Depression of 1920 and 1921. But not too long afterward he was being described in newspapers as one of the three biggest independent oil operators. To an offer of $100,000,000 for his holdings, Mr. Cosden was supposed to have replied:

"Sorry, gentlemen, my horses and the entertainment of my friends and family still leave me a lot of free time. I must have something else to keep me busy."

A real swashbuckler, this man could even pretend to regard a business worth $100,000,000 as a toy.

In 1924 Cosden achieved the social climber's dream of dreams. The Prince of Wales, during his visit to this country, consented to use the Cosdens' railroad car to travel about the country. At the end of the summer, His Royal Highness, Lord Louis and Lady Mountbatten and the rest of the regal entourage attended a party at The Cedars. There were one hundred guests at this fete.

The following week the Mountbattens stayed for several days at The Cedars. On September 11, the *New York Times* carried this front-page headline:

LADY MOUNTBATTEN
AND HOSTESS ROBBED
OF $150,000 JEWELS

The robbery had taken place two days before. For some reason the police had not been notified. First reports set the loss at a quarter of a million dollars. Lloyd's of London had insured Mrs. Cosden's jewels, and it was their American adjusters, Toplis and Harding, who asked me to investigate the loss. I went out there with my superintendent, Francis J. Farley, who was something of a lock expert. He would look for traces of a forced entrance while I talked to Mr. and Mrs. Cosden.

We found an armed guard at the gates of The Cedars. There were a dozen or so reporters and photographers waiting to get inside, but with no luck. The New York newspapers had been tipped off by someone, even if the police were being ignored. The papers had their best men there, but all they were doing was waiting. I knew some of them. Carl Helm, young reporter of the *New York American,* said, "My boss, Victor Watson, thought you'd be out here." He called me to one side, and whispered, "He says he'd appreciate any help you could give me."

"I have to find out what's going on first," I told him. The guard forced Farley and myself to display our credentials even after we told him that we had an appointment with Mrs. Cosden. "She's been informed we were on our way, and is waiting to see us," I said.

Mrs. Cosden, née Eleanor Neves, a charming, gracious woman, greeted us in the library. "I am very relieved to see you," she said.

"Is Mr. Cosden at home?"

"No, he is out. I do not expect him and the Mountbattens until ten o'clock."

"Have the police been notified?"

"Mr. Cosden decided not to notify the police until you insurance investigators had completed your work."

"Do you know why, Mrs. Cosden?"

"No," she told me.

Several odd angles developed in that investigation. But that was the first puzzler. Why *hadn't* Joshua Cosden notified the police of the loss at once? That was the first thing one would have expected him to do on learning he and his guests had been robbed by a burglar.

The night before, Mrs. Cosden said, they had given a party for the Mountbattens. The last of the guests had left by 2:00 A.M., and the two couples retired a few minutes after that. Their sleeping quarters and the British couple's were on the same floor and fairly near to each other.

Soon after Mrs. Cosden awoke next morning, the butler reported that he was unable to find a pearl shirt stud that had been in her husband's shirt. Mr. Cosden was still sleeping, and they did not disturb him. Instead, supposing it had fallen on the floor, Mrs. Cosden helped the servant look for it. While they were doing so,

Lady Mountbatten came in to say that she was unable to find the jewelry she had worn at the party and that she had put it on top of the bureau before retiring.

Mrs. Cosden had done the same thing with her own jewels. She now looked at the top of her bureau.

Her loss amounted to more than $100,000, Lady Mountbatten's about half of that. The British couple's valuables were insured by two American companies who were using another private detective, Noel Scaffa, to look into the loss for them.

Among Mrs. Cosden's missing jewels were:

A black pearl	$40,000
A pink pearl ring	25,000
Diamond bracelet	8,000
Ruby bracelet	5,000
Pigeon blood ruby ring	30,000

Both ladies had far more valuable jewels in their collections, and every professional diamond thief in the world knew it. But none of the drawers of either bureau or anything else in the two bedrooms had been disturbed. Why not? Was he frightened away by a noise? Why else would he take the risk of walking into rooms where people were sleeping and make no attempt to get all the loot?

Mrs. Cosden said that neither she nor her husband nor Lady Mountbatten had been disturbed. Lord Mountbatten had heard some sort of noise, his wife said, about 4:00 A.M. But he was inclined to think it was the wind rustling the curtains in the room. He'd turned over and gone back to sleep.

Both the master-bedroom unit and the guest unit, which included dressing rooms and baths, were on the second floor, and only a few feet from one another. Most of the servants lived in cottages on the grounds. But six of the house staff slept on the third floor.

Farley, after carefully examining the windows, doors, and outside of the house, reported that he could find not a trace of a marauder having been there. I had the same experience when I searched the two units. I told Mrs. Cosden I should like to question the servants. She explained.

"But gentlemen, it is not possible that you could have had dinner. They serve nothing on that train you came on. Why don't you eat before the Mountbattens and Mr. Cosden arrive? It would save time, don't you think?"

Farley and I were given a first rate meal. We were questioning the servants when Cosden and the Mountbattens came in. This Wall Street plunger was a brisk, impatient, fast-talking man. He was also a very fast thinker. Questioning him that evening — or trying to — was a memorable experience. He did not try to conceal his opinion that I was a nuisance and that the quicker he could get rid of me, the better.

Mrs. Cosden and the Mountbattens sat in on our session. In some newspapers Lady Mountbatten was called the "richest woman in England." Her husband, cousin and boon companion of the Prince of Wales, was then best known as a fun-loving, polo-playing member of the Prince's "Palace gang." It was not until many years later, during World War II, that this tall, aristocratic young man distinguished himself as a great naval commander and became Earl Mountbatten of Burma.

And I have often since wondered what his real thoughts were that evening in that beautiful library as he listened with an air of languid amusement to his host brushing off all of my questions. Mr. Cosden talked to me about the missing jewels for a straight forty-five minutes. He seemed to think the swiftest way of disposing of the matter was to offer his version and theories. He paused to accept a cocktail.

"Mr. Cosden," I told him, "I find everything you say very interesting. But now I would appreciate it if you would be kind enough to answer a few questions."

The oil man grimaced and put down his glass. "What do you mean, 'questions'?" he demanded. "Don't you realize that I have just got through telling you all I know of this ugly business?"

"I am, in a way, something like a doctor," I told him. "And, like a doctor, I cannot help a patient except by asking questions. I have only one purpose, sir, in being here: to locate your jewels. In fact, I may be able to save you much time — that is, if I can get tonight the details I need."

He was glaring at me, skeptically. "How can you save me time?"

"By turning my information over to the companies that insured the jewels of your guests. If I have the whole story, their investigators may find it unnecessary to question you again, Mr. Cosden."

"All right, Mr. Luisi, ask me whatever you like."

That turned out to be just talk, of course. But I had established my right to follow my own line of investigation. The Mountbattens,

I observed, were smiling. I noticed also that his wife, who had seemed distressed by his rudeness to me, appeared now to be enjoying our little exchange. Women married to domineering men often enjoy hearing strangers talk back to them.

Not that I got far. When I asked for a list of the people at the Mountbatten party, Mr. Cosden pointed out that nothing had been missing after the much larger party he'd given on the previous week for the Prince of Wales. Both he and his wife were certain none of the guests at the smaller Mountbatten party could possibly have been the thief.

Mr. Cosden said, "It must have been a sneak thief, or a second-story man who got into the house while we were all asleep." He demanded suddenly, "Have you questioned Mrs. Cosden?"

"I have."

"Then why question me."

"It is possible that she forgot or overlooked something that you might tell me."

"What did she tell you?"

I turned to Mrs. Cosden and asked whether she would mind repeating what she had told me. If so, I'd do it.

"I'll tell it all again," Mrs. Cosden said. "If I leave anything out, please let me know." And she told the whole story again exactly as she had before.

"Now, sir," I said to Mr. Cosden, "have you anything to add to that?"

"No," Mr. Cosden said quite decisively.

"Is it a fact," I asked, turning to Lord Mountbatten, "that you heard a noise in your bedroom early this morning?"

He nodded, and explained, "But I cannot say now whether the noise was made by someone walking in my room or by the rustling of the curtains."

Mountbatten explained that his wife's jewels were insured by the National Surety Company and the Federal Insurance Company. The latter company had notified him that its investigator would be at the estate next morning at ten.

"Lord Mountbatten," I asked, "did you notify the police of your loss?"

"No. I was advised to talk first to the companies' representatives, and let them decide what procedure to follow."

It turned out that Mr. Cosden was the person who gave Mountbatten this bit of bad advice. I asked Mr. Cosden why he had not notified the authorities.

"I didn't wish to have policemen running all over the place, frightening the servants," was the best explanation he gave me. It didn't seem to me nearly good enough.

I did leave with a list of the guests at his party. He also promised to get me a full list of everyone who worked for him in the house and on the estate and the information about them I needed. I said I wished to know the age, salary, position, and length of service of each, the name of the agency that sent them, and who their previous employers were.

"I will give you such a list," he told me as we left, "only on the condition that you must not disorganize my employees. They are all fine people, carefully selected, and I will not have them embarrassed or humiliated. Mrs. Cosden and I need them badly."

It was 2:00 A.M. I said: "I'll be back tomorrow about eleven. And I assure you, sir, I shall make the least trouble possible."

As we left the estate a man called out to me. It was so dark I couldn't make out who he was. Not knowing what to expect, I got ready to reach for my gun.

The man turned out to be young Mr. Helm of the *New York American*. All of the other newspapermen had gone, but he had waited there in the dark, just on the chance of getting information from me.

I would have none to give him, I said, until I finished my investigation. But he rode back to New York on the train with us, and never stopped asking questions.

Before going to bed that night I telephoned Major Otto and arranged to meet him at the office at seven-thirty. I wanted him to have men check on the whereabouts of all the country's jewel thieves and burglars. He was to make a similar check on the Cosden servants the moment I got the list the oilman promised me. When I did, the major even went down to Police Headquarters to find out whether any of them had a record.

None of them did, but it was a wise precaution. I've seen men and women with records in the last jobs in the world you'd suspect that people who have served time could get.

On getting to Sands Point I had a brief talk with Mr. Cosden. Then Farley and I went to Nassau County Police Headquarters to talk with Chief William Phillips. When he heard I was working on the $150,000 jewel robbery, he shook his head mournfully. "How long have you been working on it?" he asked.

"Since five o'clock yesterday afternoon."

"It's damn funny that a loss that big was not reported to my office," he said.

I thought it was damn funny, too. Phillips said he was not the only law-enforcement official who'd been bypassed. No state, county, or local official had been called in. But if the thief or thieves were not caught that would be forgotten. They'd be criticized. Meanwhile, they felt like fools, being hamstrung that way.

Chief Phillips said he'd cooperate with me "now that somebody has been good enough to tell me what is going on in my county." I asked him to check on the movements of Arthur Barry, the decade's most successful second-story man. His men were already doing that, the chief said. They later established that Barry was hundreds of miles away on the night of the Cosden burglary. This, though Mr. Barry's memoirs, I understand, describe the Cosden jewel job as one of his more daring exploits.

As we were leaving, I asked the chief, "Why don't you go to the Costen estate with me right now?"

"No, sir," he said. "I will go there only when Mr. Cosden or the Mountbattens invite me." I assured him I would send him a copy of any information I obtained and notify him promptly of any new developments.

At The Cedars I questioned those servants I had not yet talked to. I also wished to go over doors, windows, and the premises again in broad daylight. A second look never hurts. There is always a chance, particularly in a big place, of having overlooked something the first time around.

Mrs. Cosden welcomed us like old friends. We went over every square inch of the house and ground. There was not a trace of a marauder. Not a scratch against the windowsills, not a footprint or the sign of a ladder having been used. If a porch climber had done the job, he was so light-footed a fellow he had all but walked on air.

But Mrs. Cosden pointed out it had been warm that night. The windows on the first and second floors had been left open. But there too we could find not a sign even of dust disturbed.

During the early afternoon Mrs. Cosden came out to tell me, "Lord Mountbatten would like to see you in his bedroom."

In my surprise I looked at Farley.

Mrs. Cosden said, "I should have mentioned that he said he would prefer to see you alone."

Mountbatten was in his bedroom. He had a Martini in his hand. He said: "Mr. Luisi, there is one thing I omitted telling you last night. Some time before daylight, on Tuesday morning, September 9th, I was awakened by a noise. I had the impression that it was footsteps. But I did not know whether they were in my bedroom or outside in the hall. I was tired out, and I turned over in my bed. In a short time I was asleep again."

"Would you recognize the footsteps if you heard them again?"

"Perhaps."

I asked him if he would mind making an experiment that might help me. I wanted him to sit in his room with his back toward the door. I would then have the servants who slept on the floor above walk by in the hall, one by one, and into the room. If the footsteps of any one of them sounded like those he'd heard on the night the jewels disappeared, he was to signal me.

Lord Mountbatten agreed to do this. But while we were in the midst of this, Mr. Cosden, who had been late in New York, arrived.

"Are you making any progress, Mr. Luisi?" he demanded in his brisk, let's-get-down-to-business manner.

I had to explain what I was doing; I said it was to help us narrow down the field of suspects.

"Are you devoting *all* of your time to the possibility of proving one of the help guilty?" he demanded. "Have you not even considered the possibility that it might have been done by someone from the outside?"

"Mr. Cosden," I said, "you will be pleased to know that I have a staff of ten men who are devoting all of their time to checking on the movements of known burglars, sneak thieves, second-story men."

Mr. Cosden gave me a disgusted look. I'm afraid he did not like me.

I never won him over, either. All of my charm was lost on him.

I'd been getting calls from the Hearst executive Victor Watson, and also Carl Helm. The next day I telephoned to Watson that I'd like to come down and see the clippings they had there on Joshua Cosden. His actions from the start had been that peculiar.

Not only did Watson and Helm show me the clippings. They

had a whole dossier on Mr. Cosden's current financial situation. His Cosden Oil Company was about to be taken out of his control, if that hadn't already happened. He was on the brink of ruin. Bankruptcy was staring him in the face. The clippings showed he'd been in tight spots before. But this time it looked as though his finish as a Wall Streeter was at hand.

We discussed the case. I did not mention Louis Mountbatten's strange story about the footsteps he'd heard or thought he heard, just before he fell asleep again. I kept quiet about it for policy reasons even though I never dreamed they could make a story of so slight an incident.

I was forgetting several things — Lord Mountbatten's social importance as cousin and best friend of the much worshiped Prince of Wales; the degree of public interest the visit of the Prince's party had aroused everywhere in the country, and finally, Mr. Hearst's unending war on the British Empire, its rulers, and everything they stood for.

There was a story in next day's *American*. It was immediately picked up by the other papers. As though this was not enough, Arthur Brisbane ran an editorial implying that Lord Mountbatten was a coward for not getting up when he heard the footsteps in his room.

I was out there at the estate the day this was published. As I talked to one of the servants, Mrs. Cosden, obviously agitated, approached.

Calling me to one side, she whispered: "Mr. Luisi, Lord Mountbatten is very angry about something. He wants to see you. He is in his room."

I went to the room. Mountbatten was fighting mad all right. Without greeting me, he handed me a copy of the Hearst paper. I read the comment, and then looked up.

"Did you give that information, making me sound like a coward, to Mr. Brisbane?"

"Aren't you a little hasty about asking me that question?" I said. "Wouldn't it be much better if you made inquiries at the *American?*"

"I think I will sue the blasted paper!" he shouted. Hearing the noise from the hall, Mrs. Cosden came in.

"I will find out immediately if you did or not," he said, and walked out, shutting the door behind him.

Mrs. Cosden made a face. "I wish someone would kick that man in the ass," she said.

Coming from her, the words shocked me. But I was happy indeed to have her on my side. In a few minutes Lord Mountbatten rejoined us. I do not know whom he called, but whoever it was must have convinced him that I was incapable of being responsible for inspiring such an editorial as Arthur Brisbane had written. And the charming titled Britisher was over his rage at once. He held out his hand to me, and smiled as he said: "Sir, I wish to apologize. And I do think it's time we all had a Martini."

I do not drink on the job, but I broke my rule that day.

Not long afterward the Mountbattens' claim was settled. Lloyd's had me continue investigating the Cosden loss, but one day an order came from London to close the case. I was not told why. And it was neither my business nor my custom to question such decisions.

"I told you, Luisi," Cosden gloated on being told the news, "that I'd get all the money from Lloyd's that I'd asked for."

I thought that he had taken the jewels himself. And I have always believed that Mountbatten, far from being a coward, suspected it had been his host's footsteps he heard, and kept quiet because of embarrassment. But that Mr. Cosden had to rub it in was a little too much to stomach. I thought I'd give him something to think about. As he signed the claim, I said:

"Lloyd's of London, Mr. Cosden, pays all claims, unless fraud is *proved*."

Arnold Rothstein told me that Cosden had just lost a fortune gambling. The oil man's financial situation *was* desperate. Within a year he had to get rid of the $350,000 private railway car, the yacht, the villa in Palm Beach. Even his wife's jewels, people said. What must have been the worst wrench was selling The Cedars, his showplace, to Vincent Astor, who gave him $100,000 for it, just one-third of the money Cosden had spent on improving the property. The name of his Cosden Oil Company was changed to Mid-Continental Oil Company.

But there was some resilience still left in this remarkable man. The oil industry's rubber ball bounced once or twice more before he died on a train in 1940.

*

I'M told that you will also have to walk for a long time up and down Broadway to find anyone who will say a good word about Arnold Rothstein, the gambler who was shot to death during a card game in 1928. The murder was never solved, though George (Hump) MacManus, who'd been in the game, was arrested.

The general opinion was that Rothstein was killed for welshing on gambling debts. That may be true. I do not know. But I do know that Rothstein, who was accused of being New York's biggest fixer, never welshed when it came to paying off on two favors I was able to do for friends of his.

The first favor was done for Dandy Phil Kastel, the bucketeer and badger-game worker, who now runs the New Orleans branch of Frank Costello's gambling empire. With Assistant District Attorney John T. Dooling and a squad of detectives, I one day raided Dandy Phil's hotel room. We were looking for stolen bonds. I was alone with him for a moment, and he slipped me a gun he was carrying.

"If they find this rod on me," he whispered, "they'll throw the book at me."

I put the gun away. We found no stolen bonds in his room. I told Mr. Dooling about the incident before we left. "Keep it for a souvenir," he said. "After all, we raided his room to find some stolen bonds. We weren't looking for a gun."

The story of the other favor is one which Damon Runyon might have written. For it proves, I suppose, that the big bad boys of Broadway have their sentiments just like everyone else.

William J. Fallon, the so-called Great Mouthpiece, saw me on the street one day, and said he'd like to talk to me. I was not eager to do business of any kind with him. At the time, Fallon was at the peak of his fame as a man who could charm juries into freeing almost anyone, no matter how guilty. People who knew their way around the courts were beginning to call attention to the many 11-to-1 hung juries he was getting in cases that seemed impossible even for him to win.

When a lawyer has too many cases that end that way, with eleven voting guilty, one voting not guilty, the presumption is that the holdout was bribed.

"What's it about?" I asked.

"Well, Luisi, I guess it's a little out of your line. A friend of mine and of Arnold Rothstein has been arrested for a crime he didn't commit." I must have looked skeptical because he added, "Have I ever lied to you?" I had to admit he never had.

It did sound out of my line, but I was curious about it. I said I'd be up at his office to talk about it later in the day. That office — Fallon and McGee — was always jammed and jumping with clients, day and night. It was in the Hotel Knickerbocker building at Forty-second Street and Broadway, which recently had been converted to office use. You could see Broadway stars there on some days, and the underworld's elite and riffraff every day.

This day there was the usual mob waiting, but I was shown in without delay. With the redheaded lawyer was Rothstein and Nicky Arnstein, the gambler who married Fanny Brice, the comedienne, and was later convicted as the master mind of the theft by Wall Street messengers of $5,000,000 worth of bonds.

Arnstein and Rothstein listened as the Great Mouthpiece told me of the dilemma of Roy Gibson, a con man with a long record. Gibson, determined to go straight, had met a wealthy society girl. She fell in love with him, and he did the decent thing by telling her of his numerous arrests and the prison time he'd done. Her family had not yet been told about his past, but had accepted him as the man she would marry.

At the end of the summer there had been a $20,000 jewel burglary in the summer home of a Pittsburgh woman named Daniels, at Bradley Beach, New Jersey, then a fashionable shore resort. Her maid had walked in on the thief. He jumped out the window and got away. But Mrs. Daniels at that moment approached the house, and saw him. Both women later identified a Rogues' Gallery picture of Roy Gibson as the burglar they'd seen.

By the time Gibson was picked up, Mrs. Daniels and the maid were home in Pittsburgh. Gibson was indicted but was now out on bail. The women had promised to come back for his trial.

"What's his alibi?"

"At the time of the robbery," explained Fallon, "Gibson was having dinner with his girl and her mother in their suite in the Biltmore Hotel. Naturally, he prefers not to ask them to testify in his defense. What he really wants is a dismissal of the case before it gets to court. And you are the one man we think can clear him."

I looked from Fallon, who had flaming red hair and was even more irresistible to women than to juries, to the other two characters. I couldn't imagine what they were trying to pull. The way to find out was to let Fallon go on talking. They must know that Lloyd's of London had insured Mrs. Daniels' jewels and that I worked for Lloyd's on case after case.

They did know. For Fallon abruptly asked, "Are you handling this investigation?"

"No," I said, "but I know something about the case. Lloyd's has an adjuster in New Jersey working on it right now. Are you asking me to perform a miracle?"

"No," he said, "I just ask you to do your best for Roy Gibson."

"And do you really think that this guy, this con man with the long record, is innocent? And please level with me, Mr. Fallon."

"I absolutely do think he's innocent," he said.

I must say the whole proposition intrigued me. If Gibson was going straight, he certainly deserved a chance. We made a tentative arrangement conditional on my seeing this victim of circumstance and becoming convinced he had not committed the burglary. I also told Fallon: "If I take this case, I am going to submit copies of my report to Lloyd's of London, the other company, and also to District Attorney Charles F. Sexton, of Monmouth County, New Jersey. And if Gibson is guilty in my opinion, I shall report *that* to them. I want you all to understand that clearly."

The three men nodded. "Fair enough," said Fallon.

A couple of days later, Gibson, a short, chunky man of thirty-five or so, came to see me. I had got his record from Police Headquarters. It showed twelve arrests between 1910 and 1921 for burglary, larceny, extortion, obtaining goods under false pretenses, passing phony checks, and impersonating an officer. One arrest, and in Chicago, of all places, was listed as "on general principles." He'd also run into trouble with the law in New York, Philadelphia, Milwaukee and Paterson, New Jersey. He looked enough like a con man for any cop to pick him out of a crowd.

However, he was cool, and answered my questions promptly and directly. He had established himself as a stockbroker, he said, and had not been in trouble for two years.

On the whole Gibson made a good impression on me. But I have known few professional thieves with so long a record to go straight. And in this, as in my other cases, there was no necessity for me to make up my mind about a man's guilt or innocence before I had the facts.

I called upon Lloyd's representatives, Toplis and Harding, to find out whether they had any objection to my attempt to establish Gibson's guilt or innocence. They had none whatever, they said, so long as I did not interfere with the work of the New Jersey adjuster who was working on the case. I next went to see District Attorney Sexton at his office. We knew each other because we'd worked together on previous cases.

On learning what my mission was, he threw up his hands. He was not handling the case personally, but he sent for the dossier on the case. He looked the papers over. When I told him I was interested in establishing the accused man's innocence, he was astonished.

"You baffle me, Luisi," he said. "This guy's an ex-convict. Two women were shown his Rogues' Gallery picture. They have identified him as the burglar. That's why we have indicted him. Why are you so eager to prove him innocent?"

"I'd just as soon prove he is guilty, if he is. My interest is in making a recovery. I work for Lloyd's, as you know."

The next day I sent one of my best investigators to Pittsburgh. He had with him pictures recently taken of Gibson, and these he showed to Mrs. Daniels and the maid. They both were positive that the man photographed was not the burglar. They signed affidavits saying just that.

Armed with the affidavits I returned to Sexton's office. He read them, looked at the photographs that I'd attached to them, then asked, "By the way, did you get these yourself?"

"I sent one of my most trustworthy assistants," I told him.

Then he surprised me. "I will drop the case, Luisi," he said, "only if you go to Pittsburgh yourself. Take Gibson with you. If the women, after seeing him in person, still say, in front of you, mind you, that he's not the burglar, have them make out new affidavits. Then only will I ask for a dismissal of the charges against this man."

As soon as I could, I went to Pittsburgh with Gibson and the assistant who'd made the first trip. Gibson was so nervous on the train that I began to wonder about his innocence myself. But, on seeing him, Mrs. Daniels and the maid declared at once and very firmly that he was not the burglar. They signed a second set of affidavits. After being shown these, Prosecutor Sexton, true to his word, moved for a dismissal of the case against Gibson.

And from that time until his death Arnold Rothstein proved

a frequent and sometimes invaluable tipster to me. I recovered merchandise again and again with the help of his information. During the Prohibition Era Edward Tinker, the banker, was in Europe one summer. When he returned to his home on Long Island he found that $20,000 worth of fine wines and bonded whiskey had been stolen from his wine cellar. He had no insurance on it, since he'd bought it from bootleggers. Because it was an illegal sale, the insurance companies refused to insure it. But Mr. Tinker asked me to see what I could do about recovering it. He'd notified the police of his loss.

At that time Rothstein was running a nightclub on Long Island that he'd won in a crap game. After a week, I went to see him and asked if he could help me. "As well as being a client, Mr. Tinker is a particular friend of mine," I said, which was certainly the truth.

"Drop around tomorrow," he said. "I may know something by then."

The next day he gave me the name of a warehouse in Long Island City. "That's where the liquor is," he said. I told Mr. Tinker I would ask the Syosset police to pick up the liquor in a truck.

It was the only safe and legal way to move it. In a few days the police called Mr. Tinker up with the good news that they had found his stolen whiskies and wines. When it was delivered, there were only a few cases missing, and he was very happy about it.

When I thanked Rothstein, he just said, "Oh, forget it."

I came to the gambler again when I found myself stopped cold in my search for $50,000 worth of antiques and precious figurines. A few days later a reputable corporation lawyer called me up.

"I'm mystified, Mr. Luisi," he said. "In today's mail I got a letter that had a key in it. The letter, which was unsigned, asked me to get in touch with you and give you the key. It explained that the key will open the door of the rear room of the first floor of an address which, I would guess, is in Hell's Kitchen. You will find something there that you have been looking for."

I went to his office, got the letter and key, and showed them to the New York detectives who had been assigned to the case. They suggested I consult Inspector John D. Coughlin. I was very glad to. I wanted to be told that by transporting the antiques I would not be compounding a felony — under the circumstances.

Inspector Coughlin asked me a few questions about the lawyer, who apparently had been sent the letter because he had nothing to do with criminal cases and had an impeccable reputation.

"With a lawyer of that type, I don't think there can be any reason for not accepting his word. Certainly there is no question either of your compounding a felony by picking up the antiques — that's if they are still there."

I went to the room — and there the antiques were, in barrels and trunks. How Rothstein acquired the information I don't know. The police believed the job was the work of boys, beginners, who knew neither the value of their loot nor where to find a fence to sell it to.

I dined at Rothstein's home with him and his wife, Carolyn, several times. On one such evening he asked me many questions about the insurance business. I answered his questions as fully as I could. And that is the only thing I ever did personally for Arnold Rothstein. Some time afterward he bought an insurance business, which he retained until his death.

Those cynics who knew Rothstein would laugh at the idea of his doing anybody a favor unless there was something in it for him. But if he benefited in any way, I never knew it. No one, of course, was told where I was getting the tips that Rothstein kept giving me down through the years. I think the police understood the reason for my secrecy about the origin of all that information. They themselves had learned early, as reporters do, that sources of information must be protected at all costs.

And until he died, Rothstein kept helping me. Sometimes the loot was in pawnshops, warehouses, loft buildings, unoccupied homes and buildings.

The most important single bit of assistance he gave me concerned a case involving $175,000 in jewels that were reported stolen from the beautiful young wife of a Chicago industrialist.

This man, a Swede whom I'll call Oscar Prentice, was then about forty-six. His wife was twenty-eight, and a vivacious Texas beauty. They'd been married three years but had no children.

Mr. Prentice, like a lot of successful men who wait until middle age before marrying, had fallen head over heels in love, and showered his wife with luxuries. The jewels had disappeared from their suite in the Ritz-Carlton, then the flashiest expensive hotel in New York. They'd checked in only the morning before, with her personal maid.

On discovering her loss, Mrs. Prentice telephoned her husband, who was working at his New York office. He hurried to the hotel suite, bringing a secretary with him just in case her services were needed. With the maid and Mrs. Prentice they'd made a thorough search of the suite. Unable to find the jewels, they called the hotel manager, who notified the police. Mr. Prentice then called the St. Paul Fire and Marine Insurance Company, which assigned me to the investigation.

When I arrived, the detectives were questioning the members of the hotel staff who had been in the suite between the time the jewels were last seen and their absence was discovered.

Before joining them, I interviewed the Prentices. They lived in Chicago and had arrived only the morning before on the Twentieth Century. Just before leaving, Mrs. Prentice explained, she had taken her jewels from the wall safe in their home and put them in the case she kept them in when traveling. The case was about eighteen inches long and six inches wide, and she slipped it into its canvas cover.

The case was not out of her sight on the train. They ate in their drawing room. When the New York Central crack train pulled into the Grand Central Station, she picked up the case and kept it in her hands until they got to their suite and the porters had brought the last of their luggage. Then she put the jewels in a bureau drawer.

She was tired after the trip. They dined in their suite, decided not to go out, and retired early. After her husband left next day to go to his New York offices, she decided to go shopping. She took three pieces of jewelry from the case, a diamond pin, wristwatch, and clip. She closed the case, slipped it again into its canvas cover, and put it back in the bureau drawer.

Mrs. Prentice told her maid to press her clothes and then take the afternoon off. The maid, who had gone to see her sister, was not there when Mrs. Prentice returned to the suite at two-thirty. Exhausted from her shopping, Mrs. Prentice decided to take a nap. Taking off her jewelry, she opened the bureau drawer. The case and her $175,000 worth of jewels were not there. That's when she telephoned her husband, who helped her search the room.

When the maid arrived she described how she had seen Mrs. Prentice get out the jewel box that morning while she was helping her dress. She watched her put on the three pieces and then slip the case into its canvas cover and replace it in the drawer. She had taken two hours to press Mrs. Prentice's clothes, which had become rumpled on the trip. During those two hours the hotel's chambermaid and the bath maid had come in to do their work. But neither one, she declared, had been alone in the bedroom for one moment. She had remained there, in the bedroom, from the time they came until they left. The personal maid, the two who worked for the hotel, and the Ritz-Carlton's other employees were later investigated. Nothing to arouse suspicion was discovered about any of them.

A careful canvas by the police of New York's pawnbrokers and fences also yielded not a clue. When working on such a large loss, I invariably used an undercover man. Even the staff in my own office was not aware of who he was. He did not telephone. He wrote me a letter when he had collected information I wanted. We usually arranged to meet someplace where no one was likely to overhear our conversation, or we'd have our talk in a taxicab. But he'd not had a whisper from his underworld contacts about this fortune in hot ice being offered around. This meant that whoever had them was taking his time before disposing of them.

A few days after the jewels' disappearance the insurance company's general manager asked me what I thought of the case.

"It's not complete," I told him. "I haven't a clue."

"All right then," he said, "close the case."

His motive for hurrying was the vast amount of insurance business the company got each year from Mr. Prentice's many businesses. In closing a case the first step was to get a proof of loss. I telephoned Mr. Prentice and asked when I could see him and his wife.

"There's no use my being there," he said. "Mrs. Prentice can tell you everything you wish to know."

When I called her at the Ritz she made an appointment for the following morning at ten o'clock. On arriving at the suite, I got a big surprise. The personal maid admitted me and told me that Mrs. Prentice would see me in the bedroom.

I went in, thankful that I'd developed enough of a deadpan to fool most people when I was surprised by something like this. I sure needed the deadpan that morning.

Mrs. Prentice, her light-brown hair down and in a low-cut nightgown that only half concealed her snowy white breasts, was sitting up in bed, rouged, perfumed, and ready to do business. I was not then nor am I now fool enough to imagine she wanted anything else than to look so appealing and seductive that I would be bedazzled.

I pulled out the paper for her to fill in. Giving me a cuddly look, she said in a baby voice, "You will help me fill it out, won't you?"

"Of course," I told her. "But these forms are easy to fill out. You need only describe the lost or stolen articles, tell how much they cost, where and when they were bought, and how much you are claiming for them."

But when she told me she had bought some of the more expensive jewelry from Louis Duprez, I could hardly write down the name.

Louis Duprez, who had a shop on Madison Avenue, was a known fence, and was among the first receivers the police squad hit when a big jewel robbery was pulled off. Duprez, of course, had legitimate customers who hadn't an idea that his legitimate business was just a front. Sexy-looking Mrs. Prentice might be one of these innocents, but the matter was well worth exploring.

"I know Louis Duprez," I said, "he's been in business for a long, long time, Mrs. Prentice."

"Yes, I know. I have bought many other things from him," she said. "Even before I was married, in fact."

I went straight to Rothstein on that one. I said, "I'd like to ask Duprez what he knows about this woman."

"If Duprez is involved in the loss, what happens?"

"Unless he stole the jewelry himself, no one will be told he ever talked to me."

"Go to see him at his office tomorrow morning at eleven — unless I call you."

The call did not come. Duprez talked freely about Mrs. Prentice. If half of the things he told me were true, she had crammed as many adventures in her short life as had Moll Flanders. Duprez said that she had been a call girl and an inmate of a whorehouse. She'd been arrested as a jewel thief, and was a reckless gambler. She had undergone plastic surgery on her face to improve her looks. He'd heard that she once had her fingertips sliced off in an attempt to alter her fingerprints so that she could not be identified through them. She had been married, he believed, at least four times.

"That dame," he said, "would steal a dime off a red-hot stove if she needed it to get into a crap game around the corner. She's got the gambling bug bad."

Duprez also gave me a lot of leads on places where Mrs. Prentice had been. This was pretty much all over the West, Montreal, Canada, Mexican border towns like Juarez and Tia Juana, and in the East, New York, Philadelphia, and Boston.

On leaving Duprez, I telephoned the president of the insurance company. "I don't think you'll want me to settle this case so fast now," I said, and told him a bit about the millionaire's young wife. "I sure don't," he said. Bulk business or no bulk business, his company was not paying out $175,000 with such a character as Mrs. Prentice on the receiving end. At least not until I checked on Louis Duprez's statements about her. If he was lying, I'd soon find out. If he was telling the truth, I might have lots of work ahead of me. I wrote to my representatives in every city and state Duprez had mentioned to me. I described Mrs. Prentice, told what little I knew about her past — for Duprez had been quite vague on most points, including the names of her various husbands. I pointed out that gamblers, if they would talk, might provide the most fruitful leads.

Several times after that the Prentices invited me either to have cocktails with them or to dinner. My original impression had been that the Swedish-American industrialist was head over heels in love with his bewitching young wife. But now that I had a better chance to observe them, I began to wonder. There were moments when she would say something, and he'd get a questioning, wary look in his eyes.

I was having to stall whenever they asked me when I would be ready to make a settlement. After a couple of weeks went by, he began to suspect, as any smart businessman would, that something he didn't know about had come up and was delaying the payment of the claim.

I purposely made an appointment with him alone. If the opportunity to ask him tactfully how well he knew his wife presented itself, I intended to do so.

The moment we got together, he asked, *"Now* what's holding up the settlement?"

"Oh," I said, "there are still a few details to look into, sir." And then, trying a roundabout approach, I said: "You and Mrs. Prentice seem to be very happy together. Did you know each other long before you married?"

I suppose that made it possible for him to blurt out something that had been worrying him terribly for quite a while.

And I suppose what he told me was easier to confide to me, a stranger, than to a friend or old business associate. His suspicions about his wife had first been aroused when she talked him into giving jobs to her brother and several other men. They all proved shiftless and lazy, and reports had reached him that two of the men she recommended were suspected of dishonesty. He also noticed that she was reckless with money. Each time he asked about it she tried to distract him or changed the subject. Also, once or twice she had stayed out until late at night. He'd found out afterward that her explanations of where she had been weren't true.

He was a simple man. He almost cried as he told me the story of his life. He'd come to Chicago from Sweden an uneducated boy. For years he'd worked at all sorts of menial jobs. But one day his industry and shrewdness got him his first big chance — and he'd become a millionaire by the time he was twenty-five. Now he ran a dozen factories and plants. Thousands of people worked for him.

"I still have enough love for that beautiful girl I married," he said, "to hope that my suspicions of her are unjust. Nothing would make me happier. But lately there have been far too many small incidents that hint strongly that she is not all she should be. I must know, however, one way or another. I cannot stand the suspense of not being sure any longer."

He looked down at his hands, the hands that had done so much hard manual labor in his early years. He seemed to brace himself.

"I will tell you something now, Mr. Luisi, that may surprise you. I am interested in recovering the money for the jewelry." He looked straight into my eyes. "But right now it is much more important to find out the truth about my wife.

"If you can prove to me that she has anything shady in her past, I will drop the claim. I will pay all of your expenses, whatever they may be. I will pay you double the salary you are receiving — "

He could not go on. It was obvious that he would prefer to pay anything for a report that could relieve him of his doubts of her.

"Do you realize what you are suggesting, Mr. Prentice?" I asked.

"I didn't have any intention of bribing you," he said. "I had every intention of getting the permission of your company. But if you undertake this commission for me, you must keep the investigation secret. I understand that the company officials you work with will have to know about what you are doing. But I am sure they can be trusted to be discreet."

I told Mr. Prentice that he was right: the first thing I must do is to get permission of the insurance company to make any such arrangement with him. That evening I telephoned Mr. Frederick Russell Bigelow, president of the St. Paul Fire and Marine Insurance Company, at his home in St. Paul.

Mr. Bigelow was flabbergasted. "I have been in the insurance business for more than fifty years, and I never have heard of a proposition like this one," he said. "But I will consent to it on one condition. The condition is that you are to check up on every lead you have. And if the loss is bona fide, we'll pay it."

Before long I had reports from correspondents in twenty-seven communities Mrs. Prentice had graced with her presence. But these reports, like Mr. Duprez's information, had few concrete details. The woman had changed her name many times. There was apparently somewhere in Mexico a record of a divorce she had obtained, but under one of her numerous aliases, which one we did not yet know.

This was one of the most exhausting, expensive, and exasperating cases I'd ever been on. Mrs. Prentice was a whiz at covering up her tracks. For months, I traveled about the country on her trail. Undercover men had done the preliminary work, interviewing gamblers, jewel thieves, police officials, and fences everywhere we were able to trace her.

And as I was still working for the insurance company as well as Mr. Prentice, I had to proceed with extreme care. There was always the danger of alerting Mrs. Prentice. There was no question in my mind that Mrs. Prentice was a thief and had been a whore, crazy about gambling. But proving it was something else. She'd been married to a gambler named John Twist, and nicknamed Jew John. With his purported wife, a woman who gave the name of Mrs. Belle Hennessey Twist, and three other men gamblers, he'd been arrested in Dallas in connection with a jewel robbery.

One of my men interviewed Jew John, but he denied that his wife was the woman now married to Mr. Prentice. But her age and physical measurements tallied. Mrs. Prentice's handwriting also appeared to be identical with Mrs. Twist's. Her face was not quite the same as in the picture at Dallas, but then Louis Duprez had mentioned that she'd had plastic surgery to change her appearance.

There were a few other clues. Mrs. Twist, alias Miss Belle of Dallas, Miss Belle of Fort Worth, Miss Belle of San Antonio, had given Waco, Texas, as her home town. People in that Texas city remembered hearing she'd married during the First World War a Lieutenant Jerome Schultz of the U.S. Army Air Force. Also, that she had worked in bordellos in half a dozen Texas towns.

We got a list from Washington of the Lieutenant Jerome Schultzes who had been Army fliers during that war. There were more than a dozen of them, and practically all of them had put in their training periods at Texas flying fields. It was 1924, and only half a dozen years had passed since these men had left the service, but they all seemingly had become restless wanderers. I chased one after another of them from Minnesota to Mexico, from California to Connecticut, interviewing each ex-officer, trying to learn if he'd married at one time the woman whose real name we believed now to be Belle Malloy.

This was the longest investigation I'd ever given my full time to. For different reasons, both Mr. Prentice and my insurance company became increasingly impatient before I was through with it.

St. Paul was apprehensive that somehow, if I failed, Mrs. Prentice would turn and sue the company for a great fortune for ruining her reputation by my exhaustive efforts to prove her a crook.

That honest soul, Mr. Prentice, was dismayed by the necessity of living with a woman whom he pretended to love even while he was having her past investigated. He was doing this at my suggestion, by the way.

In St. Louis, while talking to the nineteenth Jerome Schultz and finding out he was not the ex-Army flyer who had married Belle Malloy, I decided to give up. I'd never been so exhausted in my life, and I had not had a good night's sleep for weeks. My company and Mr. Prentice both seemed eager that I give the whole thing up.

On getting back to my hotel I found a wire from Riverside, California. An adjuster living near there had located one more ex-Army flyer named Jerome Schultz. I still wanted to quit. And I did something I'd never done before or since. I flipped a coin, saying: "Heads I go. Tails I forget the whole damn thing." The coin came down heads. Groaning, pitying myself, feeling utterly washed out and beaten, I took the next train that left for the Coast. I didn't expect to win. I was beginning to think our informants in Waco had got the lieutenant's name wrong, or something like that.

And there, in that pleasant California town, I had one of the greatest thrills and emotional experiences of my professional life. This Jerome Schultz was a tall, thin, gentle-looking man in his early thirties. He was in the real-estate business, and was alone in his tiny office when I walked in.

I didn't beat around the bush. I introduced myself, and then asked:

"Did you, Mr. Schultz, once marry a woman named Belle Malloy?"

His face went gray, his eyes glassy. He tried to speak, but made only a strange, animal-like noise. He staggered, and I was afraid he was going to faint. I stepped forward to help him to a chair. But, putting his hand over his eyes, he pulled himself together. And it was a very strange thing indeed that he said then, and in a most solemn voice:

"I will not talk to you unless my spiritual adviser is present."

"I understand perfectly," I said quickly. Actually, I was bewildered. "Why not call him up?" I asked after a moment or two.

His behavior was so strange that I feared his spiritual adviser might turn out to be a leader of one of those crazy cults that infest southern California.

He asked me to step out so that he could talk on the phone to his spiritual adviser. In a moment or two he joined me. He explained that his spiritual adviser, on being told my name, had suggested we go to my hotel room where he would join us very shortly. As we waited, Mr. Schultz began to pace the floor.

I felt rattled. It was one of those tormenting moments when you feel, without being at all sure, that you may have a great prize within reach. At the last moment you may do or say the wrong thing, and lose it. Worst of all, the decision rests in the hands of someone else. In this case it was a person of whose existence I was unaware until that afternoon.

And there we waited, he pacing the floor faster and faster, I sitting with my eyes glued on the door.

And when the spiritual adviser did appear, it was I, the tough old kid out of Harlem's Little Italy, who almost fainted — but with joy. For I knew the man who walked through the door that day. He was an old friend, Father Keating, a Catholic priest and a one-time honorary chaplain in the New York Police Department. We'd met at New York Headquarters many years before and had become firm friends. In years before, he'd eaten in my house many times.

"What in the world are you doing here, Luisi?"

When I explained, he turned to ex-Lieutenant Schultz, and with a beaming smile, demanded: "Didn't I tell you to have faith in God? I was sure that something wonderful would happen. Why, this is a miracle, my son."

I was still completely in the dark. When I said that, Father Keating, with a laugh, asked Schultz to tell me his story. During the First World War, the veteran said, he had been stationed at an Army airfield near San Antonio. One night, with some fellow officers, he went to a brothel where he met and fell in love with Belle Malloy, who was one of the girls there. The house was run by her aunt, a woman named Pearl Yorke. Belle Malloy, who was only nineteen, was beautiful, soft-voiced, and wonderfully gay. He had a good family background, but in spite of the sordidness of their meeting he became infatuated with her. He returned again and again to the brothel to see her. On the day before his detachment was sent to France, he married her. He was a Catholic, yet they decided to postpone having a religious ceremony until after the war.

But he never saw her again after their wedding day. She had sent a loving letter or two, a few postcards, and then he'd got a notice from Mexico that she'd divorced him. He'd almost gone out of his mind. All of his dreams had been of going back to her after the war, having a family, and giving her the decent life she deserved.

On coming back he'd headed straight for San Antonio. She was gone. The brothel was out of business. Schultz, in his grief, had become a drunken bum, a ragged, wandering vagrant, moving around the country, hardly knowing where he was or what he was doing. He wanted only one thing, he said: to find Belle, take her into his arms, and never let her go.

One morning, Father Keating found the wreck of a young man lying on the stone floor of his church, the famous Riverside Mission. He undertook Schultz's rehabilitation, and slowly brought him back to something approaching health. But it was long months before the priest got his protégé into a mental state where he could do even the simplest work. When he thought Schultz was well enough, Father Keating prevailed upon a local real-estate dealer to give him a chance as an office boy. Soon the flyer was selling real estate, and making a fair living. Three years before I saw him, he opened his own small office, and prospered in a modest way.

But ex-Lieutenant Schultz's greatest trial lay ahead. This came when he fell in love with a respectable young woman, a good Catholic, like himself, but because of the uncertainty of Schultz's marital status Father Keating was unable to perform their marriage ceremony. They were married in a civil ceremony, and now had a baby daughter.

A sincerely religious man, Schultz was greatly distressed because he had not been married in a Catholic church. He loved the church he'd been born into more than ever because of all Father Keating had done for him. He wanted nothing in the world so much as having the priest perform a religious ceremony.

That night I went to my hotel and made a long-distance call to San Antonio. Then I phoned Schultz. I said: "I don't want to give you any false hopes, Mr. Schultz, but I may be able to prove that you were never legally married to Belle Malloy. I have reason to think that before you knew her she was married to a man from whom she was never divorced. I may possibly be able to prove it within the next few days."

His mention of the name of Belle's aunt, Pearl Yorke, had rung a bell. Back in one of the early reports that had come in before we knew much about Belle Malloy, the name Pearl Yorke had been on a list of Texas border brothel keepers. Her place, I recalled, was on the outskirts of a little border town not far from San Antonio. I learned later the reason why Lieutenant Schultz on his return to San Antonio after the war had not found this madam. Local reformers had temporarily forced Aunt Pearl to shut up her joy house and leave town.

My call to San Antonio was to an adjuster I knew there. He told me that Aunt Pearl Yorke was back in business on the outskirts of the city. He said he was a good friend of Aunt Pearl's sweetheart, and was positive that this man could get her to talk to me with complete frankness.

That night I slept like a dead man.

In the morning, before leaving town, I got an affidavit from Mr. Schultz which related in detail the story he'd told me. When I got to San Antonio the adjuster was at the station to meet my train. I checked in at the Hotel St. Anthony. While I was washing up in my room, the adjuster surprised me.

"Don't faint, Mr. Luisi," he said, "but Aunt Pearl's sweetheart is the president of one of our local banks. I've already explained to him what you were coming here for. He laughed. He said, 'Pearl will talk her old cotton-picking head off about that wild-riding niece of hers.' "

The San Antonio banker, a strapping man in his late thirties, and with a twinkle in his eye, took me to Aunt Pearl's establishment personally. This was a beautiful colonial style three-story house with no other homes within blocks of it. Surrounded by well-kept lawns, it was beautifully furnished. Two gambling rooms and Miss Yorke's office were on the ground floor. I suppose her girls were still sleeping. On the way over, Aunt Pearl's banker-sweetheart told me that there were ten girls on the staff and that their prices started at $5, which was not a bad price for such services in the mid-twenties.

A colored maid showed the banker and me to Miss Yorke's office. This was furnished with an antique desk, three or four easy chairs, and a divan. There was an Oriental rug on the floor, and some paintings on the wall that looked like originals.

At the desk was Aunt Pearl. Though she was in her forties, she was still shapely and pretty. She had the sort of exciting, vivid red mouth that long afterwards became Marilyn Monroe's trademark. She began by explaining her reason for exposing the niece, who had once been one of her house's superior attractions.

"I've been waiting for years to get even with that little bitch," Aunt Pearl sighed with malicious pleasure. "As anyone who knows me will tell you, Mr. Luisi, I did everything in the world for that ungrateful girl. When I took her in here she didn't have a rag on her back. She was a little tramp, and looked it. But I took her in, bought her hundreds of dollars' worth of clothes, and showed her how to wear them, and how to behave with men so they wouldn't know what a guttersnipe she was. And she actually tried to gyp me out of my rightful 50 percent of her earnings.

"How she got all of those men to marry her, I'll never know. After she married each of her first two husbands, she came back crying to me and begging me to support her. Belle was always a two-timer — not like my other girls, believe me. They're grateful poor things, most of them, anyway — particularly ones that never made any money until I taught them how to be nice and refined."

With that off her chest, Aunt Pearl gave me all the facts I'd been searching for during the last five months. Mrs. Prentice's maiden name (she said) had been Mary Genevieve Alexander. Born in Hoxie, Texas, a small border town, Belle was such a wild girl that she was sent to the local Catholic House of Refuge when she was thirteen. She escaped, and in 1913 became the bride of one Robert L. Kent, of Waco. He divorced her the following year. It was believed that later during that year she married John Twist, alias Jew John, in El Paso. Aunt Pearl did not know the date. But Miss Yorke recalled that Belle had shown the certificate of that marriage both to her and to one of her cousins. On October 23, 1918, without divorcing Twist, she married Schultz in San Antonio, under her real name, Mary Genevieve Alexander, and got a divorce by default from him in Mexico on March 6, 1920. She then married another aviator, Captain Jeremy Rose. Like Schultz, Captain Rose met and fell in love with Belle in Aunt Pearl Yorke's busy whorehouse.

If she'd divorced either Jew John, the gambler, or Captain Rose, she'd never mentioned the matter to Aunt Pearl. Belle had met Mr. Prentice in a Houston hotel lobby. He was attending a national manufacturers' convention there.

"It was a pickup. That girl just batted her eyes once, and she had that old squarehead floored. What gets my goat is that she came to me for a big stake. 'I got this Swede ready to marry me, Aunt Pearl,' she said. 'All I need is a few good wardrobe numbers, a few pieces of jewelry.'

"I came through with $1,500 for that brat. And after she got married she never paid one cent back or even wrote to me. Once, when I was a little squeezed for cash, I wrote to Belle and asked her for the money I'd loaned her. I didn't even get an answer.

"And she was two-timing that middle-aged Swede even before they were married. She'd meet some old friend on the street, and he'd ask her, 'What's this I hear, Belle, about you quitting the turf?' So she'd take them to some other house, not mine.

"The minute I heard about that $175,000 jewel disappearance, I figured right away she had a hand in it — she was always a sucker for gambling anyway. I bet you she sold the ice to pay off the guys who run some game.

"But I always swore I would get even, and now I have my chance.

I will make a trip to Chicago or New York in case you need me. I'll close this place and pay my own expenses. It will be worth it." I thanked her and told her I'd let her know if we needed her.

As we drove back to town I asked the banker, man to man, if I could rely on the statements she made.

"You can, believe me," he said. "She's told me most of that stuff about Belle before. I've also sat in on some of their fights."

It turned out that he was not only Aunt Pearl's lover but her business partner and backer in the combined brothel and gambling house.

With all the data she'd given me, I was able to go on and find the certificate of her marriage to Jew John and enough other information to convince any court in the land that she'd never been divorced from him. This meant that both Lieutenant Schultz and Mr. Prentice had not been legally married to her at any time.

I sent copies of my information to Father Keating. He wrote me later that he'd married Schultz and his wife at the Mission and had never seen a happier man than the former flyer was that day.

After arranging to have all of this information documented, I started home, but with mixed emotions. I hated to tell Mr. Prentice that all of his suspicions were justified. And when I did, he broke down and cried like a baby. He looked at his wife's police record, and told me he did not want to see anything else.

I was with an official of the St. Paul Company. He said not a word until we left, and I asked him why. "I was afraid if I opened my mouth, I'd burst into tears. I never saw anything so pitiful as that man."

"I'll get rid of that bitch," Mr. Prentice had said, but with little conviction. When we confronted Mrs. Prentice with the evidence, she kept trying to lie her way out; but at last she said: "Well, all right, you have the goods on me. I lost too much money gambling, and sold the jewels to raise the cash I needed to pay off."

I began to ask her where she had sold the jewels. But Mr. Prentice waved me down. He was sick of the whole business, and didn't want to hear another word. He released the company on the claim for $1 and never made an effort to find the jewels he had given the wife he'd adored.

After he divorced her, Mr. Prentice asked me to come to his office with all the documents. He had me burn them, while he watched. A year or two later he married again. I hope he finally found the happiness he deserved. As for the first Mrs. Prentice, she went back to her old life. A couple of years later I got word that she'd been arrested in Mexico as a jewel thief.

*

HOWEVER, not all of my complicated investigations that led me into the private lives of our richer citizens ended with such satisfactory solutions.

Consider the $300,000 jewel robbery in the brownstone mansion of Mr. and Mrs. Myron C. Taylor. The financier, who later became the first United States Ambassador to the Vatican, and his wife went to the opera on the evening of November 1, 1926. It was the opening performance of the Metropolitan Opera House season. That evening Mrs. Taylor wore a pearl necklace valued at $175,000, two platinum bracelets set with diamonds, and several other beautiful pieces of jewelry.

On returning home she removed her jewelry and put it on a shelf in her bedroom closet. The next morning her personal maid took the jewelry from the shelf, placed it in Mrs. Taylor's jewel box, and put the box in a chest in a closet in another room on the second floor of the three-story mansion. This was the customary procedure. This room was kept locked, and on locking its door Marie, her personal maid, removed the key.

On the following afternoon at 4:40 P.M. the personal maid went to the room, found the door ajar and the key in the lock. The jewel case was gone. The maid told Mrs. Taylor, who notified the insurance company.

The police detectives assigned to the case worked under the direction of Inspector John D. Coughlin, one of the greatest of all New York detectives. He and his squad worked on it night and day. The insurance company I represented had less of a stake in the loss than another company. I was assigned to the case after both the police and another investigator, Noel Scaffa, had been trying to solve the mystery for some days. By that time all doors and windows, through which a burglar might have entered had been photographed and dusted for fingerprints. The five servants had all been questioned.

On seeing Mr. Taylor in his library I told him I was aware of how much work had already been done. "However, I would like to talk with Mrs. Taylor for a few minutes, if I may." The steel man was a little doubtful. "She is very tired after having talked so much to the police and Mr. Scaffa." He had the butler go to his wife's room where she was resting to ask if she felt well enough to talk to still another man from the insurance company.

"I will discontinue questioning Mrs. Taylor at any time you wish me to," I assured him.

When she came down, I had her tell the story I've written above. The purpose of this was the hope that she might recall some small detail she overlooked when talking to the others. But this did not happen. I then asked and was given permission to have two of my assistants search the house.

On being introduced to the assistants, who were both women, Mr. Taylor said he was surprised. He had been unaware that there were women insurance detectives. I explained that they were not, strictly speaking, detectives. "Their specialty is finding lost or misplaced articles. And they have found thousands of dollars' worth."

"I am afraid," said Mr. Taylor with a sigh, "that Mrs. Taylor's jewels were neither lost nor misplaced."

"That seems very likely, Mr. Taylor," I agreed. "But it is not at all unusual for thieves to hide articles they steal in the house. They reason that the home is the last place anyone would think of looking for them."

"The theory of Edgar Allan Poe in 'The Purloined Letter,' eh?" he asked.

"I don't think many thieves have read Poe. They just have hit on the same idea that the most obvious place is the last one detectives think of looking."

The next day Mrs. Taylor watched for an hour or more while my two assistants, with Marie, searched her bedroom and sitting room before going on to the other rooms. She told me later that she was surprised at their efficiency, and even more so the care with which her possessions were handled. None of the girls and women who had worked for her as domestics, she said, were their equals.

Unfortunately, they found nothing. Neither did our careful check of pawnbrokers, receivers, and underworld tipsters reveal anything. I questioned the servants — nothing.

There was one servant whom I didn't question — at Inspector Coughlin's suggestion. This was not Marie, but a woman the Taylors had hired only a week before. The police records revealed that she had been arrested and convicted of shoplifting in a large New York department store four years earlier and fined $50. This meant that she'd been caught in the act twice. New York department stores had learned that arresting anyone for shoplifting could cost them a fortune — in the event that the store detective had made a mistake or the case was dismissed on some technicality. Then the arrested man or woman turned around and sued the store for false arrest. As with insurance companies and other "soulless corporations" juries invariably were generous in handing over big chunks of money to persons so humiliated.

In self-defense, the stores adopted a self-protective device against such suits. Whenever a shoplifting suspect was picked up, he would be taken to the offices of the chief store detective for questioning. If the suspect agreed to sign a confession, he would be freed. But the next time that man or woman was picked up, there was no danger of his suing — as the affidavit could always be produced in court.

This is what seemed so ironical about what happened after this convicted shoplifter was arrested by Inspector Coughlin for the $300,000 jewel robbery. The inspector was certain that he could get a confession from this maid and that she would implicate whoever her confederates were. So just a week after the robbery, Coughlin arrested her. But it turned out to be one of the worst mistakes of his brilliant career.

She did not confess. No jewels were found on her. In fact, they never were recovered. On being freed for lack of evidence the maid sued Mr. and Mrs. Taylor for $100,000, charging them with false arrest. On advice of their lawyers, the Taylors made a settlement out of court.

*

I HAVE known millionaire couples to become so dependent on a servant that they will disregard all evidence that he has robbed them. This was the case with Joe and Muriel Roth, as I'll call them here, and their Negro butler, Jason James. One winter day their summer home at Woodmere, Long Island, was looted of some antique lamps, a radio, a couple of lighters, and much of Mr. Roth's wardrobe of summer clothes.

I suspected Jason James, the butler, because there were no signs of a forced entry (he had a key) and the robbery took place while he was away for several hours from the Roths' Park Avenue apartment. There was also the matter of his surliness toward me when answering my questions. Sometimes he pretended not to hear what I said. Other questions he asserted he did not understand. Once in a while he retorted irritably, "You already have asked me that."

Once he started toward me in a menacing manner. I pushed back the right side of my coat, which allowed him a fine view of my .38 Police Positive Colt. He backed up.

He was a tall, handsome man but with effete ways. The articles that disappeared — antique lamps, expensive sport clothes, flashy-looking lighters — were the sort of thing, it seemed to me, that an effeminate man with his aesthetic tastes would take.

But Julius Salinger, Mr. Roth's general manager, told me: "You are wasting your time questioning that man. Mr. and Mrs. Roth depend on him for everything. He is their combined butler, social secretary, and chauffeur. They've trusted him with large sums of money, jewels worth thousands of dollars. They consider him indispensable, feel almost as though he's a member of the family."

I didn't say anything. After a couple of minutes, Mr. Salinger asked, "Do you suspect Jason?"

"I'd like to concentrate on him for a while."

But Julius Salinger proved to be right. In the next few days more little clues pointed to Jason James as the thief. But I had nothing conclusive when Mr. Roth asked me my opinion. I told him I was working on the theory that his butler had taken the missing articles. Mr. Roth insisted that the idea was impossible.

"That leaves me no choice," I said. "I have to reject your claim. Although I cannot yet prove it, I think James is guilty."

"Well, the claim is for less than a thousand dollars. Mrs. Roth and myself think Jason is worth ten times that."

I was sorry. They were nice people, the Roths, and I would have bet, if I was a gambling man, that the butler would rob them again.

Four months later that happened. Fifteen thousand dollars, in tens, twenties, and hundreds, were taken from the wall safe. Jason James had the combination. However, the cash was kept in a compartment they locked. As far as they knew, the butler was unaware of where they kept the key to it.

This time they had no doubt that Jason James was the thief.

He'd flown the coop. The claim was paid in full. Seven years later James was picked up in California on a charge of stealing a car from his employer there. That boss not only forgave him but also gave him his job back. Whatever Jason James' shortcomings were, he knew how to hypnotize the people he worked for and how to convince them that he was indispensable — whether their belongings disappeared mysteriously or not.

Of course, neither the Roths nor the insurance company pressed charges — after seven years almost any larceny rap is easy to beat. The insurance company technically had the right to insist he prosecute. If he failed to do that, they could demand that he return their money.

But Mr. Roth's company gave us much more than $15,000 a year in premiums — so the matter was forgotten.

*

THE Japanese butler employed by Mr. and Mrs. Edward Tinker in their New York apartment was another servant who adopted a menacing attitude when I questioned him about a valuable ring that had just disappeared.

The night before, Mrs. Tinker had worn the ring to the theater. On coming home she had put it on a tray on the dressing table next to her bed. She was certain she had taken it off and put it there. In fact, her husband, who was then president of the Chase Securities Company, had picked it up and remarked she should send it to the jeweler to be cleaned.

But at eleven in the morning, or ten hours later, the ring was gone. She and Mr. Tinker had searched the room thoroughly before sending for me. Three of their servants had been in her room that morning: the maid who did the cleaning, her personal maid, and her Japanese butler. The women had worked for the Tinkers for years, the butler for only a few weeks. Nevertheless, I questioned the maids first. They gave me frank, direct answers, and made an excellent impression.

Before I asked the butler to come in, I had Mrs. Tinker explain once again exactly what he had done on bringing in her breakfast that morning.

The Japanese evaded questions. Either he said "I no understand" or pretended not to hear me, as Jason James did. I had to ask five questions to get one answered. Also, like James, he twice got up, and approached me in a threatening manner. Each time I was forced to get up and tell him "Sit down!" The second time he did not obey until after I put my hand in my pocket. I merely pulled a handkerchief from my pocket. But I pushed back my coat far enough to give him a chance to see the .38 nestling on my hip. I had made an appointment to meet the two police detectives who had been assigned to the case. But I was spending so much time questioning the butler that I went to the phone and called them, saying I'd be delayed, and explained why. They said maybe they'd better come over to the house and see what they could do with him.

I resumed questioning the butler, but with no more progress than before. I was interrupted again by the arrival of Mr. Tinker. He sent one of the maids in to say he wished to see me. I left the butler in the library, telling him to wait there. Practically everybody is interested in detective's working methods, but I've met few persons so fascinated by every detail of my work as was this powerful banker. And for him I made now an exception of my rule about not telling anyone whether I'd made up my mind about a person's guilt till the proof was wrapped up and ready to deliver.

"I think your butler took the ring, Mr. Tinker," I said, "but I need more time to prove it."

We were discussing the matter when the two detectives, both of them burly two-hundred-pounders, arrived. I introduced them to Mr. Tinker and resumed talking to him.

"Where is the butler now?" asked one of the detectives.

"In the library," I replied.

"Let's see what we can get out of him," he muttered. With that, he and the other man walked into the library while I answered the banker's questions. But before I answered many of them, we heard a commotion in the library. At that point, one detective ran out to us. He said of the little butler, "He hit me first."

With Mr. Tinker on my heels, I rushed into the library. The Japanese was flat on the floor. The other detective was standing over him.

"Save me!" wailed the Japanese. "Save me! Me tell! Me tell!"

I whispered to the detective to leave me alone with him, and told Mr. Tinker the same thing.

The terrified little butler lost no time in confessing how he'd stolen the ring. He'd seen it on entering. As he put the tray down on the bedside table, he nudged a spoon so that it fell near the dressing table. While picking it up, he also palmed the ring and straightened up, his back to Mrs. Tinker.

"Where is the ring now?"

He led me to the basement and showed me the hiding place — back of the electric meter.

Mr. Tinker's hobby was breeding fine cattle and importing rare and exotic birds from all over the world. Like most gentlemen farmers, this banker liked to sell the products — but encountered difficulties most professional farmers are usually not troubled by.

He was shocked one day to get a warning that the milk and cream given by his pedigreed Angus cows had been rejected by the Syosset (Long Island) Board of Health inspectors because of contamination.

Mr. Tinker, who had the habit of summoning me if anything larger than an acorn was missing from his acres, asked me to investigate. The man in charge of scouring the tin cans in which the milk and cream were sent to market had been neglecting that part of his job.

My services were also called for when about forty exotic birds vanished from his carefully guarded aviary. Gerard Luisi, though just a city boy, noticed holes outside and inside the enclosures. Rats — who'd just as soon eat a rare bird of fine plumage as a much more palatable fat duck of undistinguished lineage.

In 1931 Mr. Tinker's $50,000 barn burned to the ground. This time one of the new hands proved to be a firebug. I found evidence indicating this in his rooms, where he kept clippings of an even more expensive fire in another New York suburb.

He confessed to me, was tried for arson, and convicted.

*

MR. Tinker admired these feats as though I was a twentieth-century Sherlock Holmes. But I did a job for at least one millionaire banker who admired me not at all. Early each June this gentleman and his wife closed up their Park Avenue apartment and moved for the season to their summer home at Locust Valley, Long Island.

This year, as usual, the last thing they moved was his wife's jewelry collection, which included a $100,000 diamond necklace. They took it out of the apartment's wall safe, which was behind a picture, and his wife put it into a traveling bag. She turned this over to her personal maid to carry out to their car. The maid rode in the front with the chauffeur, and the banker and his wife in the rear seat of the limousine.

On getting to the country home the banker's wife had the maid bring the bag to her bedroom where she transferred the diamond necklace and the rest of the jewelry to the wall safe there. A week afterward the banker suggested his wife wear the diamond necklace to a dinner party they were attending.

The necklace was gone!

But none of the other jewelry was missing.

When I got to the house in Locust Valley, detectives from the local police force were questioning one of the gardeners.

The banker was a chesty-looking man in his forties. He had obviously taken over the running of the investigation. Without hesitation he led me into the library where the detectives were questioning one of the gardeners. They were concentrating on him because he'd admitted he had a record.

They stopped asking questions when we walked in. I apologized, said I would not interfere with their work, and led the banker out again. "I'd like to speak to your wife," I said.

"Come downstairs," he yelled, "and bring the maid with you." His wife, a timid-looking woman, appeared with the maid. I was beginning to get the hang of things. I had not asked for the maid. But he was doing it his way.

"You don't have to talk to either of them," he said. "I can tell you the whole story. I know as much about it as my wife does."

"I'd rather speak to this young lady later," I said, indicating the maid. She thereupon left the room. The banker then plunged into his account of the disappearance of the necklace. It was the story I've related above.

"Who," I asked, "opened the jewel case before you put the necklace in?"

"What difference does that make?" he blustered. When I didn't reply, he said: "That was eight days ago. But as long as you want to know, I opened it myself."

He glared at his wife. "Didn't I?" he demanded. His wife hesitated, then answered, "Yes, dear."

Later, when the maid was present, he roared the same question at her. The maid looked at her mistress questioningly, and also replied meekly, "Yes, sir."

This banker, according to his story, also unpacked the bag on getting to Locust Valley, opened the case the necklace was in, and showed it to his wife and maid before locking it up in the wall safe there. Again he used a bullying tone to get the wife and the servant to confirm this.

As I excused myself, to join the detectives who were questioning the man downstairs, the banker told me: "Those detectives say that fellow they're talking to now is the thief. They expect to break him any time now." As I walked out, I couldn't help noticing how upset and nervous both women seemed.

I asked one of the detectives to examine all doors and windows, but there was no sign anywhere of a forced entrance. The gardener had not confessed, but the detectives seemed certain he was the thief. We quit at 2:00 A.M. to get some sleep — and also some dinner, for the banker had not offered us a morsel. The gardener was instructed not to leave the premises. We arranged to return at 10:00 A.M.

But in the morning, as I dressed, I recalled that the missing necklace had been bought at Tiffany's. I was there when they opened, and I asked to see the general manager.

"I would like to get a description of a diamond necklace." I told him who had bought it, and the price and the date it was purchased. He rang for the foreman of his workshop. When this man was asked for a description of the necklace, he looked bewildered.

"Perhaps you would like to see the necklace itself? It's here right now. The clasp is being repaired. The lady who owns it brought it in only two weeks ago."

"I wonder if you could make a photostat of it for me?" I said when I got over my surprise.

While they were having it made, I went to an outside phone and told my superior at the insurance company that I had located the necklace and was bringing a photostat of it to show the banker at his office.

The banker had me ushered into his private office, but he did not interrupt signing papers to greet me. When he had finished this, he said, "What can I do for you?"

I showed him the photostat. "Is this your wife's necklace?"

His steely eyes widened in amazement. "Why, yes, that's her necklace. Have you got it?"

"No, but I've located it at Tiffany's. It seems your wife brought it there to be repaired. That was two weeks ago, before you moved to Locust Valley for the summer."

For once he lost his composure. "You know, I would have sworn I saw it when we left Park Avenue and again when we got to the country."

He said he would insist on paying my expenses, and was going to ask the insurance company for a bill.

"Now, what can I do for you, Luisi?"

"There is one favor I'll accept," I said. "That gardener they've been questioning has been given a bad time. He volunteered the information to the police that he had a record. I think he wants to go straight. Give him that chance."

"That's the favor you want?" he asked.

"It is."

"The favor will be done."

I couldn't have had a bigger reward.

CROOKS IN HIGH PLACES   8

THE district attorney is the most powerful man in any community. His office can arrest and indict his fellow citizens almost at will. It is a rare occurrence indeed when a grand jury develops a will of its own and, as the newspapers term it, runs away.

I can recall meeting very few prosecutors whom I could not trust and cooperate with. But the two of them I write about here really shocked me.

*

MY first shock of this kind came after a $24,000 burglary in the home of Matthew Wilson, a manufacturer, in Syracuse, New York. Only jewelry was taken, the most valuable piece in the lot being a $10,000 pearl necklace.

The burglary occurred one evening, between eight and eleven, when the family was at a friend's house. The Wilsons came home to find the front door unlocked. Feeling a draft from the kitchen, Mrs. Wilson walked back there and found a window open. Concerned about her jewelry, she hurried to her bedroom on the floor above and found that her jewelry had been taken from the dresser drawer in which she kept it. The bureau drawers were all pulled out. The thief in his haste had thrown the clothes on the bed and on the floor.

The adjuster expressed doubt that there had been any burglary.

A burglar might have crawled in through the window undetected, as the nearest house was quite a distance away. What aroused the adjuster's suspicion was Mrs. Wilson's statement that the kitchen window was open only about eight inches. Also, he believed Mr. Wilson was having money troubles. The manufacturer had not been paying his bills on time, though creditors were pressing him.

I was in Syracuse the following week on other business, and talked to the detectives there who'd worked on the case. Though they'd found no evidence of forced entry, they accepted Mrs. Wilson's story. They pointed out that the burglar may have started to close the window after climbing through, then changed his mind, fearing he'd make a noise.

I also believed the story. I found newly made shoe scratches under the window. And a quick check proved that Mr. Wilson was in no financial troubles. He was just one of those businessmen who perversely delay paying their bills though they have plenty of funds on hand.

I recommended holding up the settlement, but for another reason. The burglary seemed to me the work of an amateur. No professional would have taken the crazy risk of leaving by the front door and being seen by someone walking by or in an approaching car. And if he was an amateur, he might not know a fence. He might try to sell his loot to a pawnbroker or even to a jewelry store, not knowing of the New York State law that compels them to report what they've purchased to the police. So it seemed reasonable that the jewels might turn up soon.

My recommendation was accepted. But the jewels, when next heard of, had a condition attached to their return that astounded me.

A man who claimed to be the district attorney in a large city in Ohio had visited the office of the company that insured the Wilson jewels. He told its superintendent of the Claims Department, "I can help you get back those jewels stolen last week in Syracuse."

"Fine!" exclaimed the superintendent.

"There is a prisoner in our city jail who swears he knows the man who has that stuff, but he wants a reward."

"We'll give him the usual reward."

"How much is that?"

"Ten percent."

"Only 10 percent!" said his caller, shaking his head. "I guess I've wasted my time coming to New York to see you. The least this man in jail says the thieves would consider is a 50 percent reward."

The claims man, of course, was flabbergasted at the idea of any district attorney making such a proposition. Of course, he could be an impostor. But it made no sense. What possible advantage could a thief obtain by posing as a prosecutor?

The problem was turned over to me. The Claims Department man gave me the alleged district attorney's card and a good description of him. I called a friend in the Ohio city whom I thought would know the local prosecutor. I read the description.

"That's our boy," he said.

"Is he well thought of out there?"

"Not exactly," he said. "Nobody has been able to pin anything on him, but there's been a lot of dubious rumors about him. I'd say his reputation was most questionable."

I told him that if he could meet me I'd take the night train to Cincinnati, which was only two or three hours from his town. What I had to discuss I preferred to discuss outside the district attorney's jurisdiction. I wanted to play it safe.

When we met in Cincinnati, my friend told me of various fixes and crooked deals the D.A. was believed to have engineered, though nothing had ever been proved. The district attorney was quite crafty and sly, he said. He also told me of a well-respected lawyer who would be the right man through whom to approach this grafter.

The lawyer readily agreed to introduce me to District Attorney Watterson. The lawyer was told nothing of the purpose of my visit and asked no questions about it, assuming it was a routine matter. A luncheon date was arranged.

I was taken to the prosecutor's office to be introduced to District Attorney James Watterson. He had the flamboyance and some of the physical look of Bill Fallon, Broadway's greatest jury charmer — bushy hair, the manner of an actor, handsome face, eyes that could smile even as they looked right through you. But Watterson lacked the thrilling voice and flashing wit of the red-haired Fallon. They were both schemers, but Fallon, unless it served his purpose, did not talk like one. This prosecutor did. He sounded like a man born on the wrong side of the tracks who should have stayed there. He'd guessed what I was there for on seeing my card.

The jewelry, of course, wasn't mentioned during the lunch. Instead, Watterson told dirty jokes that weren't very funny. After we'd eaten, the lawyer left us. The district attorney and I returned to his office. My plans had all been made in Cincinnati. The first thing I had to do was to convince him that I was a complete dope, a stupid blunderer. This might get his guard down. If so, he might take chances with me that he'd never take with a man who impressed him as smart.

The moment we were back in his office, the prosecutor closed the door and took up the matter of the jewelry. "You mean to say this stuff was stolen by a burglar?" he asked. "And in Syracuse, New York, you say?"

I acted as though I was taken in, believed every word. He insisted that he didn't know who had the jewelry or how much it was worth. When I told him its value was $24,000, he said that every cent of the 50 percent reward would go to the man who turned it over. He himself was acting as go-between only as a favor to the insurance company.

I nodded and smiled, as though I not only believed that whopper but considered this proof of what a fine public servant he was. But I dickered a little about paying 50 percent. I thought he'd expect me to. He finally said he'd find out if 45 percent would be acceptable to the man who now had the jewelry.

"As soon as you can get the jewels to me, I will take them to Syracuse to show them to the couple who owns them."

"Have you got the money with you?" he asked.

I smiled. "As prosperous as I may look, sir, I never carry as much as $10,800 around with me at any one time."

He stared at me, appraisingly.

"But naturally," I added, "I can get the reward money either from the insurance company or my own office immediately — when and if the owners agree."

"Why must *they* agree?"

"Forty-five per cent of $24,000 is $10,800," I replied. "How can I ask the insurance company to pay out so much money, a small fortune like that, unless I am absolutely sure that we're recovering the stolen stuff? Suppose the owner looks at it and says, 'Oh, no! These are not my jewels'?"

"I guess you have a point," he said, rubbing his chin.

Then to my surprise he admitted that he had the $10,000 pearl necklace right there in his office. Going out of his office for a moment, he came back with a man he introduced as Detective Warren Finnegan.

"He's one of my staff men," said Watterson. He told Finnegan to show me the necklace.

"Look at those," the prosecutor said as Finnegan handed me the pearls. "You can see for yourself that they're the real thing."

"Beautiful. And they look valuable," I said, "but I'm not an expert on pearls. And I never saw the Syracuse jewels, anyway."

The prosecutor took them back and held them up to the light. "Real beauties, aren't they?"

I said, "Yes, but you're not a jeweler either, are you?"

"Now if I send Finnegan with you to show those people the pearls, would you have the $4,500 reward money there in cash?"

"Yes. I can get the money in cash either from my own office or the company. I'll arrange for that right now if you'll let me use your phone to call New York."

With an amused smile, he said, "Of course."

I called my office and instructed Major Otto to bring $4,500 in cash to me next day at Syracuse. I'd be waiting at the hotel where I always stopped, I said.

When I hung up, District Attorney Watterson said, "If this works out all right, we may be able to deliver the other jewels to you in the same way."

Finnegan and I and a representative of the insurance company took the train to Syracuse that night. I got a compartment for the insurance man and myself, a lower berth for Finnegan.

Finnegan asked me to take the pearls from him overnight. He said, "I'll be nervous in a lower with $10,000 worth of pearls on me."

"As I told Mr. Watterson," I said, "I'm not a jeweler, certainly not a pearl expert. I don't know yet whether it's the real thing you have or a string of phony pearls. I won't touch them until the owner has a chance to identify it." When he looked at me suspiciously, I added, "I don't want to be accused of switching them on you."

I wanted him to be nervous about the pearls, so nervous that he wouldn't be able to figure out what I was doing. Finnegan accepted my excuse. But I had a much more important reason for insisting he keep the pearls as we traveled on that train to Syracuse.

We had hardly checked in at the hotel next morning when

Major Otto was announced. He'd come himself. I introduced him to the D.A.'s man. "You have the $4,500 with you?" I asked.

"Yes, sir," said Otto.

"Give it to me."

"Right away?"

"Right now. This man here," I pointed at Finnegan, "doesn't want any mistakes made. He's dealt with crooks all his life. Why should he trust us — or anyone else? Why shouldn't he make sure the money is all here, every cent of it, before he turns over a $10,000 pearl necklace to us?"

But Major Otto just looked at me pleadingly.

"I'm going into the bathroom," he said.

"Never mind that!" I told him. "Finnegan and I don't trust even you, Dick Otto."

I was having fun with both him and Finnegan. Now I didn't have to care what that flatfoot was thinking. I figured I had him and his crooked boss right where I wanted them.

Blushing as I'd never seen him blush before, Major Otto turned his back and opened his fly. He took out a wallet stuffed with forty-five hundred-dollar bills that he'd pinned to the jockstrap he'd put on just for this occasion. He had taken a leaf from the story he'd heard about Peggy Joyce's jeweler. But he had not expected to be forced to share that bashful fellow's embarrassment.

We all laughed at that, even Detective Finnegan.

"Now, Finnegan," I said, "watch me count this money. I want you to be convinced I have the money with me before we do anything more."

He watched me count the forty-five bills with dewey eyes.

"Okay?" I asked.

"Okay," he said.

We phoned the Wilsons that we were coming over. Mrs. Wilson said she and her husband would be there.

While she was looking at the pearls, Mrs. Wilson cleared up a little mystery that had been puzzling me. How had the district attorney known what company had insured the jewels? Mrs. Wilson mentioned that a few days after the burglary she'd had a long-distance call. A man, who hadn't identified himself, asked, "What company insures your valuables?" She told him, and he hastily hung up.

Mr. Wilson was fairly certain the necklace was the one he'd

bought. His wife was inclined to think so, too. "But I'm not quite sure that two or three of the center pearls haven't been changed," she said. "They look to me just a little different."

That gave me an excuse to suggest something I'd intended to do anyway: have the jeweler from whom she'd purchased the pearls make a positive identification of them.

Finnegan couldn't suppress a groan. He became more nervous than ever when I insisted that he again carry them as we all approached the jewelry shop. It was on Syracuse's busiest shopping street. On being told what we wanted, the jeweler got out an old record book in which he'd written down the size, weight, and color of the individual pearls in her string. He unstrung the pearls to weigh, measure, and examine them. He compared the new figures he wrote down with those in the book.

"Yes, Mrs. Wilson," he said as he started to restring the pearls, "this is the string I sold you three years ago." When the string was back in its box, I told the jeweler, "Please hand the pearls to my friend, Detective Finnegan here." I asked the jeweler to sign a statement certifying that they were Mrs. Wilson's pearls. Then I paid him his fee and we left. Outside the shop, we said goodbye to Mr. and Mrs. Wilson, who thanked us profusely.

"I'll see you before long," I told them.

Finnegan had started to sweat.

"Is there still some doubt in your mind that these are her pearls?" he asked.

"Not a bit," I said. "Let's go back to the hotel room."

Finnegan stopped sweating, and relaxed. When we were once more in the room, he took out the box. "Boy, will I be glad to get rid of this thing! Now, give me that $4,500 and I'll catch the first train out."

I looked at him. "You're a nice fellow, Finnegan, but I'm afraid I can't do that. You're going to have to go right back to Ohio and return the pearls to the man you got them from."

"What?" he wailed. "What are you pulling *now?*"

"Why, Finnegan!" I said. "During the night it occurred to me that once the necklace was identified as the one stolen, we would have to notify the police here in Syracuse. It's a felony not to tell them we have this stolen property, where it was recovered, and by whom."

Poor Detective Finnegan held his head with both hands. "But

my instructions are to turn over the necklace to you the moment you gave me the $4,500."

"Now, now," I said, patting him on the back, "we're all sure that it is stolen property. If I take the pearls I'd be receiving stolen property. Mrs. Wilson, the jeweler — even Dick Otto here — could be forced to testify to that against me, if I was indicted and put on trial. For the moment we won't worry about any action the federal authorities might take against you for carrying stolen property across state lines. So you just take it back to your boss and tell him what I have just said."

As he picked up his hat, I told him, "If we don't receive every piece of jewelry that was stolen from Mr. and Mrs. Wilson in seventy-two hours, I will have to report the matter both to the police here and to the federal authorities."

At the door, Finnegan said, "I think you've won *this* round."

The district attorney from Ohio must have run to catch the first train to New York after Finnegan described the discouraging results of his trip to Syracuse. He turned up at my office a full thirty hours before the deadline.

District Attorney Watterson now resembled Fallon at the peak of a long binge. He had not shaved in a couple of days, his eyes were bloodshot, and he was as nervous as a cat. Before I could say anything at all, he started taking the stolen jewelry out of his pockets.

"Now, I am not going to accept this jewelry if we're expected to pay 45 percent of its value," I said, still playing the innocent boob.

"I never wanted any compensation, any part of the reward," he declared in a righteous voice. "I return these jewels because it is my duty. I want you to remember that."

"I'll remember it."

Before I left, I had Major Otto bring in the policy on the Wilson jewels. Together we studied the descriptions of the jewels listed on it. They seemed to be all there. There had been no switching, as far as we could determine. In utter misery the district attorney watched us as we studied the $10,000 pearl necklace, a $4,500 diamond bracelet, a $2,500 diamond brooch, and three rings worth $7,000. He must have been thinking of the $2,400 he believed the company would have paid him if he'd asked only for the usual 10 percent reward.

And a horrible thought struck him. He'd been spending his own money! "What about my expenses here on these two trips?" he asked in a pleading voice.

I gave him $200, and he was glad to get it, I must say. "If I can ever do you a favor out in my neck of the woods," he said, "just let me know."

Later I learned how the jewels had come into his possession. County Detective Finnegan had accidentally seen a seventeen-year-old youth on a street late at night. The boy was acting suspiciously, so Finnegan stopped him and searched him for a gun. Instead he found the Wilson jewels.

Instead of taking the lad to the nearest police station, the usual routine, Finnegan brought him to the district attorney's office. On hearing this was his first theft, between them they cooked up the scheme for getting the reward. The boy was glad to accept the prosecutor's kind offer to permit him to plead guilty to vagrancy, for which he was sent away for thirty days. That put the thief out of the way until the jewels could be disposed of. After that, even if he told the story, who would take his word against that of the district attorney, particularly when he was backed up by one of his detectives? The boy remembered the Wilsons' address. Either Finnegan or the district attorney had telephoned Mrs. Wilson to learn what company had insured the jewels. Then the district attorney had made a trip to New York. Being a crook, he thought that the insurance company would do anything to save money.

But he was like any crook in or out of public office — he'd overestimated his ability to get away with it, and underestimated, if I may say so, my acting ability.

*

FAR more reprehensible, in my opinion, was the double cross attempt by another prosecutor. He was the Assistant Federal Attorney in Seattle, Washington, and was also seeking a reward.

The crime in this case had been a holdup of two Seattle jewelers who claimed two bandits had taken from them at gun's point loose diamonds worth between $50,000 and $60,000. They were wholesale dealers, and each of them was insured by the St. Paul Fire and Marine Company for $75,000. The company offered a $5,000 reward for the return of the jewels. The Seattle police offered an additional $2,500 reward for the arrest and conviction of the stickup men. One of these had been identified by one of the jewelers as Jimmy (Lefty) Malloy, a mediocre middleweight prizefighter whom he had seen perform in the ring.

But neither Malloy nor the other man was picked up. Nor were the loose diamonds traced. The company, after a while, had paid the two jewelers in full for their losses.

Eight months after the holdup a big, imposing, smooth-spoken man of about thirty-five walked into the Manhattan office of L. Weitz and Company, general agents in New York for the St. Paul Company. He sent in his card to William Boylan, the manager:

PATRICK J. JARNEGAN
Assistant United States Prosecutor
Seattle, Washington

Shown into Mr. Boylan's office, the visitor mentioned the holdup and asked if the St. Paul Company had withdrawn its offer of a $5,000 reward.

Bill Boylan said he did not imagine so and asked what Mr. Jarnegan's interest in the matter was. The man from Seattle said he had a friend who knew where Lefty Malloy, the holdup man the jeweler had identified, was now hiding. He added: "Malloy told this friend of mine that the holdup was a put-up job, a fake. He insists he got no diamonds. He says the jewelers put $2,500 cash in the wallets as the payoff to him for pulling the phony holdup."

"Where are you stopping, Mr. Jarnegan?"

"At the Hotel Astor."

"I'll get in touch with the home office in St. Paul," the insurance executive told him, "and let you know what they say in a day or two."

The home office told Boylan to ask what I thought of the matter. I'd just finished an exhausting job and never had felt so tired in my life. I intended to go home early that night and get a real night's sleep.

But his account of his talk with this odd fish of a prosecutor intrigued me so much that I told Bill Boylan to set up a dinner date for the three of us so I could see and listen to Mr. Jarnegan for long enough to form some opinion of him.

"Have him meet us in the Astor lobby," I said. "I want to put a couple of undercover men on this guy's tail and find out what he's up to. The Astor lobby is a perfect place for me to spot him for their benefit." I told the two shadows that I'd blow my nose after shaking hands with their subject. I didn't want them to make the mistake of following some acquaintance who might see me in the lobby and greet me with a hearty handshake. We'd eat in the hotel, I told them, and instructed them to tail him if he left the hotel that night.

Mr. Jarnegan proved to be a confident, smooth-talking character. Along with nerve he possessed that intensely earnest and forthright manner that lawyers who master it find so effective in courtrooms. His command of language was magnificent. I did not doubt that he was a lawyer or that he might be, as he said, the chief assistant of the Seattle Federal Attorney.

Jarnegan talked to us for almost an hour. And this time, I noticed, he went quite a bit farther than he had in his first talk with Boylan. He made no mention of the friend who knew where Lefty Malloy was hiding. The fighter, in fact, was right there in New York, he said.

"I have investigated his story of the holdup being a fake, gentlemen," he added, "and I believe every word of it."

"Well, then, Mr. Jarnegan, all Malloy has to do is to surrender himself to the Seattle police."

Jarnegan smiled and replied, "He feels, and with some justice, that the police will give him a better deal in Seattle if someone from the insurance company accompanies him there."

"Do you plan to represent this fighter when he surrenders in Seattle?"

For the first time the man from Seattle seemed a little hesitant. "I don't think I will," he said. He explained that at the moment he couldn't very well.

"Why not?"

Jarnegan took a deep breath, and said: "There's no use in my trying to conceal anything from you fellows. Any company man of yours who mentioned my name to the Seattle police would be told I'm under indictment." A frameup, he explained, on the part of insanely jealous and unscrupulous political rivals. They were trying to destroy him by claiming he'd had a part in a bribery scandal. Not that they'd get away with it.

I gave him the sympathetic smile I reserve for smart men like him when I wish them to tell me more. "Bribery!" he said. "Boot-leggers! Who'd take money from those double crossers?"

"If you are not going to be Lefty Malloy's attorney," I asked, "what role are you going to play in this case?"

"I want 50 percent of the reward your company offers," and he added, "and I want it regardless of whether Malloy is convicted, or the two jewelers."

"The jewels have to be returned. That's a stipulation of the reward."

"Oh, I suppose I won't get anything unless the jewelers reim-burse the St. Paul Company for the money given them for the fake holdup. But on the other hand, Malloy may be convicted. If so, I'll get *that* reward."

I was glad that I had developed the trick of concealing my feel-ings. Because I was shocked. Here was a cold-blooded conscience-less schemer, a lawyer advising a man to give himself up, and trying at the same time to get the reward money in case he was convicted. Talk about playing both ends against the middle!

"If Malloy gave himself up would you personally take him to Seattle?" he asked.

"Yes."

"Malloy has no money. Will you pay his fare to Seattle?"

"We will." I told him to bring the fighter in to see me at my office.

After we said goodbye to this ornament of the American bar, Boylan said, "What do you think of him?"

"I know exactly what you think of him, Bill. I think the same thing. He's a guy who would sell out his mother. It would serve him right if Malloy found out that he is only advising him to turn himself in so he can collect the reward. He'd kick him from here to Seattle!"

Next morning I had the report from my shadows. Jarnegan had walked from the Astor to the Hotel Taft, less than a mile away. In the lobby he met a man who looked like a fighter and who answered Malloy's general description. They went upstairs to-gether. After an hour Jarnegan came down alone. He went back to the Astor and up to his room and did not come down again that night. One of the shadows remained at the Taft to tail the man the prosecutor had met. When Malloy didn't come out of his room by 2:00 A.M., my man went home.

Jarnegan was sure in a hurry for his blood money. He had Lefty Malloy in my office before ten. After we talked for a couple of minutes, I asked Malloy if he wanted to tell me his story. He nodded. "Would you have any objections to me having my secretary in here to take it down?"

He looked at Jarnegan, who told me, "We have no objection." It was pitiful to see what faith that poor club fighter, who appeared more than a bit punchy, had in the man who couldn't wait to turn him in. When the secretary came in, Lefty told this story.

In September he was broke, hadn't had a fight in a long time, and his manager had nothing lined up for him. He was sitting in a poolroom in Seattle when a man he knew only by sight approached him and got him to go out in the street with him.

"Didn't want none of them wise guys in there to hear about this deal I have to offer you. Wanna make some easy dough?" Lefty said he thought he was going to be asked to throw a fight. But it wasn't that.

"I know a guy who's a jeweler," this poolroom acquaintance explained. "He's a practical joker. Got a whale of a sense of humor. He has a friend he wants to throw a scare into — so he wants me and somebody else to get toy guns and stick the two of them up. We'll take two wallets away from them. They are supposed to be full of diamonds, these wallets, but they'll be empty except for the money's he's giving us for the stunt."

"How much money?" Lefty asked.

"Twenty-five hundred."

"Just for that?" Lefty asked. It sounded like a very fishy proposition to him. "Suppose this guy he's playing the joke on starts to holler? The cops come and we're grabbed. Then I'd be in a fine jam."

"Everything is taken care of," said the other man. "The joker is gonna tell his pal: 'You wanna get killed? Didn't you hear 'em warn us to give them ten minutes or else — ' "

"I don't know," said Lefty, thinking of all the left jabs and uppercuts he'd have to take for that much money — if and when he could get some fights.

"I'll be with you all the time, won't I?"

Lefty had reluctantly agreed. On the appointed morning he met the other man in front of a downtown office building in Seattle where the fun-loving jeweler and his victim shared an office on the fifth floor. With the toy guns in their pockets, they waited in the lobby. As the other man had told him, the jewelers at night kept their diamonds in safe-deposit boxes in the basement vault of the bank that occupied the ground floor.

The jewelers entered the bank, and the two "bandits" rode to the fifth floor and hid in the corridor until the jewelers came up in the regular elevator. When they had the door open Lefty and his companions followed them in, toy guns in hand. They snatched the wallets that each jeweler carried in the right side pocket of his coat, ran down the stairs, and out through the rear entrance. They went straight to the poolroom, and opened the wallets. Just as his partner said, there were no loose diamonds in them, only the $2,500 he'd been promised.

Lefty offered to split this, but the other fellow refused, saying he'd been paid already. The fighter congratulated himself on making the first easy money of his life. But the headlines about the robbery in next morning's newspaper sent him out of town in a hurry. The jewelers had reported that between $50,000 and $60,-000 were in the wallets taken from them at gun's point. The taller bandit was recognized. That meant him.

He hopped the next bus East, intent on getting to New York. But he stopped off a couple of times en route. In one town he'd lost some of his money in a crap game. What little he had when he reached New York was gone by the time he ran into Jarnegan whom he had known in Seattle.

"What a break that was!" said Lefty Malloy. "I was at the end of my rope. No money, no job, no friends. Scared to write to any of my friends for help. I was afraid to go near a promoter and ask for a fight. I knew that's the first place the cops would be looking for me. So I run into this man. He was a prince, like a big brother to me. He even staked me to a room in the Taft besides some eating money while he was fixing up things with you people so I can get home and clear myself."

I couldn't help sneaking a look at Patrick J. Jarnegan. He had a dreamy smile on his face. I've noticed a peculiar thing about double crossers of his type. Their vanity is so great that they take it for granted that you admire their sneaky tricks. Jarnegan was unaware how monstrous it seemed to other people that he was taking such cruel advantage of this punchy fighter who probably hadn't been too bright in his pre-ring days.

When the girl came back with his statement, I asked Lefty to sign it. He looked trustfully at Jarnegan, who nodded. I then had the fighter sign a second one attesting that he was returning to Seattle with me of his own free will. No threats had been made to him and no promises. The St. Paul Company was paying his fare and traveling expenses to Seattle with the understanding that he would surrender himself to the police there and do all he could to assist me in my investigation of the alleged diamond robbery.

As I've hinted, I had just been through one of the most grueling adventures of my career. My associates were shocked at the idea that I planned to travel alone by train across the country with a punchy young prizefighter. My doctor gave me an examination and said I needed a rest desperately, and pressed me to delay the trip, send an associate West with Lefty Malloy or at least bring along another man with me.

I guess I should have taken his advice. But I've always had inordinate pride in my stamina and I saw the trip as a real test. I wanted to travel with Lefty alone because it was a great challenge in another sense. Could I win his confidence? Could I get him enough out of Jarnegan's influence to get him to tell me the truth about the holdup, so I'd know whether it was a fake or not?

As the time approached for us to leave, Patrick J. Jarnegan said he'd go out for a day or two ahead of us to make sure of getting a good lawyer for his protégé. He asked me to lend him $100, and I did.

Malloy seemed so eager to start for Seattle that I began to suspect he might be planning a break for freedom somewhere along the line. It didn't make much sense, but I was dealing with a man with a befogged brain. He was scared and had been hungry in New York. But once he was fed and comfortable and realized he was getting closer and closer to Seattle Police Headquarters he might panic and want out.

Nevertheless, as soon as I got the necessary permission from the New York and Seattle police to take him across the country, we started out. I booked a drawing car all the way. We would have an eleven-hour layover in Chicago, which meant it would be five days before we got to Seattle.

Stubbornness again stopped me from changing my plans. It would have been easy to have a strong-armed male assistant on the train, just in case Malloy made trouble. I still don't know why I didn't arrange for that.

And I began to wish I had brought a helper the first evening of the trip. It soon became clear that the poor fighter didn't know that a reward had been offered for him. His kind friend on whom he depended so utterly hadn't told him that.

But he was wondering about it all. I could almost see that dull brain turning the question over and over. His mind was elsewhere. I would talk to him and he'd not answer. I suggested gin rummy, and let him win, but he could hardly remember what card he had just played. Talk about his ring idols, Dempsey, Benny Leonard, and Harry Greb, brought him out of the fog for only a moment.

At dinnertime I thought it might cheer him up to eat in the diner. But he said he'd rather eat where we were. He ordered a steak, but when it came he scarcely touched it. When a club fighter can't eat a big free steak that's a real warning signal. He did go out with me to the platform while the porter made up the berths. We came back and played a little more desultory gin rummy. At ten he said he was tired and wanted to go to bed. I told him to take the upper berth, I'd sleep in the lower.

"I'm going to the washroom," he said, suddenly.

"You don't have to go to the washroom, Lefty," I told him. "You can use the one we have here in our drawing room."

"I forgot we had one here," he said, but in a disappointed voice.

It was obvious that he was already regretting his decision to go to Seattle, where he would have to face criminal charges. He got his pajamas from his bag.

I thought it was a good time to say: "Lefty, you don't happen to have your toy pistol or any other kind in your pocket — or your bag. Do you?"

"Search me — and the bag. I haven't any kind of pistol."

I didn't mind doing that at all. But I reminded him as I made the search, "Remember, Lefty, you told me to do this."

But he was clean.

I thought it well to remind him before he went to sleep that he was returning to Seattle of his own free will and for his own good. "You don't want to disappoint Mr. Jarnegan, do you? He will be waiting for you in Seattle. And I've promised that the insurance-company officials and I will do whatever we can to help you out."

I took off my coat so he could see that I had a .38 Colt Police Positive. That didn't stop him from putting his clothes in a neat pile. A man would do that if he planned, when I fell asleep, to climb down, snatch them up, put them on, and get away fast. His shoes and socks were on the couch near his trousers.

I waited until he was up in his berth. Then I switched off the light, and announced I was going to use our washroom and would be out in a minute. I took no longer than that.

I was taking no chances with this husky young scrapper.

I did not undress, took off only my coat and shoes, then I loosened my shirt collar and lay down.

I don't suppose I slept an hour altogether that night. Each time I was about to doze off, Malloy would move, and his bunk would make a creaking sound, waking me up. Once, though, I heard a different sort of noise.

I held my breath, grabbed my gun, and waited as the fugitive, trying to make as little noise as possible, came down the ladder. I sat up with my left hand on the electric-light switch, the other holding the .38.

On reaching the floor Malloy slipped his coat off the hanger, threw it over the trousers and picked up them and his other clothes. As he did so, I switched on the light and pointed the gun at him.

"Please don't shoot!" he cried. "I don't know what I'm doing."

"Oh, I'm sorry," I said. "I didn't know it was you. I thought somebody got in here." When he calmed down a bit, I asked, "But what are you doing with all your clothes over your arm?"

From the first I'd treated him as I might an erring son, and this made it easier, I think, for him to say what he did next.

"I'm afraid to go back to Seattle," he whispered. "I'm afraid that the cops there won't believe me. They'll send me away."

I started talking to him. If he was not involved in a real stickup, we could help him. At this, the big fellow burst into tears.

"I lied to you, Mr. Luisi," he sobbed. "That wasn't no fake holdup. But I got nothing like $50,000 to $60,000 out of it."

"Who was the other man?" I asked.

"His name was Bernstein."

"First name?"

"That's all I knew him as: Bernstein. I never heard him called nothing else. When I took the wallets from those two fellers, I gave them to Bernstein. He gave me $2,500 for my share."

"Did you tell that to Mr. Jarnegan?"

"Please don't force me to answer that," he pleaded. He felt caught between two men, either of whom could save him. It is difficult for most people who haven't had experience with uneducated men like this fighter to comprehend the depth of the fear they have of educated men, particularly lawyers, and also their exaggerated idea of the power of such persons.

"But you are telling me the truth *this* time. You say the holdup was on the level, not a fake, at all?"

"Yes."

"Do you want to give me a statement on that?"

"Yes."

With that he sat down and wrote a statement. "You are treating me as my own father would," he said. We talked for a while longer. When he started up to his bunk again, it was three-fifteen. During the rest of the night I dozed off only fitfully. I got up at seven-thirty. Lefty, having come clean, seemed to feel better about everything. He went off with me to the dining car and ate a double breakfast.

I was surprised by the hearty appetite I had that morning after so troublesome a night. Not that I relaxed my vigilance. I was aware that Lefty was so unstable that he could compulsively swing back to the opposite way of thinking in a minute. One of St. Paul's men met the train. He had other business to discuss with me.

"Watch him," I told the Chicagoan, as Lefty walked to the newsstand to get a magazine. "He's punchy and may decide to take off at any minute. Don't refer to crime, or use that word in his presence."

We all went to the Hotel La Salle where the Chicago man and I discussed business. Lefty seemed at ease, leafing through magazines and looking out of the window.

The Chicago man was still with us when we boarded the train that night for Seattle. A minute after we got aboard, Malloy said he was tired and wanted to go to bed as soon as his bed could be made up. Again we stood on the platform, smoking.

"Do you really want to go to Seattle?" I asked him. "If you do, I may be able to help you."

"I'm ready to go back," he said, and I believed him.

And he didn't make another false move. But I, not being sure of him, would awake every time I heard him move in the berth above me, or turn over. However, the train noises, the whistle, squeaks, howls and groans of the wheels, the stops at stations in the small hours, also kept me awake.

When we reached Seattle at last, I felt punchy myself. Captain Charles Tennant, Chief of Detectives in Seattle, and Jarnegan, posing as the hero who'd talked Lefty Malloy into surrendering, met us there. I never was happier to turn a prisoner over to a police officer.

Tennant was amazed on hearing that I alone had brought the fighter from New York. "He was very quiet," I said.

Captain Tennant replied: "He is also a professional stickup man. This wasn't his first job."

Lefty, faithful to his promise to me, confessed and told the true story. He implicated two other men, both jewelers. One said he didn't know what the fighter was talking about. The other man was arrested and later freed for lack of evidence.

The end of the story is pretty sad. Malloy, the dupe, did his best to help us recover the jewelry. I stayed in Seattle ten days; but though I had the fullest cooperation from the Seattle police, none of the loot was found.

Yes, sad is the word. Malloy was convicted and got from six to fifteen years in Walla Walla Prison. Mr. Jarnegan, the ex-Assistant U.S. District Attorney who double-crossed him, beat the charges against him on a technicality.

But he never asked me for the reward. The only compensation he got was the $100 he had borrowed from me, and kept.

*

THE truth is that I was far more often moved to pity when I solved crimes by white-collar people, executives, clerks, or salesmen for big mercantile firms. They had so much more to lose than men like Lefty Malloy. When they went wrong they wrecked everything that they had been building up all their lives. They destroyed themselves, hurt so many more people, their families and their associates at the office. But the man most deeply hurt was the man himself.

There used to be a saying about criminals: they never come

back. The man that I've found does not come back is the white collar thief. Even if he has been stealing from his employers for years, his is not a thieves' or outcasts' world or one on the fringe of poverty and hopelessness. So he is lost when exposed.

There are exceptions to this rule, but I've found them very rare. I'd like to discuss briefly half a dozen such cases where the motives were different in each instance. You will observe that in most of these cases the white-collar thief gave himself away.

Let's start with one of the top executives of the old P. F. Collier and Son Company, which ran a flourishing book business as well as publishing *Collier's*, the weekly magazine. All its employees were bonded by Ocean.

I had done so much work for the firm that I considered the three men who ran the company as much friends of mine as clients. By that time, the early twenties, I had left Ocean but remained on retainer. Anything that seemed complicated to the company or involved a great deal of money was assigned to me. Sometimes Ocean, like the other seventy insurance companies I worked for from time to time, handed me cases when dissatisfied by reports from their own investigators.

I also had investigated many matters for Collier that had nothing to do with its bonded employees.

On this particular day it was Frederick Stephenson, the company's secretary and assistant treasurer, who phoned me. He said that Thomas A. Beck, the head of the company, wished to see me on an important matter right away.

I got there to find Mr. Stephenson, George Kennedy, the vice president, and the company's insurance broker all on hand in Mr. Beck's office. Mr. Beck suggested that Mr. Stephenson tell me the story. I couldn't help noticing how terribly nervous Mr. Stephenson was both when he greeted me and as he explained what had happened.

There had been $5,000 in the petty-cash drawer when his assistant locked it up in the old-fashioned bank vault the night before. The money was still there when the assistant, William Knowles, checked it that morning on taking the box out of the vault. A couple of hours later one of the *Collier's* magazine staff writers was given an out-of-town assignment. The editor made out a $750 expense voucher, which he brought to Knowles.

It was while handing over the cash for this that Knowles discovered that $3,000 of the $5,000 in the box had vanished. He reported the matter to Mr. Stephenson. Another assistant, Bertram Johnson, the cashier, who ordinarily worked with Knowles in the cage where the money was kept, happened to be away on vacation.

I'd known Knowles from the day four years earlier that he'd started working for the company. He was a pleasant, smiling young fellow of twenty-two.

But he was scared to death of me when he was brought in to see me this day. I gave him a cigarette, which he took with trembling hands. Then I lit it for him, and waited. He confirmed what his superior had told me. I did not know until later one reason he was so nervous. Mr. Stephenson, in a rage at the loss, had already threatened to fire him. Knowles came from a respectable family. To be fired under such circumstances — the day $3,000 disappeared from a cashbox he was in charge of — must have appalled him.

Nine persons, it appeared, had access to the cage, including clerks and bookkeepers who kept coming in and out to get or bring back the company books they were working with. Knowles said that as usual duties had called him away from the cage three or four times that morning.

That meant that all nine had to be fingerprinted, along with Knowles and Stephenson. But when this was done the only fingerprints on the box proved to be Knowles'. With the cashier away, Knowles and Mr. Stephenson were the only persons authorized to handle the money in the box. This was on a shelf in the cage clearly visible to half-a-dozen other employees.

I talked with Mr. Stephenson, after I finished with Knowles. Mr. Stephenson expressed no suspicion of the young man. Instead he advanced the theory that a burglar had stolen the money from the vault some time during the night.

The Collier Company was then housed in an ancient downtown building. Its vault was almost as old, the kind cracksmen boast they can open with a can-opener. There was no question of any pro thief being able to get in that building and clean out the vault. And the secretary-treasurer seemed just a little too eager that I accept his theory.

There were two absurdities in the theory, of course. Unless Knowles had lied about the $5,000 being there when he first checked it in the morning, it had not vanished during the night but after the office opened in the morning. And what sort of thief would take only part of the money in the cashbox?

I began to wonder about Mr. Stephenson, particularly after I'd learned he had threatened to fire Knowles without even giving his assistant cashier a hearing, and later had dropped that idea.

There were no signs whatever of a forced entry or traces of the lock being tampered with.

I got from Mr. Beck the information about all persons who had access to the vault, and put tails on them. Like Mr. Van Cleef, the Fifth Avenue jewel merchant, Mr. Beck was far more interested in finding out whether one of his employees was a thief than in getting Ocean to pay the claim.

"If Ocean tells you to drop the investigation," Mr. Beck said, "I'll pay your fee and expenses to go on with it." Later, I must say, he became impatient, and tried to get me to close the matter.

In all, I investigated fifteen employees. This gave me all sorts of information, and answered my questions that would show whether they had immoral tendencies. Had each one given the same name and address the company had? What did they do in their spare time? Who were their friends? What was their family status? Were they habitués of nightclubs, gambling houses, poolrooms? Did they gamble? Have a police record? Did they have a car? Did they pay rent, board, or did they own their own home? The answer to any of these questions might give a clue.

I must say that the employment manager had a good eye for decent, clean-living, honest men and women. There was only one person among those he hired who seemed to be living above his means. That was the vacationing cashier. But my real suspect was a man whom the employment manager had not hired. Just the opposite. The employment manager had been hired by the man who now became my Number One suspect. He was, of course, Mr. Frederick Stephenson, the secretary and assistant treasurer of the company. He had worked for P. F. Collier and Son for twenty-nine years. And those persons who naïvely take it for granted that salaries in the twenties were anything like those paid today might ponder the salary of Mr. Stephenson, the third in command of this publishing empire. He got $6,200 a year.

On going over the company books, my accountants were uncovering some extraordinary discrepancies. There were dozens of shortages, dozens of unexplained withdrawals. Materials of various kinds had been bought that had never been delivered. The false entries and other fradulent tricks went back over a period of several years. It seemed to me impossible that Mr. Stephenson, the secretary and assistant treasurer, who supervised the cashier's department, could have remained blissfully unaware of all this.

He was a smart man, knew his job.

I was only partway through my investigation on the day that Mr. Beck called me into his office. Mr. Kennedy, who was with him, was terribly upset. With utter sincerity he told me that Mr. Stephenson had repeatedly complained that my investigation was disrupting the entire office force. The employees resented having their private lives and private affairs invaded.

"They all feel that they are under suspicion. They do not like your men making inquiries of their friends, relatives, everyone who knows them. One girl said to me 'I'm no criminal, but I never thought that I'd have to prove it when I came to work in this office.' "

"Well, gentlemen," I said, "I still have some work to do. Do you want me to complete it or not?"

This was the point at which Mr. Beck went over to his executives' side. "Luisi," he told me, "we want you to wind it up, bring the whole thing to a head. If you can't, I'll have to ask you to discontinue your investigation."

He took me to his house for dinner that evening. He pointed out something I didn't know. Kennedy and Stephenson had been best friends since boyhood, and had entered the employ of the company as office boys at the same time, twenty-nine years ago, and had risen together from the ranks. Furthermore, Mr. Stephenson had much more importance in the company than I seemed to realize. In addition to his job, he also audited the Collier Estate's funds.

"It so happens that I have great faith in Mr. Stephenson. Do you suspect him, Luisi?"

"I will be able to answer that question better in a few days," I told him.

He knew, of course, that meant I did. And Mr. Beck sighed. "Makes no sense. You may as well suspect me as Mr. Stephenson." The next morning I was handed a report on Mr. Stephenson that caused me to put a day-and-night tail on him.

What we found out was that Mr. Stephenson, with no income

but his salary, was managing to live it up somehow. He lived with his wife in a $125-a-month apartment, had two sons in expensive colleges, another in a good private school, and owned a Cadillac. His wife needed this, so he took taxis to and from work. But his big expense seemed to be the beautiful young mistress he was keeping. He had found her right there in his office.

This came to light when the undercover man reported that several nights a week Mr. Stephenson did not go home. His taxi instead stopped off at another apartment house on the way. That's where his girl friend lived. Until he set her up in an apartment, she had worked for him right there in the cashier's cage. Lillian Durand was twenty-two, just half of Stephenson's age. She had confided to her neighbors that the sad, kind-faced middle-aged gentleman they saw going into her apartment so often was her father, a widower.

Day after day Mr. Beck and Mr. Kennedy had been pressing me so hard that I decided, against my better judgment, to inform them that I had learned enough to say that it was definitely possible that Mr. Stephenson might be one of the guilty persons. This literally threw his old friend into a wild rage.

"You're crazy, Luisi!" he shouted. "You don't know what in hell you are talking about when you say a thing like that!" He looked like a man about to have a stroke.

Both Mr. Beck and I tried in vain to calm him down. But he kept raging that I was just like all the other detectives. I was suspicious of everyone, never happy unless I was stirring up trouble. Why didn't I accuse him, instead of his best friend?

The poor man was near tears. He and Mr. Stephenson had gone through life together since they were little boys. "I was the best man at his wedding and he was best man at mine. I watched his family grow up. I'm proud to be his friend and the friend of his wife and children!"

It was a really painful scene. "You are now on the spot, Luisi," he said. "You have put yourself there. And you will either prove these absurd charges in front of me, or apologize to — " Unable to go on, he rushed out of the office.

I still wanted to continue my investigation. But Mr. Beck said: "We have to respect Mr. Kennedy's wishes. I have never seen him so distressed."

As I've mentioned, I prefer not to tell a client of my suspicions and other theories until I am satisfied that I've gathered all the facts. But I had no other alternative this time than to give Mr. Beck some idea of what we'd learned so far. A very short time afterward I had all of the facts about Mr. Stephenson I needed. I believed he would confess and also implicate the others who with his knowledge and consent were stealing from the company.

Nevertheless, I thought a little shrewd staging would be of some psychological value. Mr. Beck permitted me to use his office for questioning Mr. Stephenson. I had two of my assistants there with me, as stage dressing. Also, Richard Davisson, the company's attorney. With difficulty I had pledged Mr. Kennedy to silence, and I had him and Mr. Beck remain in the former's office until I sent for them.

When ready I sent for Mr. Stephenson. It was shortly before the end of the business day at Collier's. He looked at the attorney and the two assistants, neither of whom he knew.

"What's going on here?" he said looking from one man to the next. "What's all the mystery about?"

No one said anything. We all stared at him. Our faces were expressionless. When I had him good and nervous, I said in a very low voice: "I thought you'd be happy to know, Mr. Stephenson, that I'm closing my investigation tonight. So please tell young Mr. Knowles to remain after the usual time."

"What do you want me to do?"

"I'm glad you asked that, Mr. Stephenson. I want you also to remain tonight."

"Why didn't you at least give me a chance to call my wife? I could have told her that I'd be late for supper tonight." I just looked at him, and he went on to say many other things.

I let him say all he wished to say, without interrupting. But he seemed unable to look at me. He would look everywhere about the room, but not at me. He kept wetting his lips, and you could see perspiration forming on his forehead.

When he was finished, I merely said: "You have seen me question other employees here at Collier's, haven't you, Mr. Stephenson? On other matters, as well as this one? So please guide yourself accordingly. There is one thing you forgot to complain of."

"What's that?"

"You said I didn't give you a chance to phone your wife. But you said nothing about having a date tonight with Lillian Durand, your so-called daughter. Wouldn't you like to call her, Mr. Stephenson?"

He looked as though he were going to faint.

"In case you've forgotten her number," I went on, "I have it right here." I mentioned the girl's number.

Now, cruel as it may seem to keep pounding away, an investigator has no choice. He has to move in for the quick knockout that will bring a confession. The thief who has a chance to think sometimes changes his mind about confessing.

I said, "You have been living far above your means, Mr. Stephenson." I started telling him about the extravagances he couldn't afford, the Cadillac bought on time, the expensive clothes his wife was forever splurging on, school fees, weekend trips with his wife to see the boys, vacations with the family that only a rich man could afford.

"In addition to all of this, you have been spending plenty in keeping your daughter, Miss Durand, in an expensive apartment. Then there are her Fifth Avenue clothes. She must cost you more, much more, than your entire salary. Or doesn't she?"

"Please, Luisi," he begged, hysterically, "stop. I'm convinced you know everything, or at least enough to send me to prison. I'll tell the truth and, believe me, I'll be glad to get it all off my chest.

"During the past week I've been calling up just about every friend I have in the world. I've been trying to see if I can raise enough money to pay back every cent I've taken."

"How much does the shortage amount to?" I asked.

He calculated briefly, then said, "More than $70,000. But that's not including the money I took from the Collier Estate."

I pointed to the desk of Mr. Beck's secretary. "Why don't you go over there, Mr. Stephenson, and write out your whole story, everything you did, everything you remember? Put it in the form of a letter to Mr. Beck. And I'd appreciate it if you would make a copy for me."

"I'm too nervous," he said. "I don't think I could typewrite."

"Well, we have all the time in the world," I said, "and I'm a very patient man."

He smoked a cigarette, talked of other matters. Then he seemed to gain enough control, and went to the desk. And, once started, he typed with the speed of a champion.

Mr. Stephenson was still at it when the phone rang. It was a call from the man waiting outside Miss Durand's. I told him to go to her apartment and bring her to the office. "If she argues, tell her Mr. Stephenson is waiting to see her."

He had stopped typing to listen, and was now as pale as death. "Please, for God's sake, don't bring that girl here!"

"I am going outside for a little while," I told him. "When you have finished the letter to Mr. Beck, please send for me."

I instructed my assistants not to let him leave the building under any circumstances. With Mr. Davisson I went to Kennedy's office where the executives had waited for me. It was no fun telling them the truth. Before I had half finished, Beck began to blow his nose and Kennedy broke down and wept. "I never thought he would do that to me," he kept saying. "And after thirty years! Thirty years!"

The next event of that crowded evening was the arrival at the office of Miss Durand. She was a snub-nosed, rosy-cheeked, whole-some-looking Irish beauty. She readily admitted that for three years Mr. Stephenson had been keeping her, paying the rent of her apart-ment, and buying her clothes and jewelry. She later gave us about $5,000 worth of the jewelry and $2,800 in cash, what she had left of the $3,000 she'd talked him into stealing to keep her quiet.

It was quite a contrast, after Miss Durand left, to meet Mrs. Stephenson, his stout, unlovely-looking wife. She was indignant at being hauled down there to the office in what she described as the middle of the night. She didn't seem at all concerned about her husband's dilemma, or to feel any responsibility about it.

I finally got her to admit that she knew what his salary was. "And do you really believe, Mrs. Stephenson," I said, "that $6,200 a year is enough to buy and maintain a Cadillac, pay the rent you pay, buy the fur coat and clothes that you have on right now, and also support three boys at school who live away from home?"

She just stared at me, haughtily, and did not reply.

This made me so angry that I pointed to the diamond brooch on her dress. "Who gave you *that?*" I asked.

"Who do you think gave it to me?"

"My guess is that Mr. Stephenson gave it to you. Is that correct?"
"Yes."

"Well, madam, you can take that right off. It was bought with stolen money and does not belong to you."

"What evidence have you of that?"

Just then Stephenson came out of the office with the signed statement he'd just completed. When he saw that I was talking to his wife, he just dropped, open-mouthed, into the nearest chair. I asked him, "Mr. Stephenson, isn't the brooch your wife is wearing something you bought with money that did not belong to you?"

"It certainly is."

After that, she handed it over. But she still did not have any feeling for him, the man whose three children she'd brought into the world. And I felt then that he was like a great many white-collar thieves who are married to women who have no consideration or affection for them. I may be wrong, but it seems to me that such a man does not love the other woman in his life, even though she is invariably more sexy than his wife. The wife just did not give him whatever he wanted of a woman. It could be passion that he found lacking. But just as often it was, I think, that lack of consideration which the woman he kept either felt for him or pretended to feel.

Mrs. Stephenson, not heeding her husband's protests, had plunged into a way of living that he could not sustain. A weak man, he began stealing, and when the vivacious Miss Durand started to work for him he could see no reason not to start stealing enough more to support her in the style she'd never been able to afford on her clerk's salary.

Mrs. Stephenson had not once asked, "Can we afford it?" She had just gone ahead and bought what she liked, to impress her friends and neighbors.

The amount Stephenson had stolen over a period of years came to exactly $78,924.59. I don't know how much he embezzled from the estate. Since becoming Miss Durand's "sponsor," he had been embezzling each year about twice what he earned.

There were two unforgettable oddities in this case, by the way.

From the day he started appropriating the company's money, Mr. Stephenson seemed to have hypnotized himself into believing that he would someday be able to put back every cent of it. At home he had kept a precise account of his thefts, adding the amount and the date each time he took more.

The other oddity was that the cashier who was vacationing had caught on to this, and had began stealing smaller amounts himself. His take amounted to $3,500. Next, his rosy-cheeked assistant, Mr.

Knowles, in turn became aware of the thievery of the other two and began stealing small sums himself. His thefts were modest. He swiped only $500, and took money when he wanted to take his girl out for a very big evening.

None of the three went to prison.

Relatives and friends, I was later informed, gave the Collier Company everything the three men had stolen. I never asked later what became of the three semipartners in crime. Not that I was not curious about them, and the two women, Mrs. Stephenson and Miss Durand. But I have found that clients are happier if I do not inquire about the fate of men they trusted and who took advantage of them. They preferred to forget them, just as we all like to forget our past mistakes.

WHITE-COLLAR THIEVES, BLUE-COLLAR THIEVES

9

THOUGH I usually felt sorry for white-collar men who turned to stealing, I cannot say my heart was twisted by pity for Mr. Stephenson. I could understand a man being so weak he could not stop his strong-minded wife from spending too much money, or turning to a young mistress because whatever he wanted from a woman he did not find at home. It was letting his devoted friends front for him until one of them made a spectacle of himself that made me despise the man. The loyalty of Mr. Kennedy and Mr. Beck should have been better rewarded.

But who wouldn't feel sorry for some of the others?

The mild-mannered hat salesman who worked for years for Rogers Peet Company, the New York men's clothing store, is a good example. After he was trapped with marked bills, I asked:

"Why did you do this?"

He burst into tears.

Three years before, his son (he said) had been in a terrible accident. His doctor told him that one surgeon alone could save the youth's life. But the clerk could not scrape enough money together to pay this surgeon's $3,000 fee. He asked one of his superiors if the firm would lend him what he needed, and was turned down. Another less expensive surgeon was hired. The boy died on the operating table.

Nothing could convince the little salesman that the first surgeon also might not have been able to save his boy. He began to hate the store in which he'd worked for so long. Not knowing how else to revenge himself, he began to steal.

The sales checking and accounting systems in the store at the time were very inefficiently run. Whenever he saw the chance, he kept the money after selling a hat. But he did not spend one cent of this money. Instead he put everything he took in this way into a safe-deposit box.

I pleaded against his being arrested. I had to plead. His superior, the one who had refused to pass on his request for a loan to the heads of the company, was intent on his being taken to the station house, but this man agreed that the final decision must rest with the higher-ups. The salesman was allowed to go home that night.

The next day he took me to his bank, opened the safe-deposit box, and handed me all the money he'd stolen — $2,870. Mr. Frank Turnbull, president of Rogers Peet, was shocked when he learned of the case. Not only did he refuse to bring charges against the salesman; he got him a job in another department store.

Down through the years I had hundreds of cases in which little people who felt frustrated, defeated, utterly unhappy, stole from their employers. Bank tellers, always underpaid, handle thousands of dollars every day. It seemed only human to me that some of them would take a little of the bank's money to bet on a long shot, and then get in deeper and deeper up to the very day they were caught. Cashiers in theaters, restaurants, and other businesses who handled large amounts of cash were also often tempted for what usually began as a small flutter.

Again and again I felt sorry for white-collar thieves who almost fainted in astonishment when caught because they were so cocksure they'd covered up their tracks.

One of the most pathetic of all was the manager of an Austin-Nichols branch grocery. He stole petty sums from the company for about fifteen years, amassing $60,000 before he was caught. He also kept the money he stole in a safe-deposit box. But his reason for stealing was different. He was a miser with a phobia about going hungry in his old age. This nightmarish fear drove him into robbing his employer — all it got him was disgrace and loss of his job. I was able to save him from prison, getting the consent of the local law authorities after he made complete restitution.

But I could not feel sorry for Ed McIntyre, the shipping clerk of the same Rogers Peet Store at which the hat salesman worked. He had only one purpose in stealing: to live like a king, and, I must say, he managed it for years.

McIntyre was a big man who had such a big head that he had to wear a size nine hat. McIntyre worked for the store for fifteen years, and had started as a fourteen-year-old errand boy. He was considered a scrupulous, honest, and hard-working young man. At twenty-nine he was still a bachelor and lived in the Bronx with his widowed mother. McIntyre earned $150 a month, which at the time was more than enough to support a fairly large family.

As you will see, McIntyre's larceny of a fortune, like the smaller thefts of the hat salesman, was possible only because of the store's loose-jointed accounting and inventory systems. Most Rogers Peet deliveries were made by truck. But the store also had ten delivery boys who rushed purchases to those customers who were in a hurry.

McIntyre was the boss of these boys. They turned over to him the money they collected on C.O.D. orders and also any merchandise that was rejected. In making out his daily report, the shipping clerk included these transactions. After the report was approved by Ronald Widdicomb, the store's manager, he gave the report and the C.O.D. money to the cashier. Persons with charge accounts had the charges for whatever they returned deducted from their bills. The C.O.D. transactions were marked canceled. McIntyre also had charge of putting the rejected articles back in stock. He filled out individual cards that described the merchandise customers had sent back. Mr. Widdicomb approved the cards by punching a hole in each one. The shipping clerk then brought the cards to the bookkeeping department, which filed them.

By the time he had become a shipping clerk, eight years earlier, McIntyre had figured out how he could swindle the store. Some of the C.O.D. cash the boys brought to him he began to pocket. These thefts he covered up by listing all such items on his daily report as returned merchandise.

Soon Ed McIntyre was really living it up. And with him, generosity began at home. He told his mother he had been made an officer of Rogers Peet Company, and increased her house money to $200 a month, $50 more than the store was paying him. Mrs. McIntyre's old biddy friends envied her because she had so freehanded and successful a son. Ed confided to his mother, his girl, and his friends that as an officer of Rogers Peet and Company his salary was $450 a month, plus bonuses.

McIntyre was engaged to a pert, pretty Irish girl who was the envy of all *her* friends. The $2,000 diamond ring McIntyre had pledged their troth with was the talk of the office she worked in. When they went out on the town, McIntyre always spent a lot of money. They would have dinner at some expensive restaurant, then buy tickets from a speculator for one of the Broadway musicals, and would finish up the night with a visit to a nightclub. McIntyre was lavish with tips to headwaiters, waiters, and cabdrivers. He spent about $50, or more than his weekly wages, on each of these dates. The girl, a sweet, respectable young person, tried in vain to induce him to take it a little slow.

Once again it was pure chance that eventually brought about this thief's exposure. One day, while passing through the suit department, Mr. Widdicomb was hailed by one of the salesmen. He said: "Mr. Widdicomb I'd like to have you meet George Evans, a neighbor of mine, in Nutley. I only wish I had a thousand other neighbors like him. He just bought two suits from me."

While in the shipping department down in the basement a few days later, Mr. Widdicomb noticed half a dozen suits lying on a counter. He asked McIntyre what they were there for. "They've been returned," he said. On the shipping clerk's report that day the store manager happened to notice among the suits listed as "Not Wanted" the two that had been sent C.O.D. to George Evans of Nutley, New Jersey.

On seeing the salesman next day, Mr. Widdicomb asked, "Why did Mr. Evans return the suits you sent him?"

The salesman seemed astonished. "He didn't return them, sir. Why, I met him just this morning on the train coming to work. He had one of the suits on, and told me how much he liked it."

The puzzled Mr. Widdicomb sent for his shipping clerk. "Do you recall shipping two suits to a George Evans in Nutley last week?" asked the manager.

"No, I don't," said McIntyre.

"It was a C.O.D. order. And the customer refused delivery."

McIntyre promised to check on it. Mr. Widdicomb assumed a mistake of some sort had been made which the shipping clerk would explain. But Ed McIntyre did not come back the next day, nor the one after that. Nor did he have anyone call up to say he was sick.

A little belatedly Mr. Widdicomb became suspicious, and telephoned McIntyre's home. His mother sounded frantic. She said she was worried to death herself about Ed. He hadn't been home for two days, nor had she heard anything from him.

Like most of the store's other employees, the shipping clerk was bonded by the Ocean Company for $10,000. On being notified of McIntyre's disappearance, I sent a man to his neighborhood in the Bronx to find out everything he could about the man.

Meanwhile I went to the store. After discussing the matter with Jesse Brundage, the store's treasurer, who liked to work with me personally on investigations, we interviewed the salesman, Mr. Widdicomb, McIntyre's assistant, and others who worked with him in the shipping room. The sixteen-year-old boy who delivered the two suits to the Evans home recalled that errand very clearly. The reason was that Mrs. Evans gave him a one-dollar tip when paying for the two suits. On going back to the store, he had given the C.O.D. money, as usual, to Mr. McIntyre. A routine check later cleared this boy of any suspicion of collusion.

Edward Rapp, McIntyre's assistant, had been working for Rogers Peet for only a brief time. He said that if there had been irregularities in the department he knew nothing about them. The others who worked with McIntyre said the same thing. But Rapp told us one thing that indicated the shipping clerk's swindle might turn out to be a very big one. "I often would hear him make bets of as much as $250 on the phone," said Rapp. "And now I think of it, there *was* one guy who knew him on the outside that I did see, even though I don't know what his name is. This was McIntyre's bookmaker. He'd come in here almost every day, either to pay off Ed or to collect. It seemed to me that he collected about three times as often as he paid off Ed."

The best way to start finding out just how much McIntyre had stolen was to check the record of merchandise returned to the various departments against the items marked "Not Wanted" on the shipping clerk's daily reports.

That was where the officers of Rogers Peet got the shock of their lives. None of the department heads had kept any such records. Mr. Widdicomb was horrified, and admitted he should have checked up on the shipping clerk. "But I trusted that man," he said. "He worked for the store as a boy, as I have." Mr. Widdicomb also pointed out that he was doing the work of four men in the store.

This could not be denied, though it was still no adequate excuse for such astonishing inefficiency.

It seemed impossible that Ed McIntyre, the man who wore size nine hats, could have worked this lucrative racket without help of other employees. But this, as far as we could ever find out, was the case. We investigated everyone in the store who had anything to do with his operations, including Mr. Widdicomb. All proved to be beyond suspicion.

The deeper accountants dug into the records, the more losses attributable to McIntyre were uncovered. It soon appeared that he had stolen at least $25,000 with his faked-returns trick. Later the books showed the sum was closer to $50,000.

His mother, an honest, humble old Irishwoman, was heartbroken. She feared that Ed would kill himself rather than go to prison.

But she begged us to find him. Just to know he was alive would be a relief to her mother's heart, she said. As an honest, God-fearing woman she also believed it right that he should return and face the consequences. One day the poor old woman brought out to me some pieces of jewelry her son had bought her.

"They belong to the store, that they do," she said. "And there is $700 I saved, like the thrifty woman I am, out of the money that my poor misguided lad gave me for the house. This, too, belongs to the store, and I will thank you to take it. And I will also work as a scrubwoman, night and day, and get a little more each week to give them back."

I told her that I was sure the store wanted neither her jewelry nor her small savings nor any part of her wages for scrubbing floors.

The girl, a true Irish beauty with rose-petal complexion, tip-tilted nose, and a pretty figure, was less surprised at the disaster than Mrs. McIntyre had been.

"Oh, he spent so much money I was afraid that something like this would happen," she said, after she got over her first crying spell. She offered to give me the $2,000 engagement ring to sell to apply to the store's losses.

I told her exactly what I had told Mrs. McIntyre: that the store would not take it. And my guess was correct. It was the store, by the way, that was going to have to absorb the largest part of the loss. We had bonded their shipping clerk for $10,000. Any loss above that, the company had to pay.

One day I got a tip that McIntyre was living in a boardinghouse at Revere Beach, a suburb of Boston. I took the train to Boston and wired a company claims agent to meet me at the station. Before going to the address, we went to the Revere Beach police station, which sent a policeman along to help us with the arrest.

McIntyre knew me, so I kept out of sight while the other two men went to the door of the boardinghouse. An old Irishman answered their ring and said, "No, no Mr. McIntyre is living here."

I'd given the claims agent a good description of the shipping clerk, and mentioned his size nine head. On being told about that, the boardinghouse keeper shouted: "We have a man with a watermelon of a head here, but you got the name wrong. He's Ed Ryan, the feller you want, and you'll find him right now in the room on the first floor back."

The claims agent and the policeman raced to the room, but it was empty. Mr. McIntyre-Ryan may have heard the conversation and left by the back door. We sent out an alarm for him, but he never was apprehended.

However, Rogers Peet paid tribute to his ingenuity by installing a bookkeeping system which made such thefts impossible.

*

ANOTHER horny-handed son of toil right after World War II accumulated $100,000 by an even simpler trick. Before he was caught he managed to stop cold an army of investigators, including F.B.I. men, state and local policemen across the country, and the combined detective forces of the Railway Express Company and several railroads.

He did it by stealing cartons, bales, and bags of raw furs en route from fur-breeding farms in the Middle West and Southwest to eastern dealers. I got into the act fairly late, following the disappearance of a $10,000 consignment of mink from the Triple C. Fur Farm in Fort Atkinson, Wisconsin, to the New York Fur Auction Company. The latter firm was insured by St. Paul under a policy that covered all such shipments from fur ranchers it dealt with.

I spent a busy week following the route over which the furs had been sent. I started from Fort Atkinson, went to the first junction point at Janesville, and on from there to Chicago and New York, and ended with no clues whatever. The thief could have been anyone who handled the furs. That included workers on three railroads, the Railway Express men, the truck-company men at the various terminals where the cartons of mink were transferred from one of the freight cars of one railroad to another. It could have been an outsider. Or, for that matter, employees of the New York firm itself. I was investigating the auction company's people when I was informed that the F.B.I. office in Cleveland had nabbed a long-sought fur thief there.

The arrested man, Anthony Alan Fusco, was another caught by accident. An Ohio farm rancher who'd recently lost shipments en route to New York came to the big town on business. While visiting a dealer who was an old customer, he was told that a Cleveland man named Anthony Alan Fusco was selling furs far below market prices.

"I don't know how he does it," the New Yorker said.

The fur rancher asked if he could see the furs. On examining them he observed that some of the pelts had been stamped with his farm's trademark. He got Fusco's name and address. And on getting back to Cleveland, he reported the matter to the F.B.I.

The F.B.I. obtained a search warrant and raided the suspect's home. Fusco confessed at once. He explained that he had struck on his original idea in 1945, three years before, soon after he got a job working for the Railway Express as a freight loader at the Cleveland Union Terminal. He saw that many raw-fur shipments were coming through on trains, mostly from points in the Southwest. Other shipments of pelts from Ohio fur farmers were being shipped from Cleveland.

Fusco stole cartons of pelts by taking off the tags and replacing them with ones addressed to his wife. At night he broke up these shipments, removed all tags and labels, and repacked them in cartons of his own.

He then sold these to dealers in the East who advertised for pelts in the "Furs Wanted" columns of a trade paper.

Fusco swore that neither his wife nor anyone else helped him or had knowledge of what he was doing. The fact that he was a very methodical crook saved the F.B.I. a great deal of work. From the day he went into business, he had kept complete records of all his transactions. These gave the names of the dealers and the amounts they'd paid for his hot furs. For some reason Fusco also kept a careful record of the shippers, consignees, and what sort of furs had been in each lot. In two years he had taken in $117,000 selling at bargain prices. He had also stolen in the same way a Scott Atwater Outboard, an electric roasting oven, and a Mixmaster for his own use.

What pleased his victims most of all, though, was Mr. Fusco's thrift. He had in his house $57,000 in cash and $11,000 in United States Government bonds, not to mentiton $500 worth of traveler's checks. He and Mrs. Fusco also maintained joint bank accounts in banks and savings and loan associations all over Cleveland, its suburbs, and in Columbus, Ohio. Fusco, a frank chap, admitted that only a tiny fraction of these savings had been honestly earned.

There was also $8,000 due him from dealers. The only honest fur deal he'd made, Fusco said, was the purchase of about $500 for pelts he bought from part-time trappers in Ohio. Fusco had amassed a fortune of $93,800. All of it went back to the firms he had robbed. Fusco pleaded guilty in Federal Court to the theft of interstate shipments, and was sentenced to two years' imprisonment on each count. I visited him there in 1948. With me were two lawyers, one from the St. Paul Company, another from Railway Express. We questioned Fusco for several hours, but he insisted that he knew nothing about the vanished Fort Atkinson shipment. And that lot was never traced.

After men are in prison for a while they like to talk. Fusco answered all of our questions freely, but kept to the line that his was a one-person operation. He was a very tough man, Mr. Fusco, and showed neither remorse nor bitterness at being caught and in prison. His attitude was that he'd taken a smart gamble, and lost, and that there was no use complaining about it.

What the Tony Fuscos of this world never seem to realize is that in such gambles they have to lose. The accident that enabled the law to catch up with him was inevitable, and would sooner or later have happened under other circumstances.

I was once asked to investigate the disappearance of thousands of gallons of cider from the Wayne County Cider Company in Brooklyn. Its plant occupied an entire four-story building.

The loading platform seemed to me the most important place

to be watched. The owners replied they had been watching the men who worked there and also in the other departments without catching anyone. I arranged for the firm to hire three of my under-cover men. One was given a job in the receiving department, an-other became a general utility man, and the third was on the plat-form as a loader.

This last man, Jake Breslin, looked the part, being a powerful man though short. He was bald and a born actor. His one short-coming as a detective was his curious superstition about beggars. He believed that if three beggars in a row asked him for a handout, it was certain to bring him bad luck. While shadowing someone on a busy street, this sometimes happened. Whenever it did, Jake would lose control of himself and all but throttle the third beggar. This, of course, drew so much attention to him that he had to be replaced.

The combination of Jake's looks and acting talents was most valuable in jobs that brought him into contact with roughnecks. His favorite role was that of a deaf man. It was not an easy part to play, because his fellow workers often prankishly tested his hear-ing by exploding firecrackers behind him. Or they would suddenly yell, "Fire!" or "Look out! That steel beam is going to hit you!"

Jake had nerves of iron, however, and never gave himself away. At the cider factory the other employees soon became accustomed to the idea they must holler at him in order to be heard. They got in the habit gradually of talking freely before him.

Before he'd been on the job for very long, he saw how the steal-ing was done. It was simplicity itself. The thieves put more jugs of cider than had been ordered on the trucks of the drivers who were in on the swindle.

I had my men tail these trucks each day. Their instructions were to make a note of each stop and the amount of cider delivered there. By comparing these deliveries and the actual orders, we soon knew who the receivers of the stolen cider were.

As always, I had informed the police in that precinct what I was doing. When I was ready to arrest the dishonest loaders and drivers, I asked a detective to go to the cider plant with me. I thought the smart move was to arrest Jake first. We grabbed him right there on the platform and belted him around a bit. We yelled our lungs out at him. "Don't tell us you didn't steal all that cider!" we kept saying for the benefit of the other loaders. "We have proof of it."

When we took him off to the station house, he ruefully rubbed his jaw. "You didn't have to be that realistic, Chief," he told me.

At the station house Jake told the desk lieutenant the names of seven men he believed composed the cider-stealing ring. He believed one of the loaders, Bill Ward, was the weakest of the lot and would be the easiest to break. Bill Ward was arrested, but proved a lot tougher than Jake imagined he'd be. For two hours he refused to admit under intense questioning that he had stolen any cider or knew about such thefts by his fellow workers.

We were running out of steam when I thought of taking him to Jake's cell.

I yelled through the bars at Jake, "I want you to tell the truth now, Jake."

"What's that? What's that?" he asked, cupping his ear.

"This man here thinks we'll beat him up if he tells us the truth about stealing the cider. So tell him what happened to you. Did we lay a hand on you, Jake, after you confessed stealing over twenty jugs of cider?"

"No," said Jake, "I'm glad I spilled it to you."

I turned to Bill Ward. "What do you say, Bill? Shall we put you in one of these cells — or do you want to talk?"

Bill looked around the filthy, desolate-looking cell. "I'll talk," he said. He confirmed Jake's story that if forty jugs of cider were ordered, fifty would be hauled from the stockroom to the platform. The checker was in on the swindle.

We brought the three other dishonest loaders to the station house and the two drivers later on. Each man was questioned separately. At three the next morning we had confessions from all of them. By that time Jake had been out of his cell for hours. During the evening he became so sick that he had to be rushed to a hospital. It was his greatest acting job, as I told him.

None of them had police records. And though they admitted that they had stolen thousands of gallons of cider, which they sold at a reduced price, they could not be charged with grand larceny, only petty larceny. This because the value of the cider in none of their many thefts was worth $50 or more. The storekeepers who had been buying the jugs from them at reduced prices could not be charged with anything. Each of them claimed the same thing: he had not known that the cider he bought was stolen.

The company also decided to drop the charges against the employees, and merely fire them. But the company did devise a better system of checking outgoing orders and managed to plug up the great cider leak.

*

COPING with the streamlined methods of the gangs who hijack trucks, loot terminals, warehouses and wharves is another story.

Between 1944 and 1951, as special investigator of the St. Paul Fire and Marine Company, I tried to solve the losses of a dozen or so of the largest American trucking firms and many smaller ones. Their losses from hijacking alone ran into hundreds of thousands of dollars each year. I had very little success, was able to jail few of the crooks, and recovered little of the stuff they stole.

Hijackers have no trademark, and leave no "calling card" as a clue, as do most other thieves. They all operate in about the same way. Four or five of them in a car force a truck to stop on a lonely stretch of road. Pulling their guns, the hijackers order the two or three men on the truck to get out and make them lie on the floor or back seat of the car. One hijacker drives this away. Another keeps his gun on the truckmen. The others drive the truck either straight into the receiver's warehouse or transfer the load to another truck at some other lonely spot. The truckmen are released miles away.

Many trucks full of valuable merchandise have been hijacked in front of diners where the crew stopped to eat. Others have been stolen in front of the driver's house while he is catching up on his sleep. It is not too unusual for daring hijackers to take over trucks at gun's point on busy streets in New York and other cities.

Many additional millions of dollars are stolen every year from terminals, the manufacturer's parking lot, or the garage of the company that ordered the load but had not had time to pack it.

One reason this stolen merchandise is so rarely recovered is that invariably the thieves have completed all arrangements to sell and deliver it before they steal it. In fact, this huge and fantastic racket is so well organized that these thieves steal on order, according to the laws of supply and demand. Whatever their customers say is in short supply — rayons, cotton goods, tobacco, liquor, or drugs — these crooks steal for them.

What may surprise many people is that though the Teamsters

Union has long been dominated by thieves and gangsters, all but a few of the union's members refuse to work with the hijacking gangs. That's my experience.

I've seen figures on merchandise stolen in transit put at $65,000,-000 a year. It would amount to much more if not for the F.B.I. It is the chaotic nature of the trucking business itself that makes for such rich pickings by the underworld. The thieves seem to have everything going for them — conflicting state laws, union rules, Interstate Commerce Commission regulations which handcuff the operations of the trucking concerns and so harass them with problems that many have neither the time nor the inclination to cooperate with insurance-company investigators. Some take the attitude that they pay such high insurance rates that the insurance men can solve the crimes without their help. After many bitter experiences I came to the conclusion that unless the trucking concerns, the police of various cities and states, and the Federal authorities work together nothing can halt the continued growth of the flourishing hijacking trade and the massive larceny of goods in transit.

District Attorney Frank Hogan of New York, as honest an official as the big town ever knew, once declared that he could stop racketeering on the waterfront in short order if the shipline owners and the companies that lease the docks and the trucking magnates would cooperate.

These businessmen ignored him. Apparently all have felt that it is easier and more profitable to keep doing business in that way, paying tribute to thugs, protection money to crooked union officials and other racketeers. The men who run a hundred and one other businesses in New York and other of our great cities have the same policy, whether they are dress manufacturers, publish newspapers, or sell fish and produce. If you ask one of them why they subsidize the underworld in this shocking way, he will tell you: "I myself consider it a disgraceful situation. I'd like very much to get rid of these parasites. But as long as my competitors do it, I have to."

Ask the competitors, and they will give you the same answer.

*

BURGLARY, which is one of the oldest forms of stealing, has resisted the trend of the underworld to run in packs. It is still largely a trade that attracts individualists. I've had to cope with burglars all my life, and I suppose this is one of the reasons I resent so bitterly the legend that a fellow like Jerry Dennis is a Jimmy Valentine or has the charm of a Raffles. Whatever they steal, they are all sneak thieves who have given more men, women, and children nightmares than the H-bomb.

My war with burglars started years before my shooting match with Mr. and Mrs. Vogel in 1911, and has not ended yet. I still sleep each night with a loaded revolver at my side. So does my wife.

But I've had all sorts of experiences with them, including hilarious ones. One occurred in Englewood, New Jersey. There had been a series of house burglaries in Englewood and surrounding communities, and the losses from these amounted to more than $50,000. Thanks to Mr. Vogel, I was still limping and using a cane.

Floyd R. Dubois, Ocean's General Agent in New Jersey, who lived in Englewood, was eager that I devote a week or two of my time to an attempt to end the burglaries. The whole area had been terrorized by these crimes. The company's General Manager Oscar Ising said Ocean would pay all expenses and urged me to take on the job. "The company has insured so many homes in New Jersey that it would be well worth it to us."

I honestly thought that a limping man like me was not the perfect choice. But Mr. Dubois said that the local state detectives had failed to stop the burglaries, and so had private detectives they'd employed. He was secretary of an emergency committee called "Citizen Volunteers" which had been organized to do something about the marauders. They and Vernon Munroe, Mayor of Englewood, were eager for me to take over. I must say I was greatly flattered, and accepted the assignment.

When I met Frank Titus, the town's chief of police, he also seemed happy that I had been drafted for the assignment. As it turned out, he did not have enough men to police properly a growing community of Englewood's size. But he said he'd cooperate and could guarantee that his men would give me their wholehearted help.

In the past few months there had been thirteen homes robbed, he said. From the details of these jobs he gave me I concluded they'd all been the work of one mob of professionals. They used jimmies to open windows, took only clothes, jewels, and objets d'art of value. I got a list of these articles. But the most significant thing was that all the robbed homes were looted while the owners and their families were out of town. That sounded like someone who knew when the houses would be empty was tipping them off. It might be one of Chief Titus' men.

"Did all of these families call up Headquarters to ask that the house be watched because they were going away?"

"In practically no case."

That all but eliminated the theory that the thieves had a co-operative policeman working with them. I put the "Leech" and another undercover man to work checking on known burglars in New Jersey and also New York. I gave a copy of the list of stolen articles to police in both states, but none of the stolen stuff turned up.

Before long the Leech, always a wonder at remaining inconspicuous, had something interesting to report. He had been shadowing "The Bergen Gang," a notorious mob that worked out of the Bronx, across the river.

The Leech had observed three of the gang eating in a diner the night before. One of the burglars was reading newspaper items to the other two. When they finished eating they took a trolley to the Hudson River ferry which then ran between Harlem and Fort Lee, a town not far from Englewood. There they took a trolley to Englewood. On getting there they had walked up Engle Street, the town's main residential street. The burglars stopped before a home and looked it over for a few minutes. They then returned to the Bronx where they spent the rest of the evening in a poolroom.

The Leech had the newspaper he'd seen one of the men reading from aloud. He'd picked it up after he saw the suspect discard it. The newspaper was a copy of the *Englewood Express,* a weekly newspaper.

The Leech took Chief Titus and me to the house on Engle Street which he'd seen the suspects case. The chief said that Mr. and Mrs. George W. Hooven lived there. But nobody answered our knock. The Hoovens, neighbors told us, had gone out of town.

The chief hadn't known that. But the Bergen Gang had. We looked through the *Express* and found this item on the society page:

> Mr. and Mrs. George W. Hooven,
> of 475 Engle Street, are vacationing
> for the next two weeks at the Prince
> House in Lakewood.

Now we at least knew that the burglars were getting their tips on where to do their housebreaking next from the society column.

We lost no time in getting Mr. Hooven on the phone. We explained the situation, and advised him to keep his family in Lakewood. We told him that we thought the best place to wait for the burglars was in his home. If he'd lend us the key, we'd send a man to pick it up.

That night three of us, Titus, my assistant, Charles Gordon, and myself were in the Hooven house, waiting for the Bergen Gang to fall into our laps. We planned very carefully how to trap them. One Englewood cop was guarding the front door from behind some trees; another was concealed in the garage, behind the house, with Kaiser Bill, the chief's slashing, dashing, gnashing German police dog.

"You're sure," I asked Chief Titus, "that your four-footed Sherlock is the world's most ferocious manhunter and can catch anything alive? We have spent much time making sure that this eighty-pound Sherlock Holmes realizes what side Gordon and I are on."

"Certainly he does," said Titus. "But Kaiser Bill will rip out the throat of any thief whose scent he detects — if I'm not there to control him."

"I hope he won't scare them away by barking."

"He's too intelligent for that."

Having no such faith in Kaiser Bill, Gordon and I had spent hours petting this monstrous canine, feeding him scraps of choice meat, and otherwise trying to make sure we wouldn't get chewed up and so become victims of mistaken identity. But I stopped worrying about the police dog that night as we waited in that freezing house. It was December, and the heat had been turned off. The chief and I were in the kitchen, and Gordon was in the front room looking out of the window. He could alert us the moment he spotted our visitors approaching.

We waited until dawn. I had never been colder in my life.

The burglars didn't come.

Nor did they come the next night, which was just as cold.

So was the third night.

But at one-thirty in the morning, on our third night in that big freezing house, three members of the Bergen Gang crept down Engle Street. Gordon hastened back to tell us that they were coming down the alley adjoining the house.

With Gordon we huddled there in the kitchen, waiting for them. We got our guns out. Just in time, for soon we could hear someone skillfully jimmying open a kitchen window a few feet from us. It was pushed up, and one burglar, then another, climbed through. But Gordon had said there were three of them. We wanted all of them in the house. Then, from outside, we heard the third man say quietly, "Put on your flashlight."

A flashlight went on. As it moved around the room and close to us, Chief Titus and I both yelled, "Hands up!"

As for what happened next, I can only say I've never seen a faster getaway. Before we could move, both men jumped through the window. Despite my game leg I got through the window next, and started after them in the dark. "Stop or I'll fire!" I shouted. No one stopped. Just then I saw a flash about twenty-five feet ahead, and fired in its general direction. I heard a man fall on the ground, but the other two kept on running in the dark. Yelling, "Get the other two!" I ran up to the fallen man and slammed him over the head with the butt of my gun.

As I leaned over his prostrate form, I could hear the others shouting, and running, but they hesitated to shoot in the dark, fearing to hit one another.

"Get the others!" I yelled again. Just then a big hairy thing jumped on me, almost knocking me off my feet. You guessed it! It was the chief's wonder canine, old fierce, furious Kaiser Bill.

He ignored the two running burglars, who had disappeared by that time into a wood adjacent to the Hooven property and were making their getaway.

We thought they would head for the Fort Lee Ferry. I turned my man over to one of the Englewood cops and we headed for the ferry landing. But no one vaguely resembling a burglar showed up. After waiting there for an hour, we left Gordon and an Englewood detective to watch out for the thieves.

But on getting back to the Englewood police station to interview the captured man, we got a break. The arrested man had a lump on his head but was otherwise undamaged. I had not shot him. He explained that he had dropped to the ground on hearing the shot. But that is all he would tell us.

He had a railway ticket in his pocket. It was for a Pullman berth on a train to Pittsburgh that was scheduled to leave New York early that morning.

Now we had an explanation as to why the two missing burglars had avoided the Fort Lee Ferry. If one or both of them were going to Pittsburgh, they would have to catch that early train at Manhattan Transfer, the junction point in New Jersey, which they could reach in time.

I got hold of the Leech and had him meet us at that station. I wanted him to watch passengers get on that train with me. If we missed them, we could go through the cars, giving the Leech a second chance to identify the men.

The train came in. As the crowd surged forward, the Leech nudged me and pointed out a man. He had a deep, freshly made gash across his nose. "That's one of the guys!" he said. We closed in on him fast.

"I haven't done nothing," he protested as we placed him under arrest.

By the time we got to Englewood Headquarters, he admitted he was one of the Bergen Gang and had come to Englewood that night with two pals to burglarize the Hooven home. He'd gashed his nose while getting away from us. He'd run into a wire fence in the dark. He'd come with a gun but had thrown it away. When morning came he helped us find it.

Both burglars refused to say who the man who got away was. Both men, James H. Fay, twenty-eight, and John J. Connelly, twenty-five, later pleaded guilty and were sentenced to indeterminate terms in the New Jersey Reformatory.

The third man was never caught, but the epidemic of Englewood robberies was ended. The town gave me a $500 reward and a letter of commendation. I divided the money among the Leech, Gordon, and the other assistants who'd worked with me on the case. The letter I kept, as I have the many other letters of commendation I've received from other communities.

*

A GREAT many years later there was a similar epidemic of burglaries in another fashionable New York suburb, this one New Rochelle, in Westchester County. I entered the case after the seventh crime in the series. This burglary was in the home of Mr. and Mrs. Frank Stone, who were insured against such thefts by a company that employed me.

On this evening the couple had gone out just before ten o'clock. They returned at one, a little more than three hours later, to find their home looted of jewelry, clothing, silverware, and bric-a-brac. The thief had left a trademark, an overcoat.

Edward J. Timmons, the suburb's chief of police, told me that the coat the burglar left behind was one he had stolen in the last house he'd robbed.

"And he has done that same thing several times," Timmons said. "If an overcoat in the house fits him, he will take it and leave the one he picked up on the last job."

Timmons said the burglar didn't favor tweeds or any other particular color or style of overcoat. Detective Frank Cody, who succeeded Chief Timmons when the latter retired, was assigned to the burglaries investigation. He said he'd get in touch with me if anything else developed.

Cody called me a few nights later at my home. The burglar had pulled another job. Again he had taken a new coat, and left Mr. Stone's.

I got up to New Rochelle in a hurry. Waiting with Cody for me was Lieutenant Joseph Fanelli, who ran the detective bureau. I'd heard he was a brilliant detective and was glad to meet him. On a table I saw the coat that Mr. Stone had described in his list of articles he'd lost. I picked it up and started to go through the pockets. Lieutenant Fanelli didn't care much for this.

"Luisi!" he protested, "we have already searched the pockets. We didn't miss anything. We took everything out of them."

"Did you search the pockets personally, Lieutenant?"

"No, but I had one of my best men do it."

"I hope you don't mind my searching them," I said. Before he could reply I was started. Fanelli, Cody, and another detective who was in the room, watched me. And in the inside pocket of the overcoat I found a little rolled-up wad of paper. When I pulled it out Fanelli was incredulous. He seemed to think I'd taken it from my own pocket.

"What are you doing, Luisi?" he demanded. "Playing tricks?"

"Not in working hours," I told him as I rolled the paper flat.

The piece of paper was a receipt for fifty cents. It was for room rent at the uptown Mills Hotel in New York. This was one of two nonprofit hotels built by the Mills family for indigents who wanted to avoid sleeping in a Bowery flophouse.

The downtown Mills was near Greenwich Village. For fifty cents a night a man could get a clean room at either one.

Within minutes Detective Cody and I were on our way to the uptown Mills Hotel. Before going to the hotel, we stopped at the precinct police station. A detective was assigned to accompany us in case we made an arrest.

We got to the hotel at 3:00 A.M. The night clerk was asleep, and we had to wake him up. After looking at the receipt he said he'd made it out to a customer named Morgan. He described Morgan as a tall, slim youth of about twenty with brown hair and a fair complexion.

"He usually checks in about this time," the clerk told us, "but he hasn't come in so far tonight."

"Is there a place that we could sit around here where he wouldn't see us? We want to watch the desk and also the door." The clerk took us to a little anteroom. We could watch the desk and also the front door from there. And we'd keep the light out so he couldn't spot us.

"Scratch your head when Morgan checks in," Cody told the clerk. "And let him go upstairs to the room. We'll arrest him there."

The three of us waited all night. Morgan didn't show up. At eight in the morning the New York detective went home, saying he'd be back at six that evening. Cody and I were determined to sit it out until our man walked in. When the New York detective did come back, he told us he'd been given another assignment, and he went away. Which emphasizes the advantage I usually had over police detectives. I could stay with an investigation as long as it made sense.

Cody in this case could also stay on the one job. But this was only because the burglaries he was working on were the important crimes of the year in New Rochelle. The citizens were up in arms about them.

That morning, after the New York man left, I suggested that Cody rent a room upstairs and get a few hours' sleep, then he could spell me. But he'd have none of that. He was my kind of cop. When and if the young burglar checked in, he wanted to be there to arrest him. The result was that the two of us waited together in that downstairs anteroom all of that day, through the next night, and the following day. By the third morning Cody and I both felt licked. Our bodies felt numb. But, like two stubborn kids, neither of us would admit the other had more stamina.

At one o'clock on the third night, after we'd been sitting in that room for seventy hours, the break came. Harry Morgan walked in, carrying a suitcase in his left hand, and registered. The clerk scratched his head. He checked Morgan in, handed him a room key. Morgan took it and went upstairs in the elevator. We got the room number, which was 319. When the elevator came down we took it to the third floor.

With Cody behind me, I knocked on the door of Room 319. We were both breathless.

"Who is there?" asked Morgan.

"The clerk," I said.

"What do you want?"

"I don't think I gave you enough change, so I brought it up."

The burglar opened the door and we rushed in, forcing him back into the room. I saw the suspect reach for his hip pocket. I pulled my gun out with my right hand and with my left grabbed his right hand, which, as it turned out, was already on his gun. In no time Cody was in back of him and had wrenched away the burglar's weapon.

After that, Morgan did not put up much of a fight against us two old huskies. He readily confessed that he had committed all the New Rochelle burglaries. He had hocked most of the loot and still had the tickets. In the suitcase were the jewelry, silverware, and bric-a-brac he'd taken in that night's haul. Because of this we recovered 90 percent of the loot of his previous jobs. In these cases it is the policy of the insurance company to pay the pawnbroker the money he has loaned. This is seldom, pawnbrokers being what they are, more than a very small fraction of the value of these articles.

Morgan told us that the reason he hadn't checked in at the hotel before was that he'd been sleeping in the downtown Mills. He checked in at whatever one he was closest to, he said, when he decided to go to bed.

Morgan, who was nineteen, was the product of a broken home. When I asked him the reason for his habit of changing overcoats, he shrugged, and said, "I guess I never had enough clothes bought for me when I was a kid, and was trying to make up for it."

*

BY AN odd coincidence it was George Fanelli, the New Rochelle detective's son, with whom I worked some years later on the tracking down of Gerard Graham Dennis, the Canadian second-story man, whom the papers called the "Prince of Burglars" and the "Man in the Mask."

Personally, I never subscribed to the belief that Dennis, a Canadian, was one of the century's great thieves. But so much has been written about this man who stole $600,000 in jewels over a period of five years that I tell here only my part in his pursuit and eventual capture.

In 1945 I went to Montreal to investigate for the St. Paul Company the $75,000 robbery of Mrs. Noah Timmins, widow of a Canadian tycoon who had left her a fortune of many millions and a castle worth more than $250,000 to live in.

On the evening of October 13 Mrs. Timmins, who was in her seventies, after a visit to friends, returned home to her castle in Westmount, a fashionable suburb of Montreal.

In her bedroom she was seized by two burglars who dragged her into the bathroom, where they gagged and tied her up. The pair was either new at the business or reckless, because they did not shut the bathroom door on the old woman. Or they might have got a thrill out of the thought that she could watch them go through her wardrobe and bureau drawers. But Mrs. Timmins was terrified by something else that evening. Her personal maid would come into the bedroom with a glass of warm milk at any moment. This was a set rule in the castle. Whenever she stayed out late, the maid waited up. On hearing Mrs. Timmins come in, the girl warmed up and brought her the milk. The wealthy old woman had found this helped her to go to sleep.

After a very few minutes the girl did come in. She screamed hysterically on seeing the burglars. They turned on her and beat her unconscious. Then they calmly proceeded with their looting.

When I interviewed Mrs. Timmins, she recalled that one of the burglars had very slender ankles and small feet for a man. She added, "I was also struck by the delicate, loving way he handled my negligées, underthings, and sheer silk stockings."

The Montreal police told me later that there had been five robberies recently that they believed were the work of the same two burglars. In all they'd gotten away with $150,000 in loot. The police had no clues. I suggested that it was quite likely that one of the thieves was a woman.

A couple of years later a daring thief, who invaded homes with a black stocking over his face and a gun in his hand, committed a series of sensational crimes in wealthy homes in Westchester County, New York. Here was the description of the burglar that the Westchester authorities sent out:

> Subject enters occupied homes at nighttime, in the best suburban residential sections, by means of unlocked windows, or doors, or often climbs porches, etc., to a second floor. Is very agile. Wears black mask and usually awakens his victims and demands their money, jewelry, furs and other valuables. Usually cuts or rips telephone wires. May be accompanied by one or two accomplices. In one burglary in New Rochelle he shot the occupant and then calmly proceeded to rob him of cash and jewels.
>
> Subject frequents fashionable, high-class restaurants and roadhouses, mixes with patrons and in that way gets a line on his victims; later locates their homes from conversations with them or by checking their car license numbers.

The "Man in the Black Mask" again and again became front-page news all over the country in the months after that.

He was not identified until 1947 as Gerard Graham Dennis, a Canadian with a long record. His wife, also a Canadian, who had a baby, told police who Dennis was after they showed her a picture of a young woman and told her she was her husband's sweetheart. He'd lately been using the name of Farrell. They locked her up on finding stolen jewels in the house. They sent the baby to a foundling home until his respectable sister, Mary Dennis, came down to get the child. Here is the appeal Farrell had sent to his sister on August 5, 1944:

Dear Mary,

I have very bad news for you. I have been accused of a lot of crimes. I saw the detectives coming up to the house so I left. Eleanor wouldn't come. I guess she's had enough of me. The trouble with this society is that when a person makes one mistake you are forced through the necessity of having to live, and pay bills, to gamble and make a living the best you can. I got myself in bad company and made a few mistakes. I must ask you to excuse all the lies I told you, and everyone else, about my means of making a living.

Even Eleanor didn't know what I was doing although she suspected. I could never trust her because of what she did before. I guess I am a yellow rat for not staying — she was a perfect wife and mother, but I couldn't see that it would make things any better. I want you to go down there right away and help her with her clothes and if she still wants to see me, I'll get in touch with her when she goes home. I know you don't care for me any more but please do it for the child. She is your flesh and blood too.

Sincerely,
Gerard

Somehow it is always the same story with men like this good-looking thief: whatever he does, it is not his fault. He is the victim of society, made one bad mistake, got into bad company, wants someone who loves him to take care of his responsibilities.

And, somehow or other, he will always find a woman whose mother heart beats wildly for a sinner no matter how many times he repeats his "mistakes." These, in his case, included beating up a woman and stealing at the point of a gun.

Three weeks later, the fugitive wrote another letter, this one to the police. It read:

With reference to charges made against me under the alias of Gerard Farrell, I do admit sole ownership of all four guns, quantity of jewelry, and other articles alleged to be stolen property, and found in my possession at 628 West 227th Street on the night of Monday, Aug. 4. As to the origin of my belongings and money, I successfully lied to my wife and family as well as my closest friends with whom I spent more time than with my wife and child. Having similarly deserted a previous wife with 2 children and now causing misery and disgrace to another, I realize the extent of my sins. As evidence has no doubt proved Eleanor Farrell is a woman of fine character, a conscientious housewife, and a model mother.

This 23-year-old mother has virtually been widowed; disgraced; and left penniless, with a 2-year-old baby to support. Added to this grief and suffering I have caused, she has been subjected to further insult and injury by being held unsuccessfully as hostage for a cowardly husband, separated from her baby, and kept in prison with all its loathesome environments.

This woman, as well as all others I came in contact with, is as innocent of my crimes as is her 2-year-old daughter, who is now likewise suffering from the loss of her mother.

As my wife she was completely dominated by me, aside from refusing to break the law, she was told what to do, what clothes to wear and very often to mind her own business and look after her house.

Sincerely,
Gerard Farrell
alias Woodruff, Langstaff, etc.

His wife was later cleared because of lack of evidence.

After being identified, Jerry Dennis adopted various new aliases and moved to Hollywood, where he lived with another Canadian woman, this one a schoolteacher.

He pulled a whole series of house robberies in Beverly Hills. Some of his victims were movie stars, and he had a long list of others whom he intended to rob when he found time for it.

A handsome man, whom many women said resembled Erroll Flynn, Dennis had a weakness for having his photograph taken at all sorts of social gatherings. Gradually the police accumulated quite a collection of these taken with and without a moustache, and in all sorts of sports clothing, business suits, and evening dress. The pictures showed his face from all angles.

It was because of this weakness that I was able to contribute to his eventual capture. I had seven of these photographs of Dennis made into a montage and mounted on a postcard-size "Wanted" circular. Through the Westchester police it was sent to police all over the country.

Some time later Dennis, as Duke McKay, California jeweler, had the rashness to permit home movies to be taken of himself (with the other guests) at a party in Cleveland. A jeweler who had attended this function saw the montage on the bulletin board of a Cleveland police station the next day.

"But that's Duke McKay!" he exclaimed.

But when arrested, Duke McKay turned out to be Jerry Dennis. He was brought back to New York, where he was convicted of burglary and sent to prison for fifteen to twenty-three years. He is eligible for parole in 1963, but the Canadian police have notified New York that they will be very happy to pick him up and carry him back to Canada the moment he is free to go home with them.

In all, over a period of five years Dennis is known to have stolen $140,000 in Canada, $150,000 in Westchester, and $357,635 more in California. He had $1,435 left on him when he was picked up. But he sold his life story for $10,000 to Warner Brothers, which made a picture of it titled *The Great Jewel Robber*.

My most important contribution to the case has, I am sorry to say, not yet borne fruit. The St. Paul Company financed my suggestion that a central clearinghouse be established to furnish information, fingerprints, pictures, and all the known facts to companies facing losses because of further depredations of the Man in the Black Mask.

It is my hope that this experiment would lead to the establishing by all inland marine insurance companies of a permanent central bureau for the investigation, on a nationwide scale, of all thefts of property suffered by persons or companies they'd insured. There were about ten companies who had to pay out large sums because of the crimes of Dennis. But not one of the other nine companies asked the Lost Property Bureau of the New York Police Department for help or information.

The bureau, then run by Lieutenant Jerry Murphy, is housed in a large room lined with filing cabinets in which are thousands of 3″ by 5″ cards and slips. On these are written precise descriptions of jewels and other valuable property that has been stolen.

A ring, for instance, is identified on these cards with a description of setting, stone or stones, weight, value, and other marks of identification, and the name, address, and sex of the person who lost it.

These are classified and cross-indexed, and when the pawnbrokers' daily reports are received the items are checked against the cards.

It seems obvious that the insurance industry could save itself (and its customers) a great fortune each year by establishing a permanent clearinghouse to work with that bureau and the others maintained by police departments from coast to coast.

HOW DID I DO, POP?

10

I SIT now with Lillian in the Florida sunshine, remembering the adventures I've written about here, and many of the others. And I cannot help wondering what my father would think of what I've done with the career which he prepared me for with such care.

I imagine he would be impressed by the fact that I was elected president of the World Association of Detectives and also by the hundreds of letters of praise I have from mayors, police chiefs, and executives of great businesses for and with whom I've worked.

Pop always had a good sense of humor and he would be amused to hear how I, his shrewd, sharp-eyed son, got clipped more than once by fast-talking con men.

There was the occasion on the Albany night boat when a distinguished-looking man approached me and introduced himself as the general manager of Albany's best hotel, the Ten Eyck. He was with a young lady, was returning from New York, and had run out of cash. If I'd give him $25 he'd return it first thing in the morning. Not seeing him on deck next morning, I called the Ten Eyck. The moment I asked for Mr. Jennison, the phone operator said, "How much did he get *you* for, sir?"

The man had never bothered to work at the hotel. He merely had cards printed that said he was manager. Two months later he was arrested while plying his chiseling trade, this time aboard a Boston-New-York boat.

A respectable-looking man who said he was from Philadelphia

visited me in my home. He wanted me to shadow his wife, whom he suspected had a lover. I told him that I did not take cases of that kind. He pleaded, and when I continued to refuse, he said, "But let me leave my card — in case you change your mind."

He reached for his pocketbook, and grew pale. "My God," he said, "I've had my wallet stolen! And it had not only my money, but my railroad pass in it!" His distress impressed me as genuine.

"How much do you need to get to Philadelphia?"

"Five dollars would be enough."

"Are you sure?" I asked.

He said, "Yes." Our eyes met then, and he got out of the place very fast. Almost before the door closed, I knew I'd been taken by a con man.

One day a friend phoned and asked if I would attend a dinner to be given the wife of a surveyor we both knew. She was in ill health, he said, and leaving for California.

I went to this party and it was very pleasant. I was told her husband was not going away with her. He was financially embarrassed. Two months later this man, the surveyor, came to me.

He told me that his wife had died in California, and he burst into tears. They had an agreement, he explained. If either died the other would have the body cremated and see that the ashes were brought to New York.

He needed $500 to go out there to keep his promise. He would return the money in three months. I gave him the money. A month later I met a lawyer who also had been at the dinner for the woman. "How much did her husband take you for?" he asked the moment he saw me.

Feeling rather foolish, I said, "Write what you lost on a piece of paper, and I'll do the same."

He too had given the surveyor $500. Two others who were at the party, I learned later, had also been clipped for $500 each. None of us knew where the surveyor was. Through a friend of mine on the Coast who knew the man I had the surveyor located. The man's wife had died. She was buried in Los Angeles. I wrote the deadbeat and demanded my money. He replied without mentioning the $500, but asked me to send him $200 more. That was the last I heard from him — and vice versa.

My father would also be amused by the trick pulled by a husky man named Hoffman. He was a watchmaker who had been drawing workmen's-compensation insurance checks for more than a year. He had suffered a neck injury in a car accident which prevented him from working.

During this time he had gone to Germany and had a doctor there certify he was still unable to work. So the weekly stream of checks was uninterrupted. When he came back an insurance company at last decided I should check on this disabled watchmaker.

The shadow man I put on Hoffman reported that he went to a gymnasium two or three times a week. He wore the neck brace when he went into this place and when he came out.

Out of curiosity I went to the gym on a day he usually went there. I told the manager I wanted to reduce. Hoffman was already there, working out, and without the neck brace.

I asked him if he did any wrestling. When he said Yes, we had a short bout. I let him put me down once and I wrestled him to the mat for the second fall. I had managed to twist his neck a couple of times with no complaint or moan of anguish from Mr. Hoffman. We made a date to wrestle again a couple of days later and we went out together.

He had the brace on again.

"Why do you wear that? Did I hurt you while we were wrestling?"

"No," he told me, "I wear it for protection."

I had one of my assistants take movies of our second bout with a concealed camera. That next week Hoffman received no check. On getting no satisfaction from the company, he hired a lawyer. The company sent Hoffman and his lawyer to see me.

On entering my office, Hoffman stared at me in surprise.

"I have a movie showing us wrestling," I told him. "Would you care to see it?"

"No," he said gruffly, and left with the lawyer, who apparently didn't care to see the movie either.

I have no doubts that my father would have been inordinately proud of the investigation that required me to disappear into the underworld for weeks and live with the mobsters of the Lower East Side. For this was one case in which I worked as he'd done so often when coping with thieves and cutthroats in southern Italy.

I was seeking evidence on the murder of Jacob Rothenberg, a dress manufacturer, on February 10, 1930, during a strike. That date, February 10, 1930, was among the more tumultuous ones in New York labor history.

The dressmakers' union had called the strike the night before. That morning thousands of the striking workers paraded through the Garment District. They had not gone far before they were attacked by Communists armed with knives and sawed-off pool cues. The Reds were trying to seize control of the organization, and provoked a second riot later in the day. Twenty-three men were arrested, and dozens on both sides required medical attention.

In addition there were street fights all day between pickets and workers loyal to their employers who tried to cross the picket lines to get to work.

Shortly after nine that morning, Jacob Rothenberg, a middle-aged partner in the Anna Scheer–Rothenberg Company, one of the struck shops, got a telephone call from a woman who told him:

"A bunch of your girls are trying to get into the building. But the pickets keep calling them scabs, and are trying to scare them away."

Mr. Rothenberg was one of the more aggressive manufacturers. "Tell the girls to wait," he said, "I'll be right down. Tell them that I'll see that nobody lays a hand on them."

When he got downstairs he was assaulted by a husky man he had never seen before. According to witnesses, the manufacturer was hit across the chest and head merely by this man's arm. But Mr. Rothenberg fell as though he'd been hit with a hammer. His head crashed against the steel rim of a manhole cover, knocking him unconscious. His assailant started to run away. But on looking back he saw that Rothenberg had not got up and walked back, apparently to see how badly his victim was hurt. The traffic policeman on the corner hurried up at that point and arrested him.

Mr. Rothenberg was carried into a clothing store to wait until an ambulance got there. The officer dragged his prisoner into the same store, hoping that the manufacturer would identify him. Mr. Rothenberg never regained consciousness. He died in Bellevue Hospital three hours later.

The man accused of hitting him was Irving Ashkenas. He was booked for felonious assault, but this was changed to murder when Rothenberg died. Ashkenas, twenty-seven, was a powerfully built East Side thief and thug and had been arrested fifteen or twenty times before. Rose Rosenberg, twenty-eight, a prostitute with whom he lived, was also arrested that day and held as a material witness.

Police suspected that she had made the phone call which lured Rothenberg to his death on the street.

For some time the district attorney's office had been criticized for its failure to prosecute vigorously the vicious crimes of goons hired by labor unions. This seemed to be another one. The most tragic thing about the courageous manufacturer's death was that the strike was settled in less than twenty-four hours.

The district attorney was a seventy-one-year-old Tammany man, Judge Thomas C. T. Crain. He denounced this street murder and promised that those responsible would be punished to the full extent of the law. Nevertheless, Ashkenas was indicted, not for homicide, but for manslaughter, a much lesser crime. And the Rosenberg woman was freed.

This enraged Mr. Rothenberg's fellow dress manufacturers. With their attorney, William Klein, a group of them called on Crain and asked him for an explanation. The district attorney said that the police had found no eyewitnesses and that the case against Ashkenas was so weak that he feared the case would be dismissed for lack of evidence.

On Klein's advice, the association hired me to find the evidence for a charge of first-degree murder. They were particularly eager that I establish a connection between the dressmakers' union and the mob of sluggers that Ashkenas belonged to.

I explained to the manufacturers that I could not undertake the investigation without informing both the police and Judge Crain's office of what I was doing. The officials offered no objections. The aged prosecutor, in fact, agreed to let me see all the reports and other documents he had on the case. The assistant who was handling the case against Ashkenas would cooperate with me, he added.

I found the stenographic reports of the examinations of Ashkenas astonishing reading. There had been two of these examinations, one made by one of Judge Crain's assistants a few hours after the arrest. The assistant had forced Ashkenas to admit that he had struck Rothenberg on the chest and then run away.

Judge Crain personally had examined Ashkenas a second time the day before the committee of dress manufacturers and Mr. Klein visited his office. Present at that examination was his assistant, Ashkenas' attorney and the detective assigned to the case.

This time Ashkenas made no mention of having hit Mr. Rothenberg. What he said was: "Everybody was running on top of me. They called me a scab. I said 'What am I running about?' I stopped. I looked back and I see a man lying on the street. When I went over to pick up his head, the officer pulled my tie."

"What happened then?" Judge Crain asked him.

"How should I know? I was getting hit, punched and kicked, not only me, but everybody."

Judge Crain had not asked any more questions after that or asked about the discrepancy between his two statements. And neither his assistant nor the detective called his attention to that.

As I pointed out in my report on these documents:

"In the 32 pages that comprise Judge Crain's examination of this suspect there is absolutely nothing that would assist anyone to investigate any part of the defendant's story. He did not even ask the movements of Ashkenas, from the moment he woke up, on the day of the killing, until he went to bed. And this, as you know, has long been routine procedure in all such examinations."

No one in the district attorney's office told me, by the way, that the $10,000 bail for him had been posted. I knew that he was back in circulation only because the undercover man I'd put in the suspect's Lower East Side neighborhood had seen him there in a restaurant that Joe Ashkenas, his brother, owned.

This roper, Harry Weisenberg, was the perfect choice for that particular roping job. He'd grown up in the neighborhood, knew Irving Ashkenas and his fellow mobsters by sight, and looked like a gangster himself. Though only five feet four inches tall he was very strong, looked tough. Weisenberg, about twenty-five then, had applied for an appointment to the United States Secret Service and was hungry for experience as an investigator. Within a day or two he had met Irving, Rose Rosenberg, and some of their mobster friends. Though the gang was not called that then, they were the nucleus of "Murder, Inc.," led by Louis (Lepke) Buchalter and Jacob (Gurrah) Shapiro.

In ten years these cold-blooded men killed personally or ordered the execution of a thousand persons. Usually they had them tortured first by burning their feet and hands or stabbing them to a slow death with ice picks. Nothing like these ruthless killers for hire had been seen since the era of Lupo the Wolf.

When these contacts were established, I decided to move down to the East Side myself. I had Weisenberg rent me a room on Eldredge Street, where the mob hung out. I asked him to spread the word around that Joe Lotto, one of the Capone boys was coming to town. Before moving down there I removed all of the labels and other marks from my clothes and put a few copies of current Chicago newspapers in my suitcase. The sort of people I would have to cope with would take the first chance they got to go through my possessions. It was dangerous enough to pose as a Chicago gangster with Capone's boys, who were in and out of New York all of the time, but that was a risk I had to take.

The room Weisenberg had found for me was on the fourth floor of an ancient, sour-smelling tenement. Its iron bed was old, rusty, and rickety. Its mattress, though matzah thin, was big enough to harbor whole armies of ferocious, ravenous, king-size bedbugs. Sometimes when awakened late at night by their attacks in force, I would try to console myself by thinking of the great artists who'd lived and suffered in squalid surroundings for their art.

Manhunting is a science, but I was suffering for it just as though it were an art. There was no bath, and I tried to sneak out of the neighborhood every day to take one at a hotel. Weisenberg and I ate with those goons every day in their greasy restaurant hangouts, drank rotgut whiskey with them, shot pool and played poker with them.

The mobsters were anything but subtle in their attempts to check up on me. They didn't try to tidy up the things in my suitcase after they went through it. And I noticed that Irving and a couple of the others patted my pockets as I sat down each night to play poker. They did not bother to steam the letters I'd arranged to have sent to me there as Joe Lotto, but tore them open and left them in the box. The letters were scrawled in pencil and told the news of what was happening to my pals and members of my family in Chicago.

One night Irving, after giving me a frisk, said: "You say you are one of Al Capone's boys. I thought you guys all carried gats. How is it you ain't got no gat?"

I had anticipated something like this happening, and had figured out it would give me a chance to really impress the thugs. "Guns are for beginners," I said. "They make too much noise when you're taking out a guy." I carelessly pulled out my stiletto. "This is faster," I said. "Paste this postage stamp on the door, and watch." I handed Irving the stamp and he pasted it on the door.

I threw the stiletto, and they watched with awe as it slid through the air, hit the stamp, sank deep in the wood, and quivered. I went over and pulled it out. Wiping the stiletto on my pants leg, I carelessly shoved it out of sight. I won some money in the stud game that night. Possibly my exhibition of skill had made them too nervous to concentrate on the cards.

On learning that Rose's mother and sister lived in Newark, I planted a girl roper there. The police records there told Rose's story. An incorrigible child, she had spent the years between eight and sixteen in a reform school. On coming out she married Abe Sachs, alias Fat, a thief and fence. She was sent to the New Jersey Reformatory for Women at eighteen for receiving stolen goods, went back two years later, this time for receiving and larceny. Sachs was convicted with her on this charge and was now again in prison.

On coming out, Rose moved to the Lower East Side, took a lover, and had since been convicted and sent to prison as a prostitute and also for running a combined brothel and opium den. She was ugly, short, and built like a wrestler. Rose was very proud of her strength. Once, toward the end of our investigation, she boasted of how men would take her along on street stickup jobs to hold the victim while they went through his pockets.

Weisenberg questioned that. She leaped on him from behind, pinioned his arms to his sides, and squeezed him so tight that she broke two of his ribs. The last man she lived with before she met Ashkenas was another thief, Sam Rosenberg. He and Irving's brother, Joe Ashkenas, were partners in a restaurant where some of the mob hung out. Rose was working there as a waitress, and Irving Ashkenas met her there. He was a cruel, ignorant, loud-mouthed thug.

His whole family were thieves. His father was an extortionist who shook down the neighborhood's pushcart peddlers. His two brothers had police records. His mother sold bootleg booze in their flat. Irving's specialty as a thief was on the unusual side. As a taxi driver he picked up immigrants as they came off the transatlantic steamships. Those who were going to other cities he sold strips of subway tickets to, saying that they were railroad tickets and that they would take them to their destination in Pittsburgh,

St. Louis, or San Francisco. Sometimes he made $200 a day in this fashion.

After the police ended this racket he drove a truck, but lost this job. On falling in love with Rose he had no money. But she left Sam Rosenberg for him, though she continued using Rosenberg's name. Rosenberg, an understanding thief who was sick of Rose anyway, gave the union his blessing.

Ashkenas had no money, but Rose had $80. She spent $35 of this for secondhand furniture, and they moved into an East Side tenement flat a few doors from the restaurant hangout.

Irving Ashkenas, goon, was a crybaby whose chief emotion was self-pity. He hadn't spoken to his brother Joe for years because "he always took advantage of me." He blamed Rose for his present troubles: "That broad talked me into getting this job with the union."

In a way, it was true. Rose had urged him to go to Gurrah and ask for a job as a $10-a-day slugger. "Gurrah" Shapiro, however, didn't like him, and Ashkenas had to plead for a long time before being taken on.

Once Weisenberg and I were accepted as thieves in good standing, it was a small problem to obtain the information we wanted. There was no question, in my mind, at least, that the union had hired the Murder, Inc., mob to intimidate the dress manufacturers. Later on, it developed that Lepke and Gurrah would furnish gunmen and sluggers to the employers. Sometimes they had groups of their murderous gorillas working for both sides. In the end, Murder, Inc., obtained control of entire industries, thanks to this flexibility in their homicidal and slugging techniques.

"How do they work a thing like this strike?" Weisenberg asked Ashkenas one day, and was told:

"Well, the union puts guys like Gurrah and Lepke, Curly and Frenchy on the books as organizers, which is legal. Then they hire Greenie and the Soldier and a few others as committeemen. They are working for the union, and that can protect them from the law okay. Greenie and the Soldier lead us when we go to move around. Sometimes we don't know who we are to beat up until we get there. Then Greenie or the Soldier points them out to us. You gotta be careful in such work. You get fired if you put the slug on the wrong guy."

Irving Ashkenas's hard luck was not limited to having assaulted and killed a man during a one-day strike. Another thug had been assigned, as my reports showed. This man was nicknamed Mickey. He said that the Soldier, a professional athlete, had acted as crew manager. I quote here from one of my reports:

Micky remarked to our Assistant what a lucky break he got, saying that he was paired up with Subject and they were "laying for Rothenberg" when he, Mickey, was called on the other corner by some undisclosed person and Subject was placed on the corner where Mickey had been; that Rothenberg came along, minding his own business, and Subject pulled a piece of lead pipe out of his sleeve and said "Let him have it"; that they then ran; that they had "pulled a raw one a week before"; that they received from Gurrah, Lepke and Curly from $10.00 to $12.00 each per day for such work.

Micky again told our Assistants that it was a good break for him because he was supposed to have done what Subject did; that Subject "took a poke" at the now deceased, but did not "bump him off"; that when Subject hit the man, he fell down and struck his head; that he, Mickey, saw it all and was across the street when it happened; that he never knew Subject before the strike, that Subject would "beat the rap"; and that this case would never come up for trial.

Joe Ashkenas, Irving's brother, the restaurateur, was also full of information useful to us, the same report reveals:

That on the day Rothenberg died, his brother Irving was working on the strike with a mob and that his brother hit some man and this man fell and fractured his skull, and Joe asked Assistants if they had read about it in the paper. When they answered that they had not, Joe said that his brother Irving had a mean punch and was as strong as a bull. He further stated that Irving was in the Tombs for four weeks and that he, Joe, collects $100 per week for his brother, but if Irving was working for the Union instead of the mob, he would make them pay heavily. When Assistants asked Joe for whom Irving worked, Joe told them that Irving was working for Curly, Lepke and Gurrah. He further stated that Irving would "beat the rap" and that the case would never come up for trial because they were paying $100,000 for graft.

At the time Joe was giving this information to our Assistants, his brother Irving was serving them with drinks. Our Assistants cannot say whether Irving heard any part of this conversation or not but are unanimous in saying that they believe he did not.

Joe had advised Irving against working on the strike and he told my assistants that after Irving was arrested and held in $25,000 bail he refused to help him. But their mother came around and pleaded with him until he agreed.

Joe said that he went to the Tombs to visit Irving who said, "I'm going crazy in here." So he went to Gurrah who said he would get the bail reduced to $10,000 and the charge reduced to second-degree manslaughter but that they would not take Irving out for a few days as that might arouse suspicion that he was being aided by the union. Joe explained that the union was paying the mobsters $250 a week because of Irving's arrest. But the $200-a-week balance was being split between Curly, Lepke, Little Frenchy, Gurrah, and Irving.

Everybody but Irving himself, it appeared, was confident that Irving would beat the rap. My woman roper in Newark met Rose there through her sister. Rose confirmed the story that Irving had been hired for $10 a day, by the dressmakers' union, to do strong-arm stuff. When his bail was reduced to $10,000, she had raised $700 for the bondsman's fee and got him free. She said she was sure that Irving would get free of the whole affair as it was "fixed at the district attorney's office and with the judge."

(This talk about the "fix being in" with Judge Crain's office was heard all over town about many cases. But it is only fair to point out that when he was investigated the next year by Samuel Seabury, the man who forced Mayor Walker and many other top New York officials to resign, Seabury concluded that Crain personally was honest, but highly incompetent and inefficient. The truth, it seemed to me, was that the district attorney was already senile, which gave Tammany the kind of prosecutor it liked, one who would not interfere with the systematic looting of the city and its citizens.)

Ashkenas had been warned not to go near Gurrah, who held court in a restaurant on Fifth Avenue that the mob owned. Gurrah didn't want to be seen with a man indicted for "a labor-war crime." Ashkenas's brother went to that restaurant every Friday afternoon to collect Irving's $50 for him. Weisenberg reported that Irving really became wrought up on the day that Rose's old sweetheart, Sam Rosenberg, spoke to him in a restaurant.

"You working yet?" asked Mr. Rosenberg.

"No."

"Well, Gurrah is out of town, so your brother will now be getting your $50 each Friday afternoon from Greenie. But Greenie says to tell you to get a job, or get some businessman to put your name on his payroll so it looks like you're working for him. They can't keep paying you this money forever."

"I took a beating from the cops in the West Thirtieth Street Station," blubbered Irving. "What for? Because I was protecting Gurrah and the rest of the boys, that's why."

"A nice thing," Irving said glumly to Weisenberg when they were on the street. "If I talk the mob will bump me off. If I don't, I go to jail. I'm gonna look for that Gurrah. I don't believe he's out of town at all."

They were unable to find him, but Ashkenas was stopped by the notorious Little Frenchy, whose real name was Henry Hirshkovitz.

"How is your case coming along?" asked Little Frenchy.

"Not so good."

"Well, you don't have to go around with no sour puss, Irving. Your case will never come up, and if it ever does, what happens? You will beat the rap."

"I don't think Gurrah nor nobody else with the union is worrying whether I beat the rap or not. And if I don't beat it it means years in the can."

"That's just it," said Little Frenchy. "The union can't let you be sent up. It would cost them too much money. They have to pay your family $60 a week all that time. In most cases they pay out $100 a week — that would run into thousands."

"What way you figure that?"

"They know that if they don't pay your family, you might get sore and squeal."

"If they are afraid I'll squeal why do they threaten to stop paying me this lousy $50 a week I'm getting now?"

Frenchy was honestly appalled at this. "I have been with the union for twelve years now, and they have never yet let a man go up if they could help it."

When I had sufficient evidence to prove that Irving Ashkenas, indirectly working for the union, murdered Jacob Rothenberg, and also that Rose was the woman who lured the manufacturer to the street, I turned it over to the police.

By that time she had gone to Canada. Two New York detectives went there with one of my undercover men and brought her back. When she and Irving went on trial, it was for homicide. Both were convicted of manslaughter and sent to the penitentiary. If tried for manslaughter they could have pleaded to a lesser charge and had sentence suspended. The following year both appealed for new trials. His conviction was sustained, but a new trial was ordered for the woman rib-crusher on the ground of inadequate evidence. I do not think her case was tried a second time.

Irving Ashkenas came out of prison in 1935 and got a job driving a taxicab at a resort town in the Catskill Mountains. On September 5, 1936, he was shot and stabbed to death. The killing was done by Murder, Inc., who used a favorite torture weapon, ice picks. The mob went on to great success in other fields until the end of the thirties when both Lepke and Gurrah were sent to the electric chair.

My father would have been proud of my work on that job. I had uncovered the evidence that convicted the killer and the woman who helped him. I had also proved that the union had hired, through murderous underworld ganglords, this same killer and other goons. I certainly am proud of it.

It was my masterpiece.